CENTRAL AND EASTERN EUROPE IN TRANSITION, VOLUME 5

Central and Eastern Europe in Transition
Frank H. Columbus (Editor)

Central and Eastern Europe in Transition, 1
ISBN 1-56072-596-6.

Central and Eastern Europe in Transition, 2
ISBN 1-56072-597-4.

Central and Eastern Europe in Transition, 3
ISBN 1-5607-687-3.

Central and Eastern Europe in Transition, 4
ISBN 1-56072-932-5.

Central and Eastern Europe in Transition, 5
ISBN 1-59033-323-3.

CENTRAL AND EASTERN EUROPE IN TRANSITION, VOLUME 5

FRANK H. COLUMBUS (EDITOR)

Nova Science Publishers, Inc.
New York

Senior Editors: Susan Boriotti and Donna Dennis
Coordinating Editor: Tatiana Shohov
Office Manager: Annette Hellinger
Graphics: Wanda Serrano
Editorial Production: Jennifer Vogt, Ronald Doda, Matthew Kozlowski,
  Jonathan Rose and Maya Columbus
Circulation: Ave Maria Gonzalez, Vera Popovich, Luis Aviles, Raymond Davis,
  Melissa Diaz, Vladimir Klestov and Jeannie Pappas
Marketing: Cathy DeGregory

Library of Congress Cataloging-in-Publication Data
Available Upon Request

ISBN: 1-59033-323-3.

Copyright © 2002 by Nova Science Publishers, Inc.
  400 Oser Ave, Suite 1600
  Hauppauge, New York 11788-3619
  Tele. 631-231-7269   Fax 631-231-8175
  e-mail: Novascience@earthlink.net
  Web Site: http://www.novapublishers.com

Printed in the United States of America

CONTENTS

PREFACE

Central and Eastern Europe present more than a trivial challenge to the Developed Nations of the world as well as to themselves. Will they represent new markets, new sources of low-cost labor, or populations taking every action and avenue conceivable to emigrate to the Developed Nations? Will they be integrated into the Western economies and political structures or lose patience and wrap themselves into defensive postures and pose threats to the Developed Nations?

Chapter 1

Strategic Interactions Between NATO and Romania After 2000

Laure Paquette
Lakehead University
Thunder Bay, Ontario, Canada

Abstract

NATO is newly aware of its increased status as a force for stability in a drastically altered Atlantic community. The number of its initiatives is on the increase just as a new political, economic and military Europe emerges. The Cold War's end has wrought as many changes as there are continuities in the security environment. Eastern and central European states, especially NATO and PfP members, enjoy an increasing importance to NATO, both as trading partners and as new participants in the civil society. While the literature on relations between NATO and the East Europeans was, at the time of the writing, comparatively limited, the study of the overall posture of those states in the international system is almost non-existent, so that the consequences of their posture for NATO's renewed concept are unknown. The study of these countries' security posture and strategic interactions with Central European states in general promotes the renewed role of NATO. The study shows that the long-term relations with Romania is subordinated to the goal of entering the European Union, and that their different values will makes relations difficult. This will test NATO's new strategic concept to the limit. It also shows the importance of strategic thinking.

Part 1.

In March 1997, NATO invited to Poland, Hungary and the Czech Republic to start negotiating membership. Their accession was the fourth time NATO has added new members since 1949: Greece and Turkey in 1952, the Federal Republic of Germany in 1955, and Spain in 1982. Nine signatories to Partnership for Peace (PfP) have declared their intention to apply for membership: Albania, Bulgaria, Estonia, Latvia, Lithuania, Macedonia, Romania, Slovakia, and Slovenia.

NATO does not have a profound understanding of these new partners, given the break in relations during the Cold War and the chaotic transitions towards democracy and the market economy today. NATO is newly aware of being a force for stability in a drastically altered Atlantic community. A new political, economic, diplomatic, and military Europe is emerging, and this new Europe has as many changes as it has continuities. The economic importance of central Europe increases along with its increasing security problems. No rivalry, border dispute or ethnic conflict is likely to disappear soon: Europe will be tied to that powder keg for the foreseeable future. The inevitable changes to central European defense posture will be of great interest, even if a number of more important nations are casual about their concerns. A study of these countries' security posture in the medium and the long-term is an ideal vehicle for improving understanding of the new Europe.

The present chapter examines the national strategy of Romania, a central European state, and examines its broad interactions with NATO. This is the environment in which NATO's initiatives have encountered the limitations of slow, painful transitions to democracy and the market economy.

I. OBJECTIVES

This analysis proposes to enhance NATO's knowledge about and development of policies in Romania by investigating the new directions in national strategy. The analysis for this study uses the content of political culture of each state as an independent variable in explaining its choice of security posture. The working hypothesis is that states must make changes in defense policy, and perhaps even change overall posture, as a result of changing post-Cold War circumstances. If this is correct, then (1) the process is relatively lengthy; (2) it is propelled by domestic social malaise; and (3) it will be manifest not only in defense policy (although these changes are the earliest and the most easily observed). The framework allows for explanations or predictions about national strategy on the basis of certain permanent social characteristics. It was developed in order to determine the overall posture of a state in conditions of high uncertainty. For the purposes of this analysis, national values are defined as the accepted standards of historical or ideological origin as well as the national heritage cherished by the population as a whole. National strategy is defined as the comprehensive direction of all the elements of national power to attain national objectives, and to support and pursue the general goals provided by a nation's leaders.

The bulk of this article is therefore taken up by the determination of those two variables of the empirical hypothesis, national values and national strategy. The theory of causal relationship between the two variables has been explored in detail elsewhere, and is given here only in summary fashion.[1] Once the *type* of strategy is established, however, it becomes possible to identify the actual strategy various countries are using, and, of most interest to the policy- and decision-makers, to understand and make predictions about its tactics. It is particularly useful in the case of strategic choices made by ethno federal states such as the

---

[1]Laure Paquette, *National Strategy and National Values*, Ph.D. diss., Queen's University, 1992.

former Czechoslovakia in multiple political arenas with shifting balance of power between sister republics.[2]

II. CURRENT LITERATURE

The literature germane to this project can be divided into four categories: (1) articles about NATO; (2) articles about smaller NATO members (Greece, Turkey, Italy, Spain, Portugal, etc.); (3) articles about Central European new members (Poland, Czech Republic, Hungary); and (4) second-tier applicants for NATO membership (Romania, Bulgaria, Ukraine, Slovakia, etc.).

Since 1997, articles about NATO usually argue for or against enlargement. Detractors argue that the conceptual and operational underpinnings of enlargement are not properly developed yet[3] or that NATO is unlikely to survive such massive political changes.[4] Proponents include Richard Staar, David Calleo, David Haglund, Zbigniew Brzezinski and Robert Art.[5] Among countries hoping to become members, enlargement does not enjoy unanimous support: the rift between decision-making elites and the newly democratized peoples in Poland and the Czech Republic is both genuine and deep.[6] US control of European foreign policy led to an eastern expansion rather than a negotiated reorientation of the Alliance goals which would favor the integration of European defense policy.[7] Eastern

---

[2]Carol Skalnik Leff, "Democratization and Disintegration in Multinational States: the Breakup of the Communist Federations," *World Politics* 51:2 (January 1999), 205-235.

[3]Sean Kay, "The 'New NATO' and the Enlargement Process," *European Security* 6:4 (Winter 1997), 1-16. Joseph Lepgold argues that NATO's success in carrying out multilateral peace operations is critical to NATO's future; see "NATO's Post-Cold War collective Action Problem," *International Security* 23:1 (Summer 1998), 78-106. See Also Tom Lansford, "The Triumph of Transatlanticism: NATO and the Evolution of European Security After the Cold War, " *Journal of Strategic Studies* 22:1 (March 1999), 1-28; Hans Binnendijk and Richard Kugler, "Open NATO's Door Carefully," *Washington Quarterly* 22:2 (Spring 1999), 125-128.

[4]John Woodliffe, "The Evolution of New NATO for a New Europe," *International and Comparative Law Quarterly* 47:1 (Jan 1998), 174-192.

[5]Richard Staar, "Why NATO Should Expand," *Mediterranean Quarterly* 9:3 (Summer 1998), 25-33; David Calleo, "NATO Enlargement as a Problem for Security in Europe," *Aussenpolitik* 49:1 (1998), 27-31; David Haglund, "Les conséquences de l'élargissement de l'OTAN sur la sécurité européenne," *Revue internationale et stratégique* 32 (Win 1998-99), 66-76; Zbigniew Brzezinski, "NATO: The Dilemmas of Expansion," *National Interest* 53 (Fall 98), 13-17; Robert Art, "Creating a Disaster: NATO's Open Door Policy," *Political Science Quarterly* 113:3 (Fall 1998), 383-403; Andrew Cottey, "Central Europe Transformed: Security and Cooperation on NATO's New Frontier," *Contemporary Security Policy* 20:2 (August 1999), 1-30; Stephen J. Blank, "NATO Enlargement Between Rhetoric and Realism," *International Politics* 36:1 (March 1999), 67-88.

[6]Georgeta Pourchot, "NATO Enlargement and Democracy in Eastern Europe," European Security 6:4 (winter 1997), 157-174.

[7]Matteo Stochetti, "Flexibility or Hegemony? The Political Foundations of the European Security System and NATO's Eastward Enlargement," *Teoria politica* 14:1 (March 1998), 18-39.

expansion may move the Alliance toward genuine cooperative security,[8] but detractors fear NATO may become more of an empire.[9]

The literature about central Europe is dominated by economic issues, not military ones. To most countries, EU membership is the real goal, with NATO membership a stepping stone, an argument detractors invoke.[10] Central and East European literature also includes articles about NATO-EU relations,[11] although the bulk of it analyses the Alliance's record at the fifty-year mark.[12]

The literature about the smaller member states is sparse, unless they were involved in a conflict, as were Turkey and Greece. The literature treats most peaceful NATO members like it does Portugal: articles periodically review the armed forces; defense papers are discussed when they come out, as are relations with the US; there are also articles on participation in peacekeeping.[13] The literature on Italy and Spain is similar.[14] Greece and Turkey, which have

---

[8]Eric Bergbusch, "NATO Enlargement: Should Canada Leave NATO?", *International Journal* 53:1 (Winter 1997-98), 147-168.

[9]Gabriel Robin, "Cinquante ans après, Alliance rénovée ou empire naissant?" *Revue internationale et stratégique* 32 (Winter 1998-99), 54-58. See also Lars Skalnes, "From the Outside In, Form the Inside Out: NATO Expansion and International Relations Theory," *Security Studies* 7:4 (Summer 1998), 44-87.

[10]Karl-Heinz Kamp, "NATO Entrapped: Debating the Next Enlargement," *Survival* 40 (Autumn 1998), 170-86; Robert J. Art, "Creating a Disaster: NATO's Open Door Policy," Political Science Quarterly 113 (1998), 383ss.

[11]Guido Lenzi, "Les relations entre l'OTAN, l'UEO et l'Union Européenne aujourd'hui," *Revue internationale et stratégique* 32(Winter 1998), 77-83.

[12]Daniel N. Nelson and Thomas S. Szayna, "NATO's Metamorphosis and its New Members," *Problems of Post-Communism* 45 (Jl/Ag 1998): 32-43; "NATO's 50th Anniversary: Broadening and Redefining Transatlantic Partnership," *Congressional Digest* 78:4 (1999), 97-128; Bruno Tertrais, "L'OTAN existera-telle encore en 2009?", *Revue internationale et stratégique* 32 (Winter 1998), 121-129; Bertrand Delanoe, "Quelle OTAN pour quelle défense européenne?," *Revue internationale et stratégique* 32 (Winter 1998), 39-45; Johanna Granville, "The Many Paradoxes of NATO Enlargement," *Current History* 98: 627 (1999), 165-170; Guelner Abeyt, "NATO's New Missions," *Perceptions* 4:1 (March/May 1999), 65-75; Tomas Valasek, "NATO at 50," *Foreign Policy in Focus* 4:11 (March 1999).

[13]For branch reviews, Antonio Barrento, "The Portuguese Army," *NATO's Sixteen Nations* (Sp. 1998); Manuel Santos, "The Portuguese Air Force," *NATO's Sixteen Nations* (1998); Nuno Matias, "The Portuguese Navy 500 Years After Vasco da Gama," *NATO's Sixteen Nations* (1998); about the defence paper, Eduardo Pereira, "Debate and Consensus-Approval of Security and Defence Policy," *NATO's Sixteen Nations* (Sp. 1998); 1998); for a review of the relations with the US, see Nuno Filipe Brito, "Para a acta: o Acordo de cooperacao e Defesa Entre Portugal E os Estados Unidos Da America," Politica Internacional (Lisbon) 1 (1995), 135-57; for an overview of participation in peacekeeping, see Antonio Ribeiro, "Portuguese Participation in Peacekeeping operations," *NATO's Sixteen Nations* (Sp. 1998).

[14]On Italy, Fillippo Andreatta and Christopher Hill. "Eternally in Transition," *International Spectator* 30 (April/June 1995); René Moine and Laurent Dhome, "L'industrie de défense en Italie," *L'Armement* (May 1993), 126-38; Giuseppe Cucchi, "Italie: une nouvelle politique et un nouveau modèle de défense," *Défense Nationale* 48(Aug. 1992), 75-90 and "La défense, instrument de la politique étrangère italienne dans la période post-bipolaire," *Revue française d'administration publique* 77(Jan 96), 93-99, Matteo Stochetti, "L'attore mancante: I problemi della politica per la sicurezza in Italia," *Teoria politica* 12:3 (1996), 149-167; Carlo Jean, "L'Italia e la diffesa comune europea," *Affari esteri* 110 (Apr 96), 296-308; Francesco Paolo Fulci, "L'Italia e il consiglio di Sicurezza della Nazioni Unite," *Affari esteri* 118, (Spring 98), 320-33. On Spain, Bernard Labatut, "Les politiques méditerranéennes de l'Espagne à la recherche d'un équilibre entre l'impératif de la sécurité et l'éthique de l'interdépendance," *Études internationales* 26 (1995), 315-27; Maritheresa Frain, "A Peninsula Iberica e a Europa: uma convergencia politicas de defesa espanhola e portuguesa no pos-Guerra," *Politica Internacional* (Lisbon) 3(1997), 249-82; Antonio

been at war, had their military analyzed.[15] The bulk of the articles reexamine the situation on Cyprus.[16]

Because Poland started its reforms ten years before the rest of central Europe, it makes up the bulk of the more substantive literature about new NATO members. Most of the articles on Poland discuss the importance of security in foreign policy, and the importance of democratic civilian control to accession talks.[17] These studies of Poland remain the only yardstick available for progress and prospects for second-tier applicants. Little enough is written about the second-tier applicants to NATO, unless they have been involved in some important event with a greater power. That is the case with Ukraine, which negotiated at length with Russia about nuclear weapons and the Black Sea Fleet.[18] Beyond the odd review article about US

Sanchez-Gijon, "La defensa se defiende en las Cortes," *Politica Exterior* 56 (March 1997), 73-85; Klaus Wolf-Casado, Klaus. "Spain's Defence Industry," *Defence*lain (London) 21 (Nov 1990), 721ss.

[15]For Turkey, Peter Thompson, "United States-Turkey Military Relations: Treaties and Implications," *Kurdish Studies* 9 (1996), 1-2; Haluk Bayulken, "Turquie: une Importance renouvelée dans une région troublée," *La Revue Administrative* (Paris) 46:611 (1993); Duygu Basoglu Sezer, "Turkey's New Security Environment, Nuclear Weapons and Proliferation," *Comparative Strategy* 14:2 (Apr 1995), 149-172. Sezer, 1995; Ben Lombardi, "Turkey - The Return of the Reluctant Generals?" *Political Science Quarterly* 112:2 (Summer 97), 191-215. Ilter Turan, "The Military in Turkish Politics," *Mediterranean Politics* 2:2 (Fall 97), 123-135; Ali Karaosmanoglu, "NATO Enlargement and the South," *Security Dialogue* 30:2 (June 1999), 213-224. For Greece, Neovi Karakatsanis, "Do Attitudes Matter? The Military and Democratic Consolidation in Greece," *Armed Forces and Society* 24 (Winter 1997), 289-313; Ioannis Varvitsiotis, "The Defence of Greece," *NATO's Sixteen Nations* 37:5 (1992), 11-14, outside of NATO's own annual reviews (*NATO's Sixteen Nations*, various years).

[16]Nicholas Antonakis, "Military Expenditure and Economic Growth in Greece 1960-1990," *Journal of Peace Research* 34 (1997); Christos G. Kollias, "The Greek-Turkish Conflict and Greek Military Expenditure, 1960-1992," *Journal of Peace Research* 33 (1996), and "Greek Extended Deterrence: The Effects of the Cyprus Problem on Greek Defence Expenditure 1970-90," *Cyprus Review* 5 (Fall 1993): 88-94; George M. Georgious et al. "Modelling Greek-Turkish Rivalry: An Empirical Investigation of Defence Spending Dynamics," *Journal of Peace Research* 33:2 (May 1996), 229-239; and Christopher Tuck, "Greece, Turkey and Arms Control," *Defence Analysis* 12:1 (April 1996), 23-32.

[17]Andrezej Korbonski, "The Polish Military at a Time of Change," *RFE/RL Research Report* 3 (1994), 21-29; Prystrom, Janusz. "Questions of Security in Poland's Foreign Policy," *Yearbook of Polish Foreign Policy* 1993-94: 43-52; Wieslaw Kurzyca, "Implementation of CFE: Implications for Poland's Security," *Polish Journal of International Affairs* 3:4 (Fall 1994), 33-46. On civilian control, Pamela Waldron-Moore, "Eastern Europe at the crossroads of Democratic Transition," *Comparative Political Studies* 32:1 (Fall 1999), 32-62; Chris C. Demchak, "Modernizing Military Organizations and Political Control in Central Europe," *Journal of Public Policy* 15:2 (May 1995), 111-152; Anieska Gogolewska, "Civilian control of the Army and Post-1989 Changes in Polish Legislation," *Polish Quarterly of International Affairs* 5:1 (Winter 1996), 61-82; Elizabeth P. Coughlan, "Democratizing Civilian Control: the Polish Case," *Armed Forces and Society* 24:4 (Summer 98), 519-33. On preparations in general, see Aleksander Kwasniewski, "Poland in NATO: Opportunities and challenges," *NATO Review* 45 (S/O 1997), 4-7; Dario Tosi, "L'évolution de la politique de défense de l'environnement en Pologne: conditions, solutions envisagées et contraintes," *Revue des Pays de l'Est* 31:2 (1990), 47-91; Longin Pastusiak, "Poland on her Way to NATO," *European Security* 7:2 (Summer 1998), 54-62.

[18]Savita Pande, Ukraine's "Non-Nuclear" Option and the NPT," *Strategic Analysis* 17:2 (May 1994), 233-249; Swaran Singh,"Ukraine: an Acid Test for US Nuclear Non-Proliferation Policy," *Strategic Analysis* 16:10 (Jan 94), 1307-1322; David T. Twining, "The US-Russian-Ukrainian Nuclear Agreement: What Lies Ahead?" *Defence Analysis* 10:2 (August 1994): 141-155.

relations,[19] there is a paucity of sources regarding Bulgaria,[20] Romania, Slovakia,[21] Hungary and the Czech Republic.[22]

Outside any of the above categories are heavily ideological articles decrying US involvement in Southern Europe.[23]

III. THE CAUSAL RELATIONSHIP

The logic that gives rise to the whole process hinges on the interaction between not only national strategy and national values, but also their components.

Step 1 Treatment of Information -- Mechanism 1, Cognition

One of the most challenging tasks decision-makers face is the treatment of information. The state or government apparatus supports that treatment.

---

[19]Oleg Strekal, "Independent Ukraine: the Search for Security," *International Spectator* 30:1 (Jan-March 1995), 51-78'; Susan L. Clark, "Security Issues and the Eastern Slavic States," *The World Today* 49:10 (October 1993), 189-193; Jason Ellis, "The "Ukrainian Dilemma" and U.S. Foreign Policy," *European Security* 3:2 (Summer 1994), 251-280.

[20]Nadezda Michajlova, "Prioritäten der Aussenpolitik Bulgariens," *Südosteuropea Mitteilungen 38:2* (!998), 83-89; Galina Chuleva and Jim Derleth. "The Bulgarian National Security-Making Apparatus 1970-1994," *European Security* 3:4 (Winter 1994), 775-789; Valeri Rachev, "Combining Political and Military Considerations in Assessing Military Conflicts [in Bulgaria]," *Journal of Slavic Military Studies* 9:1 (March 1996), 45-54; Nikolay Slatinski, "Bulgarian Security and Prospects for Reform," *NATO Review* 43 (March 1995), 28-32; Veneta Monceva, "Bulgarien: die neuen Wege der veraenderten Siche," *Suedosteuropa* (Munich) 42: 11/12 (1993), 661ss; Jewgenij Alexandrow, "Ein neues Bulgarien im neuen Europa," *Europa Archiv* 45: 25 (1990), 615-622., although Stephane Lefebvre does a good survey of changes for 1992-94 and Johnson surveys the changes in military relations (1994). See Stephane Lefebvre, "A Primer on Bulgarian Security and Defence Issues," *Defence Analysis* 10:3 (Dec 1994), 243-266and M. Mae Johnson, "Civil-military relations and Military Reforms in Bulgaria," *European Security* 4:3 (Fall 95), 488-518; Kjell Engelbret, "Bulgaria's Evolving Defence Policy," *RFE/RL Research Report* 3 (1994), 19.

[21]Daniel N. Nelson, "Romanian Security," *Revue roumaine d'études internationales* 125-126 (May 1993), 185-209; Ivo Samson, "Transformation and Structural Change in Central Eastern Europe: Slovakia's Adjustment to New Security Challenges," *Revue d'intégration européenne* 20:2-3 (Winter 97), 187-200; Roxana Iorga,"Romanian Perspectives on Security Risks," *International Spectator* 29:4 ((Oct 1994), 81-105.

[22]Ferenc Gazdag and Zsolt Pataki, "La politique étrangère et de sécurité de la République de Hongrie," *Défense nationale* 53: (March 97), 97-111; W. B. Ibbetson, "Hungarian Defence Forces: New Challenge," *Army Quarterly and Defence Journal* 124 (94); Lajos Keresztes, "The Role for the Hungarian Army in Transformation of Defence and Security Policy of the Social-Liberal Government," *Army Quarterly and Defence Journal* 126 (96). For the Czech Republic, see Roman Blasek, "Perception of Security Risks by the Population of the Czech Republic," *Journal of Slavic Military Studies* 11:3 (September 1998), 89-96; Stefan Sarvas, "Attitudes of the Czech Public Toward National Security, the Military and NATO Membership, *Journal of Slavic Military Studies* 11:3 (September 1998), 56-88..

[23]Radovan Vukadinovic, "American interests in the South Europe," *Croatian International Relations Review* 5:14 (Jan/Mar 99), 11-14.

A. Information Gathering

Although it is true that the situation of states is increasingly complex, government bureaucracies play a part in overwhelming decision-makers with information. They gather more information than the decision-makers can realistically absorb, and by doing so contribute to misperceptions about crises. Moreover, a government bureaucracy is not always in a position to judge the validity, the accuracy or the significance of that information; or it might be biased in its reporting. The state perceives itself and its environment through a mechanism called cognition.

States gather raw information, i.e. information untouched and unadulterated by any processing. At this point, national values already come into play, but only to the extent that they shape how a state perceives itself and its environment. The state analyses the information using the standards that are, as already mentioned, a component of national values. This information can be of two types: either it is endogenous, i.e. the result of a state's internal operations, or it is exogenous, i.e. gleaned from the outside world. Endogenous information includes expectations formulated in previous rounds of decision-making, results of previous strategies or tactics, and conclusions drawn earlier on.[24] Exogenous information includes perceptions of outside threats or opportunities, actions of other states and actions of non-state actors in the international system.

B. Perceptions

Generally speaking, the perceptions of human beings are socially constructed.[25] That is even more true of collectively built perceptions, like a bureaucracy's. State perceptions are formed through the government's quick, acute and intuitive awareness of its environment, but understanding that information is not instant. Like a radio picking up soundwaves within its range, it may simply be passed along without any analysis.

Perceptions, like the state itself, are limited. Since the state can only pick up certain types of information, its perceptions are limited in depth. States will pick up information on military activity or economic activity, but there are certain changes in its situation to which it may not be sensitive.[26] The limitation of a state's depth of perception is inevitable, and only becomes clear when some previously unperceived phenomenon becomes important.

A state's perceptions are also limited in terms of range. Every state operates within certain practical limits, because of limited time, money, or other resources. A state's gathering of information is just as limited as any other activity. Within those limits, however, the state is free. Its choices will reflect the priority that information gathering *in toto* has, but also the areas in which information is required. Those areas reflect what the state prizes just as much. For modern states and modern decision-makers, choices about range of information are difficult: there is increasing pressure on a state's resources because the state is being forced to deal with more and more complicated situations.

This is the first time that national standards come directly into action. Here the state uses cognitive standards to judge whether any particular bit of information is accurate, relevant or

---

[24]Glenn H. Snyder and Paul Diesing, *op. cit.*, 332.

[25]As numerous social and cultural theorists agree. Peter Haas, "Introduction: Epistemic Communities and International Policy Coordination." *International Organization*, 46:1 (Winter 1992), 21.

[26]Changes in the earth's atmosphere is a good example of this phenomenon. The trends towards global warming and the implications for weather and agriculture have been available since the mid-1970s at least. Yet states did not immediately pick out information as significant until years later.

urgent. As available information proliferates and decisions complicate, cognitive standards become more and more important. ". . .[F]acts do not speak for themselves but are assessed through projections . . . two nations with very different backgrounds make highly diverse projections (that is, use quite different lenses)."[27]

If national values shape the perceptions the state has, they also shape the institutions the state creates to reach goals and carry out its decisions. As the embodiment of cherished national values, those institutions are held in high regard. Therefore, those institutions are considered assets to be promoted and protected. Since a state can focus its search for information, it can focus its attention on institutions, to detect threats against them and find opportunities to promote them. In that sense, national values also focus the state's attention on surveillance.[28] Surveillance can be affected by a variety of factors, but the most important limitation on its effectiveness is the scarcity of decision-makers' attention.[29] Given the pressure on them, it is always possible that they will miss a signal at some critical time. This obvious limitation, well beyond state control, raises the level of uncertainty considerably.

C. Information Processing

Processing starts as soon as information is available. The most important task is to identify threats to the state. The breadth of this task depends on how much information is needed. How much information is needed is determined by how powerful the state is in the international system. States are at the apex of power in the international system because and states are at the apex of power in the international system because they also have to ensure their own survival or be seen by its population to be doing so.[30] The quality and quantity of information required is proportional to that responsibility.

To be of use, the information has to be analyzed. Some information is bound to be more important or more accurate than the rest, but to know that, the state has to organize it into digestible bits that are easily manipulated. Once it is broken down, information can be compared with the state's expectations about its opponent's behavior, the various scenarios for the future of the international system, or the responses from non-state actors to its operations.[31] Once that information has been put through the mill, it becomes possible to draw conclusions.

The treatment of information might lead the state to make a decision, but it might not. If the state does make a decision, it might be a decision of tactical, not strategic, importance. If the national strategy is not changed, the information is not necessarily discarded. It can be stored and used at some later date. If the state does take some action, then it sets tangible objectives.

---

[27]Frederick H. Hartmann and Robert L. Wendzel, *Defending America's Security* (Washington: Pergamon-Brassey's, 1988), 23.

[28]On of the conclusions possible, based on John Steinbruner's paradigm, *The Cybernetic Theory of Decision: New Dimensions of Political Analysis* (Princeton: Princeton University Press, 1974), 47-87.

[29]Who would have though that the 1972 shift of anchovy banks off the coast of Chile would be part of a set of circumstances that would eventually set off a world-wide round of inflation?

[30]Zeev Maoz, *op. cit.*, 36-37.

[31]Glenn H. Snyder and Paul Diesing, *op. cit.*, 333-347.

Step 2 Diagnosis -- Mechanism 2, Appreciation

This is what Maoz, Snyder and Diesing call "problem identification."[32] This text uses diagnosis over problem identification because the definition of strategy specifically avoided making conflict the defining characteristic.

As experts in decision-making know, the framing of the question often determines the answer.[33] There are different kinds of threats and opportunities, just like there are different kinds of action. A threat is *strategic* when it puts the continued existence of the country or its values into doubt.[34] An opportunity is strategic when there is a chance to promote national values. The mechanism of appreciation shows how those threats and opportunities are assessed by a state. Appreciation has two parts - preferences and tastes. Appreciation works negatively if the process of decision-making respects a state's preferences and tastes, nothing happens. If it does not, then the state may find it difficult to implement the decision.

A. Preference

Students of decision-making often remark on leaders letting their predilections guide their decisions: preference is an analytical tool that expresses some of the non-rational components in the process. A preference is a state's inclination or bias when it comes to a particular decision in a particular area. By making repeated observations of state decisions, it is possible for an analyst to identify the set of priorities from which the decision-makers are working. If those priorities are not respected, then the state may experience some sort of dissonance or disequilibrium. If it does, then "it will tend to change some aspects of its behaviour until this disequilibrium is reduced. When the inner disequilibrium is fully enough reduced,"[35] the decision-makers can move on. In the extreme cases, implementation of an offending strategy can be prevented. Older states with documented decision-making histories eventually come to be known as having these recurring preferences. At some point, preferences become part of the state's heritage, and then they are called taste.

Preferences are shaped by national appreciative standards. The actual *production* of preferences is similar to the *application* of cognitive standards in the treatment of information. The endogenous information gathered in Step 1 also included information on prefer-

---

[32]Zeev Maoz, *op. cit.*, 36-37; Glenn H. Snyder and Paul Diesing, *op. cit.*, 333-347.

[33]The countries of Western Europe and North America provide a perfect example of that. Throughout the 1960 and 1970s, those countries greatly increased the proportion of GNP spent on providing health and welfare services. That group of states happens to be relatively similar, in terms of their political and economic systems, and their degree of development. When the budgetary crunch came, however, the question was asked in a broad variety of ways: what is a problem of inefficiency of the market system, was the state taking on a role as a capital force, was it taking on too much of a role as a capital force, etc. (Jeanne Kirk Laux and Maureen Molot, *State Capitalism: Public Enterprise in Canada*, Ithaca: Cornell University Press, 1988), *passim)*. The proposed solutions, which were to prove ineffective, largely reflected the parameters of the questions asked in the first place. Threats and opportunities are, as we have already seen, value-defined. After all, what the state protects or promotes is a function of what it prizes.

[34]Colin Gray, *Strategic Studies: A Critical Assessment* (Westport: Greenwood Press, 1982); Ray S. Cline, *World Power Trends and U.S. Foreign Policy for the 1980s* (Boulder: Westview Press, 1980); Donald E. Nuechterlein, *America Recommitted: United States National Interests in a Restructured World* (Lexington: University Press of Kentucky, 1991).

[35]Karl W. Deutsch, *The Analysis of International Relations* (2nd ed. Englewood Cliffs: Prentice-Hall, 1978), 91.

ences. Because there is so much information available, and because that information varies a good deal in terms of accuracy, it needs to be culled, or the state would waste precious time and energy analyzing everything. The information had to be organized first, then broken down into digestible bits and analyzed. At some point in the analysis, it becomes clear that the information is triggering reactions from the state as a whole, like organizational memories, collective fears or collective inclinations. Decision-makers, who feel the hegemony of national values as keenly as anybody else, share these collective reactions. The information produced by the reactions is processed along with other types of endogenous information. It is eventually compared with expectations of the state about its own reactions, and uses it to draw conclusions.[36] The state decides whether this information confirms its existing priorities and whether to store the information, change the set of priorities, or take action.

B. Taste

When analysts conclude that leaders choose options consonant with their own values more often than not, those scholars are making indirect reference to tastes.[37] Taste is a disposition, rooted in the political culture of a state, that expresses itself as an intense propensity. Taste makes a subtle but significant difference in decision-making: it works to exclude from the agenda those options which offend a society *before* the better-known, more rational operations take place. Because it appears to be permanent, non-rational characteristic of a state, it is tempting to put taste in the same category as national character, or national style;[38] indeed the three phenomena are often confused in the literature. This is the point where the risk of stereotyping some cultures, present in any study of national values, is at its greatest. A national stereotype is a perception of a particular state by others; national values, standards or tastes, can only be inferred about a state from historical observation. Taste can even influence the entire political culture, if it is prominent enough, e.g. the French taste for symbolism.[39] Once it is in place, taste can eventually become an unreflective response. Appreciation as a whole is the basis for a state's strategic approach. (See Figure 4).

Step 3 Search for Options -- Mechanism 3, Evaluation, Part I

Now, the state has to set its objectives, so that it can consider various courses of actions that will reach them. Generally, objectives reflect the desires of the population if there are no immediate or intense threats to the state, a state's first aim being the protection of the national heritage. If it is not in jeopardy, the shorter-term objectives vary according to values and desires. Although objectives are not directly affected by national standards, various options developed to meet them are.

National standards are pivotal in the early rejection of unorthodox or "impossible" options: these options are judged to be either too different from the state's usual behavior, or too unlikely to be successful. These sub-decisions in the process of considering options are made on the basis of appreciative standards. They are discounted so early that they never

---

[36]Glenn H. Snyder and Paul Diesing, *op. cit.*, 333-347.

[37]Zeev Maoz, *op. cit.*, 72.

[38]Glenn H. Snyder and Paul Diesing, *op. cit.*, 333-347.

[39]Dorothy Pickles, "Political Imperatives and Dilemmas of French Defence Policies," *West European Politics* 1:3 (Oct 1978), 115-143,121.

figure on the leaders' agenda, the winnowing being important because a state can only consider so many options at a time. The early selection of options may be unreflective or rigid, and it might eliminate from consideration some valid strategies.[40]

The next sub-decision a state faces is whether or not it will use a strategy, as opposed to a plan, a policy, a program or just "muddling through."[41] Strategic action has some very real advantages (flexibility, adaptability), but it requires a considerable investment of decision-makers' time and money. The decision about *not* using strategy can be unconscious or inadvertent: a state may have varying degrees of skill in decision-making. But no matter what happens, it is always in the state's best interest to consider a broad range of options.

After a narrow first selection, decision-makers search far and wide for strategic options.[42] Sources for these options include: the logical possibilities present in the actual situation;[43] successful past strategies;[44] individual ingenuity in office and biases or preconceived notions officials advocate or endorse.[45] The search for options occurs regardless of whether the process of decision-making is orderly (not all states use processes of decision-making that are clearly identified or determined). Even if a state is more of a firefighter than a strategist, unstated, unconscious or un-admitted national values can be at work.

Step 4 Estimation of Expected Outcomes -- Mechanism 3, Evaluation, Part II

When decisions are made in the present, they usually rely on some projections about the future. Those projections are based in part on imperfect information and analysis. Projections perforce reflect some guesswork and some biases introduced by the decision-makers's most basic assumptions about the world, including national values. National values come into play in two specific ways: (1) in judging which outcomes are acceptable at all; and (2) in judging which outcomes are the more desirable. Accepting outcomes is based on experience, while desiring outcomes is based on learning.

A. Experience

National standards develop early in the state's history and slowly evolve: they are the basis on which a state can analyze its experiences and build on its learning. Experience is the skill, wisdom, practice or knowledge gained through direct observation or participation in events, particular activity or in affairs generally. The state uses experience to draw conclusions from previous decisions that are incorporated into the decision-making process.[46]

Experience plays more or less the same role in evaluation as perceptions do in cognition. The difference is that experience uses information endogenous to the state, i.e. produced by

---

[40]Glenn H. Snyder and Paul Diesing, *op. cit.*, 333-347.

[41]Charles Lindblom, *op. cit.*, 79.

[42]Zeev Maoz, *op. cit.*, 32-40.

[43]Glenn H. Snyder and Paul Diesing, *op. cit.*, 333-347.

[44]Glenn H. Snyder and Paul Diesing, *op. cit.*, 333-347.

[45]Glenn H. Snyder and Paul Diesing, *op. cit.*, 333-347.

[46]Here a methodological observation is in order. It is significant that experience is a factor in the drawing of conclusions, an operation carried out by the mechanism of evaluation. Although this theory presents each mechanism as coming into play at different steps of the decision-making process, in fact each of them come into play repeatedly throughout the entire theory. The representation here is simplified (Zeev Maoz, *op. cit.*, 32-40).

the state's activities, rather than raw information, gleaned from the outside world. Endogenous information does not become available regularly: when it does, it is analyzed. As it is being culled, only the information judged relevant is retained. Since there is more information than the state can handle, the uncertainty comes not just from lack of the right information, but from the lack of understanding properly what that information means. The information has to be organized into digestible bits and analyzed for patterns and relationships. It can then be compared to the expectations formulated earlier.[47] Conclusions are drawn from the comparison: either they confirm the existing set of priorities implicit in national values, or they do not. The state then either stores the information, modifies its own grid or takes the decision to move to the next step.

B. Learning

Learning is a modification of a behavioral tendency by experience.[48] The phenomenon of learning has been observed in the international system: "National leaders who fail to adjust policies to changing circumstances will eventually be faced with ineffective policies and, perhaps, loss of personal authority and power."[49] But there are also obstacles to learning. Breslauer and Tetlock have identified a number of them, including a complex and constantly changing international environment, the limitations of human beings as processors of information.[50] Philip Tetlock goes on to identify more general problems in dealing with state learning:

1. observers may confuse learning with adaptation, competition, or the random ebb and flow of events;
2. observers may falsely conclude that learning occurred because they underestimated what policy makers knew in the first place;
3. observers may allow their own political biases to colour their judgments.[51]

There are several distinct theories about state learning. Cognitive theorists suggest that learning entails increased differentiation and integration of mental structures (schemata). Political scientists usually adopt this approach, although they make a distinction between what states come to know and what they come to believe.[52] The theory proposed here suggests that learning contributes endogenous information to the decision-making process. This information is internally consistent only to the extent that the state's population is itself consistent. It contributes to the creation of taste in the same way that processing information

---

[47]Glenn H. Snyder and Paul Diesing, op. cit., 333-347.

[48]Hadley Cantril's research emphasizes the importance of understanding the frame of mind of the people with whom government must deal at home and abroad. Peter Haas infers learning from policy change: policy evolves not just because circumstances do, but because states will draw lessons and conclusions from their experiences. See the special issue of International Organization 46:1 (Winter 1992), Peter Haas, ed.

[49]George W. Breslauer and Philip E. Tetlock. "Introduction," chapter in Learning in U.S. and Soviet Foreign Policy, George W. Breslauer and Philip E. Tetlock (ed.) (San Francisco: Westview, 1991), 3.

[50]George W. Breslauer and Philip E. Tetlock, "Introduction," in Learning in U.S. and Soviet Foreign Policy (San Francisco: Westview, 1991), 4.

[51]Philip E. Tetlock, "Learning in U.S. and Soviet Foreign Policy: In Search of an Elusive Concept," chapter in Learning in U.S. and Soviet Foreign Policy, George W. Breslauer and Philip E. Tetlock, ed. (San Francisco: Westview, 1991), 44.

[52]George W. Breslauer and Philip E. Tetlock, op. cit., 8 and 9.

contributed to learning, i.e. incrementally. Learning also builds reflex responses. The conclusions drawn from various individual experiences accumulate. Some similarity of circumstances in the current situation triggers a link with the past. Conclusions drawn then are retrieved, as endogenous information. The relevance of the experience is determined, and that information is included in the ongoing decision-making process. State behavior may be changed by learning or it may not. If it is, then learning is obvious; but that is not always the case. Previous conclusions may or may not be confirmed: either way that information could be retained.

Step 5 Assessment of Strategic Options

At this stage, the state looks at each option's material and nonmaterial costs and bene-fits.[53] There is no agreement in the literature about the number of options a state can seriously consider, but they do agree they are limited.[54]

Step 6 Choice of Strategy

There have been sub-decisions to be made all through this process. Now the state must decide to either adopt a new strategy or revise the old one. The choice depends on the challenge facing the state.[55] There are a number of possibilities: (1) situations that are intolerable; (2) situations that deteriorate or become intolerable over the years; (3) long-standing intolerable situations that can finally be improved; or (4) " . . . a massive input of new information [that] breaks through the barrier of the image and makes a decision maker realize that his diagnosis and expectations were somehow radically wrong and must be corrected."[56] If the state opts for revisions, it will be through trial and error.[57] If it opts for a new strategy, it moves to the next step.

Step 7 Choice of Tactics

When decision-makers opt for strategy, their needs for information become much more specific (they are not necessarily met). Options about tactics are limited only by a state's resources. Once selected, the state coordinates them, allocates resources, plans for their implementation and absorbs feedback.

---

[53]Zeev Maoz, *op. cit.*, 32-40.
[54]According to Snyder and Diesing, the best alternative is necessarily selected from an infinite set of possibilities. Amitai Etzioni is a proponent of mixed scanning, where the best alternative is chosen by scanning two or three alternatives and carefully comparing them. (Glenn H. Snyder and Paul Diesing, *op. cit.*, 333-347)
[55]Glenn H. Snyder and Paul Diesing, *op. cit.*, 333-347.
[56]Glenn H. Snyder and Paul Diesing, *op. cit.*, 397.
[57]Glenn H. Snyder and Paul Diesing, *op. cit.*, 333-347.

Step 8 Implementation of Strategy

Implementation is itself a process at least as complex as decision-making. Although it certainly deserves detailed study, it is beyond the scope of the present book.

Step 9 Confirmation, Change or Adjustment of Tactics

Information gathered and analyzed at this stage feeds back to Step 3, Search for Options. The state only re-evaluates its position once it receives feedback. Both reevaluation and change require resources, which are always committed. There may also be some bureaucratic resistance to adjustments.

Step 10 Confirmation, Change or Adjustment of Strategy

This last step feeds back to Step 6, Choice of Strategy. As the state digests the latest information, it either confirms, adjusts, or abandons the whole strategy. If it abandons the strategy, then the state starts the decision-making process all over again. It is possible that it will reach the same conclusion over again: states have been known to repeat unsuccessful strategies as much as successful ones.[58]

IV. THE METHOD

The process of analysis can be broken into four steps. The first step involves the identification of a sea-change in national policies, usually a reliable indication of the last time a new strategy was introduced. Such major shifts in direction are often accompanied by major social upheavals. Russia's, for instance, was easy to identify following the disintegration of the former USSR. Step 2 involves the identification of the new tactics introduced with the new grand strategy. These tactics are the most obvious manifestations of a new strategy. By tactics I refer to the means at a state's (or any actor in the political sphere's) disposal. This stage of the analysis looks for changes in the economic, military, diplomatic, and political spheres, and they also usually provide the material for identifying the values. Values are a key factor in determining the long-term compatibility of strategies, since my own previous research shows that they underpin the entire grand strategy. The identification of values also helps narrow the range of possibilities that must be considered.

For the purposes of this analysis, national values are defined as the accepted standards of historical or ideological origin as well as the national heritage cherished by the population as a whole. This analysis is best served by a classification adapted from Talcott Parsons' classification of social values: (1) self-orientation versus collectivity-orientation; and (2) materialism versus non-materialism.[59] The third step examines the declaratory policy or

---

[58]Glenn H. Snyder and Paul Diesing, *op. cit.*, 333-347.

[59]Talcott Parsons' classification in R.F. Bales, Edward Shils and Talcott Parsons, *Working Papers in the Theory of Action* (Glencoe: Free Press, 1953), *passim*; Michael Sullivan, *Measuring Global Values* (New York: Greenwood, s.d.), *passim*.

political rhetoric (official documents, speech, debates in the legislatures, etc.) in order to identify the goals of the national strategy.

A. Identifying Strategy

National strategy is defined as the comprehensive direction of all the elements of national power to attain national objectives, and to support and pursue the general goals provided by a nation's leaders. It can be identified by answering three questions.

(1) Is a Particular State Using Strategy? The trick here is to tell a strategy apart from a plan, policy or program. Plans, policies and programs organize means to an end as much as a strategy does. But strategy is both an idea and an action, while plans, policies and programs are not. A state using strategy is much likelier to use slogans or strong images. A state using plans, policies and programs does not rely on slogans or strong images.

(2) Is the State Using a National Strategy? A strategy is national when it uses a broad spectrum of the means available to the state, and tries to achieve objectives important to the whole rather than to parts.[60] In other words, the strategy must cut across several areas of state behaviour: economic, political, cultural, military, etc.

(3) What Strategy is the State Using? It is not easy to pick out the exact strategy a state is using from so many possibilities. The best way to proceed is to start by reducing the number of possibilities one has to consider, i.e. by identifying the type of strategy.

B. Identifying the Type of Strategy

André Beaufre's categories of strategy classify them according to their nature: direct strategy of action, direct strategy of persuasion, indirect strategy of action, indirect strategy of persuasion. The difference between strategy of action and strategy of persuasion is straightforward: the first involves physical engagement of the state's material resources, while the second involves threats, discourse, posturing -- all means and actions that require non-material resources. The difference between a direct strategy and an indirect one is not quite so obvious: a direct strategy is one that changes the opponent's direction or momentum itself; an indirect strategy changes the opponent's direction using an intermediary. Once the type of strategy is identified, then only those possibilities need be considered. The next step is to identify the components of strategy, each by its own preferred source of information:

(1)   goal, by analysis of official statements;[61]
(2)   means or tactics, by direct observation;
(3)   style, by secondary analysis; and
(4)   core idea, by analysis of official statements, although this is not always possible.[62]

---

[60]Ray S. Cline, *World Power Trends and U.S. Foreign Policy for the 1980s* (Boulder: Westview Press, 1980), 2.

[61]Although he calls it aims; F.B. Ali, "The Principles of War", *Journal of the Royal United Services Institution for Defence Studies* 108 (May 1963), 159-165.

[62]"The entirety of traditional practices and habits of thinking which, in a society, governs the organization and the use of the military forces in the pursuit of political objectives." Author's translation, as quoted by

The fourth step identifies the strategy itself, the identification of values having provided us with the type of strategy possible. It is possible that the strategy is made explicit in the declaratory policy of a state, but if not the strategy can be identified by its characteristics. Typically, a national strategy encompasses a number of spheres. It is also true that the best strategies are not made public or even explicit in sources available to the scholar. Also, some states like Canada or South Korea in the 1990s, have no particular strategy. They simply drift, rely on incremental policy- or decision-making, or crisis management.

C. Compatibility of States

A study is now necessary to develop the understanding of the small states and PFP countries' defense posture. The analytical framework used for this project is one that uses a general theory of strategy. A general theory of strategy allows scholars to explain or predict national strategies based on certain stable social characteristics. At this time, there is only one general theory of strategy, Jean-Paul Charnay's. Unfortunately, this theory is so abstract that it is difficult to use for the purposes of strategic analysis; in any event, it has been published only in French. I developed a methodology for strategic theory-building in my previous work, and used it to develop one pillar of a new general theory of strategy: the interactions between national values and national strategy. That particular section of the theory has been tested against eight case studies (France, Russia, mainland China, Canada, the ROC, the ROK, the DPRK, the US). Among the possible applications for the theory are: the prediction of national strategies, the explanation of national strategies, understanding strategic decision-making, allowing decision-makers to tailor strategies to national values or interests. The small states and PfP Countries have necessarily redefined its place in the post-Cold War world. National values can be identified through the method developed in earlier work, using sociological data, while national strategy can be identified using content analysis of interviews.

Students of International Relations are usually reluctant to work with the idea of values, because they find them too subjective. National values can be determined by inferring from history, analyzing attitudes, behavior, or ideology, using psychological insights, studying institutional and ideological norms, analyzing economic and social conditions or through content analysis of rituals, literature and films, linguistic analysis or analysis of cultural thought-systems. Historical analysis is the method of choice because it deflects traditional objections about political culture's subjectivity. Historical analysis identifies "patterns of action"[63] in state behavior by inferring from historical events, in this case from series of decisions made by states in a particular area over time. The sounder the strategy and the more established the values, the more effective historical analysis is likely to be.

National strategy is identified by gathering evidence to answer three questions: (1) Is a particular state using strategy? Plans, policies and programs organize means to an end as much as a strategy does. But strategy is both an idea and an action, while plans, policies and programs are not. Also, a state using strategy is much likelier to use slogans or strong images: plans, policies and programs do not. (2) Is the state using a national strategy? A strategy is

Bruno Colson, "La culture stratégique américaine", *Stratégique* 8 (1988), 15-82, 33. The original reads: "l'ensemble des pratiques traditionnelles et des habitudes de pensée qui, dans une société, gouvernent l'organisation et l'emploi de la force militaire au service d'objectifs politiques."
[63] Julian Lider, *op. cit.*

national when it uses a broad spectrum of the means available to the state, and tries to achieve objectives important to the whole rather than to parts. In other words, the strategy must cut across several areas of state behavior: economic, political, cultural, military, etc. (3)What strategy is the state using? Here, one identifies first the type, then the components of strategy being used.

In the case of Bulgaria, Romania, Poland and the Czech Republic, research includes both documentary sources and interviews with opinion leaders and policy-makers. It will be conducted using (a) official sources: research bureaus within the ministries of defense, of foreign affairs, of national defense colleges and any government research institutes; (b) political sources: partisan thinkers or researchers, political parties' policy wing; and (c) academic sources. Because of the framework of analysis is original, it is not possible to rely exclusively on documentary sources. The organization, selection and inclusion of information in documents reflect prevailing patterns of thought, which may or may not include information crucial to this investigation. Direct sources are therefore essential. The principal investigator is experienced in the use and assessment of these direct sources.

D. Compatibility of National Strategies

With the end of the Cold War, the prospects for improved relations between the small states and PfP countries and NATO were good. This study proposes to examine the international posture of each state, or national strategy, as a function of their long-term social characteristics, or national values, to see whether these postures are compatible, and therefore a support to future reunification, or incompatible, and therefore a drag on that prospect.

This project examines the strategic interactions between various larger NATO countries and small states and the PfP countries. It provides a number of significant insights into the stabilization of middle Europe. The study of strategic interaction focuses on the analysis, at both the global and the component level, of the national strategies of various countries. Two national strategies can interact in a number of ways: they can be neutral, identical, synergistic, cooperative, complementary, competitive, or antithetical. Table 1 (Possibilities of Strategic Interactions) discusses each of these possibilities in which detail, which can occur in varying degrees of intensity.

Compatibility exists when the two strategies are identical, neutral or cooperative, complementary or synergistic at the global and the component level. Some components' interactions are more important than others, just as compatibility of certain components is essential to the compatible interactions of strategies. Some components' interactions are more important than others, just as compatibility of certain components is essential to the compatible interactions of strategies. For instance, if the style not compatible, it is harder for strategies to be synergistic because it is harder to communicate with each other. Misunderstandings can spring up more easily, but still it is possible to work since addressing different populations. If the values are incompatible, however, then relations are quite likely to have conflict. It will also be more difficult to mobilize the population, in the case of liberal democracies at least, to accomplish the strategy. For any proposals for reunification to be successful, therefore, the national strategies must at least be neutral and preferably mutually reinforcing. So far, the proposals for reunification have not been either.

Any of the components of strategy (goals, tactics, styles, core ideas) can interact, and any of these interactions can range among the possibilities outlined above. It is easy to envisage complementary interactions if one country's goals are direct, and the other indirect, if tactics are material on one side and non-material on the other, and so on. For other components, like the core idea, the components are so central or so basic to the nature of the strategy that any significant positive interaction necessitates the strategies being mutually known and mutually understood. Problems arise when this is not the case.

The type of interaction may change if the strategy of one state changes. The type of interaction may also change if any of the components of the strategy change. Certain components change less frequently than others: values do not change frequently, but tactics can and do. The duration of various types of interactions, therefore, depends on the durability of the strategic components. At times the documentation is sketchy or the evidence contradictory, and the conclusions are more tentative.

Table 1: Possibilities for Strategic Interaction

possibility	Description	example
neutrality	Strategies do not affect each other	two countries completely isolated from each other
identity	2 strategies are identical	bloc or alliance strategy
synergy	when one national strategy reinforces the other	Franco-German proposal for joint brigade as nucleus for new EC armed forces
cooperation	deliberate, conscious common strategy addressing mutual concern	Canada-US joint surveillance of Far North
complementarity	2 strategies address different concerns but in harmony with each other	Japan and US position on North Korea nuclear issue
competition	two national strategies in a contest when combined success is impossible	PRC and ROC's policies of membership in UN
antithesis	two strategies in conflict	US and ex-USSR during early Cold War

PART 2.

I. ANALYSIS OF THE NORTH ATLANTIC TREATY ORGANIZATION

NATO policy is set by the North Atlantic Council, made up of the nineteen member states, which can meet at the level of permanent representatives, ministers of foreign affairs, or heads of state and government. The council has effective political and decision-making authority at all levels. Ministerial meetings are held at least twice a year. Permanent representatives meet at least once a week. The Secretary General of NATO is chairman, and decisions are taken by common consent, not majority vote. The council is a forum for wide consultation between member governments on major issues, including political, military, economic and other questions. The Council is supported by the Senior or regular Political Committee and the Military Committee.

The common security policy of the members is to safeguard peace through political solidarity and defense at the lowest level of military forces needed to deter all aggression. Cooperation in science and technology as well as environmental issues takes place in the NATO Science Committee. After the Warsaw Pact formally dissolved on July 1, 1991,

NATO undertook a fundamental transformation of its structures and policies to meet its new challenges.

II. INDEPENDENT VARIABLES

A. Organization Value #1: A Surprise End to Narrow Self-Interest

During the Cold War, the allies were uncommonly united. NATO's actions were always clearly limited to members' interest. Since the end of the cold War, many decisions made have been outside the immediate interests of members. Not only has the membership and the terms of reference expanded, but so has its definition of self-interest: it has moved from individualism to communitarianism.

At first, the Alliance was cautious. Even after the Soviet Union had announced substantial reductions in arms, in December 1988, NATO declined to abandon plans to upgrade or replace short-range nuclear missiles in Europe. The Warsaw Pact took the lead by publishing a detailed analysis of its military strength in Europe for the first time in its history, in January 1989. Predictably, NATO figures for Pact strength differed sharply, and Warsaw Pact officials called the NATO figures tendentious and selective. Nonetheless, at the July 1989 Council of Europe, Gorbachev announced the USSR would allow Warsaw Pact members to determine their own political future and pressed NATO to reduce its nuclear arsenal. In January 1990, senior military leaders from NATO met with their Warsaw Pact counterparts to discuss lessening military tensions in Europe. In June 1991, the North Atlantic Council announced the Partnership for Peace with the countries of Central and Eastern Europe committing themselves to:

- Organizing meetings of officials and experts on security policy issues, military strategy and doctrine, and other current topics.
- Intensifying military contacts between senior NATO military authorities and their counterparts in central and East European states, and invitations to military training facilities for special familiarisation programs.
- Including Central and East European experts in certain Alliance activities, including those relating to scientific and environmental programs and airspace management.
- Gradually expanding NATO's information programs, support for discussion of security issues in a democratic context, invitations to parliamentary, education and media groups and delegations of young leaders to visit NATO headquarters.
- Encouraging greater contacts between North Atlantic Assembly and various Parliaments.[64]

The foregoing developments show the broadening of self-interest, as do the decisions recounted below.

---

[64]*Partnership with the Countries of Central and Eastern Europe*, Statement issued by the North Atlantic Council Meeting in Ministerial Session, Copenhagen 6-7 1991, http://www.fas.org/man/nato/natodocs/bt-pfp.html.

Meeting in Sicily in October 1991, NATO defense ministers announced that the alliance would destroy 700 of its 1400 nuclear warheads in Europe. In March 1993, the North Atlantic Cooperation Council, established in 1992 as a forum where NATO members could meet with representatives from Eastern European countries and the former Soviet republics, met in Brussels. Members agreed on international mediation and possible NATO military involvement in the conflict in Azerbaijan. In Vienna, all NATO members plus Belarus, Bulgaria, Czechoslovakia, Hungary, Poland, Romania, Russia and Ukraine signed the Open Skies Treaty, allowing limited flights over national territory by foreign reconnaissance aircraft. In April 1993, Secretary General Manfred Woerner announced NATO's willingness to enforce the UN ban on military flights over Bosnia and Herzegovina, the first authorized use of force in a non-member state ever.[65]

At a January 1994 summit, NATO members established a plan for air strikes in the Bosnian war, subject to specific conditions. Among other conditions, the strikes had to be requested by UN commanders in Bosnia and approved by the UN Secretary General, Boutros Boutros-Ghali. NATO also announced plans to open the airport near Sarajevo for relief flights. A number of air attacks enforcing various agreements followed. After a peace plan was signed in November 1995 in Dayton, NATO deployed 60,000 troops from the US, France, Britain and other countries to keep the peace, taking over from UN peacekeepers in Bosnia that December.

That same month, NATO's foreign ministers approved the inclusion of unnamed formerly Communist Eastern European nations in the Alliance. The ministers also offered Russia a special charter and increased military cooperation and pledged that NATO would not move nuclear weapons into Eastern Europe. Russian Foreign Minister Yevgeny Primakov accepted the, but restated Russia's opposition to NATO expansion. US Secretary of State Madeleine Albright formally proposed NATO expansion to the east in February 1997, along with steep conventional weapons reductions in Central and Eastern Europe, and a joint NATO-Russian peacekeeping unit.

In May 1997, NATO Secretary General Javier Solana and Russian Foreign Minister Primakov reached an agreement on NATO expansion. NATO agreed to establish a special NATO-Russia council to discuss security issues. NATO also pledged not to establish nuclear storage sites in new member states. In July 1997, NATO formally invited former Warsaw Pact members Poland, Czech Republic and Hungary to join.

An exhaustive discussion of the Kosovo crisis is beyond the scope of this report. However, the crisis indicates the shift in values of the Alliance.

B. Organization Value #2: Veering Toward Dialogue

The nature of all military alliances is clearly materialistic, especially when contrasted with the more symbolic role of the UN. In recent year, NATO embraced increasing numbers of non-force related activities i.e. dialogues. Even during the Cold War, the Alliance more positive relations with the Soviet Union and the Warsaw Pact. The Harmel Report, published in 1967, established defense and dialogue, including arms control, as the dual pillars of the

---

[65]NATO Washington Summit - Fact Sheet on Defence Capabilities Initiative, http://www.fas.orgman/natodocs/99042408.html.

Alliance's approach to security. Today, the alliance pursues security through collective defense, conflict resolution and dialogue on European security and arms control.

III. THE DEPENDENT VARIABLES: STRATEGIC AND TACTICS

A. The Previous Strategy

The goal of NATO during the Cold War was to safeguard peace through political solidarity and collective defense. NATO still conducts an annual defense review to assess each country's contribution to the common defense in relation to their respective capabilities and constraints.

The initial formulation of NATO strategy was known as The Strategic Concept for the Defence of the North Atlantic Area. Developed between October 1949 and April 1950, it set out a strategy of large-scale operations for territorial defense. In the mid-1950s the strategy of massive retaliation was developed. It emphasized deterrence based on the threat that NATO would respond to any aggression against its member countries by every means at its disposal, specifically including nuclear weapons. Discussions of possible changes in this strategic approach began later in the 1950s and continued until 1967 when massive retaliation was replaced by flexible response. Flexible response concentrated on giving NATO the advantages of flexibility and of creating uncertainty in the minds of any potential aggressor about NATO's response to threats to its sovereignty or independence. The concept was designed to ensure that aggression of any kind would be perceived as involving unacceptable risks. The above strategies were enshrined in classified documents, which provided guidance to national governments and points of reference for military planning activities.

B. The New Strategy

With the end of the Cold War era, the political situation in Europe and the overall military situation were transformed. A new Strategic Concept evolved during the two years following the fall of the Berlin Wall. Bearing little relation to previous concepts, it emphasized cooperation with former adversaries as opposed to confrontation. It maintained security as NATO's fundamental purpose but combined it with the obligation to work toward security for Europe as a whole. The 1991 Strategic Concept was also issued as a public document. In 1997, NATO leaders agreed that the Concept should be reexamined and updated to reflect the changes that had taken place in Europe since its adoption.

The risks to Allied security that remained were multifaceted and multidirectional, which made them hard to predict or assess. Risks were now more likely to come from instabilities due to economic, social, and political difficulties, including ethnic rivalries and territorial disputes in Central and Eastern Europe.

C. The Prediction

The historic changes that have occurred in Europe, which have led to the fulfillment of a number of objectives set out in the Harmel Report, have significantly improved the overall security of the Allies. The monolithic, massive, and potentially immediate threat which was the principal concern of the Alliance in its first forty years has disappeared. On the other hand, a great deal of uncertainty about the future and risks to the security of the Alliance remained.

This makes NATO an excellent case study for the validity of a theory that predicts a communitarian organization will adopt an indirect strategy, and a non-materialist organization will take on a strategy of suasion. In the case of NATO, therefore, there will be an indirect strategy of suasion. As we study other countries, we will be able to determine the degree of compatibility with NATO's strategy.

D. Components of Strategy

1. The Goal

NATO's essential purpose, set out in the Washington Treaty and reiterated in the London Declaration, is to safeguard the freedom and security of all its members by political and military means in accordance with the principles of the United Nations Charter.

To achieve its purpose, the Alliance performs the following fundamental tasks:

- To provide part of a foundation for security in Europe, based on democracy and peaceful dispute resolution, in which no country could coerce any European nation through force.
- To serve as a transatlantic forum on any issues that affect members' vital interests, including risks to security, and for co-ordination in fields of common concern.
- To deter and defend the territory of any NATO member state.
- To preserve the strategic balance within Europe.

2. The Style

Common commitment and mutual cooperation among sovereign states support the indivisible security for all members. Without depriving members of sovereignty in defense, NATO's collective effort enhances their ability to realize their security objectives. This contributes to stability in Europe, and promotes cooperation between Alliance members and with others. The diversity of challenges now facing the Alliance has led to a broad approach to security, although the Alliance is purely defensive. Roles, responsibilities, and risks are shared equitably, but not equally. NATO is first and always a nuclear alliance.

The new Strategic Concept of NATO included the following five principles:

1. Effective engagement: the ability to engage effectively with appropriate assets in a number of different areas, including humanitarian assistance, force protection and high-intensity combat;
2. Deployability and mobility: the ability to move forces efficiently and effectively;
3. Sustainability and logistics: the ability to sustain engagements by delivering supplies and support equipment in a timely, organized manner, supporting prolonged operations through rotation of forces;
4. Survivability: the ability to survive and operate in a wide range of environments, including chemical, biological, terrorist, or electronic attacks; and

5. Command, control and communication: the ability to establish and maintain effective command and control arrangements and communications links, interoperable with national systems and including a deployable capability for crisis response operations.

3. The Core Idea

The new NATO has become the central player in the creation of a new security order in Europe.[66] Its core idea is to protect peace in a new Europe using three mutually reinforcing elements of Allied security policy: dialogue, cooperation, and collective defense.

4. The Tactics

Military capability is what prevents coercion or intimidation, and to guarantees that aggression can never be perceived as possibly successful. It is a condition of successful dialogue and cooperation.

(a)Collective Defense
i) The Role of the Armed Forces

The primary role of Alliance military forces is still to guarantee the security and territorial integrity of member states. In peace, the role of Allied military forces is to guard against risks, to maintain stability and balance in Europe and to preserve the peace.

In the event of military crises, the Alliance's forces complement and reinforce political actions within a broad approach to security. For this reason, the forces must have a capability for measured and timely response, for deterring actions against any Ally, and for repelling any attack and restoring the territory of member states. The Alliance's military forces are at the minimum level necessary to prevent war of any kind. The size, readiness, availability, flexibility, mobility and deployment of the Alliance's forces are strictly defensive and adapt as needed to meet arms control agreements or transparency and complementarity with the ESDI. Collective defense arrangements make more efficient use of scarce defense resources.

(ii) Characteristics of Nuclear Forces

Strategic nuclear forces are the supreme guarantee. A credible nuclear posture requires widespread participation in nuclear planning, basing of nuclear forces, command, control and consultation arrangements, flexibility and survivability. Any use of nuclear weapons is made more remote by the efforts toward dialogue and cooperation. Sub-strategic forces based in Europe linking with strategic nuclear forces elsewhere consist only of dual capable aircraft supplemented by offshore systems. There are no surface vessels, attack submarines, nuclear artillery or ground-launched short range nuclear missiles.

(b) Dialogue and Cooperation

The Alliance has been restructured in order to participate in European cooperative security structures. Its political and military structures are now adapted to peacekeeping and crisis management in cooperation with non-member countries and international organizations. The Allies support the CSCE process and its institutions. The Allies recognize that other

---

[66]Eva Feldmann and Sven Bernhard Gareis, "Poland's Role in NATO: The Significance of Foreign Assistance for the Stabilization of Eastern Europe," *Zeitschrift fur Politikwissenschaft* 8:3 (1998), 983-1003, *passim*.

bodies, including the EU, the Western European Union (WEU) and the UN may also have an important role to play. Through initiatives such as the creation of the North Atlantic Cooperation Council (NACC) and Partnership for Peace (PfP), and the establishment of a new Euro-Atlantic Partnership Council (EAPC), member countries opened up to new forms of partnership and cooperation with other countries.

i) European Security and Defence Identity

NATO supports the development of the European Security and Defence Identity (ESDI) and the Combined Joint Task Force (CJTFs)as part of adapting NATO to the new Europe. The Treaty on European Union signed at Maastricht in December 1991 identified the WEU as a ways to strengthen the European pillar of the Alliance. The WEU's job is to elaborate and implement defense-related decisions and actions of the European Union. The Alliance makes collective NATO assets available for WEU operations undertaken under the Common Foreign and Security Policy. The Combined Joint Task Forces (CJTFs) develop separable but not separate multinational capabilities which could be deployed either by NATO or the WEU.

ii) Euro-Atlantic Peace Council

When NATO and Partner countries met to inaugurate the EAPC in June 1997, NATO and Russia had just signed a historic agreement on their future relations, and the NATO-Ukraine Charter was initialed. The EAPC builds on political and military cooperation established under the NACC and the PfP. It provides a forum for consultation on political and security matters with the countries of Central and Eastern Europe, including former Soviet republics. The EAPC Council meets monthly at the ambassadorial level, and twice a year at the ministerial level. All former NACC members and PfP countries are members. Other OSCE participating states may also become members by joining the PfP. Member Countries include the 19 NATO members plus Albania, Armenia, Austria, Azerbaijan, Belarus, Bulgaria, Croatia, Estonia, Finland, Georgia, Ireland, Kazakhstan, Kyrgyz Republic, Latvia, Lithuania, Moldova, Romania, Russia, Slovakia, Slovenia, Sweden, Switzerland, the former Yugoslav Republic of Macedonia, Tajikistan, Turkmenistan, and Ukraine.

iii) Partnership for Peace

In January 1994, NATO invited NACC and other OSCE countries to join a Partnership for Peace (PfP). This partnership was designed to forge working partnerships between the Alliance and participating states. Practical cooperation expands political and military cooperation and strengthening security relationships, leading to greater stability and fewer risks. Cooperation within PfP helps transparency in national defense planning and budgets, and supports the democratic control of defense forces. Participating countries contribute to UN or OSCE operations and engage in joint peacekeeping, search and rescue, humanitarian operations and other areas. The PfP made the creation of the multinational Implementation Force (IFOR) to enforce the Bosnian peace agreement much easier. Fifteen PfP countries are also participating in the NATO-led Stabilisation Force (SFOR). The Partnership Coordination Cell plans PfP military exercises. The 26 PfP Countries are: Albania, Armenia, Austria, Azerbaijan, Belarus, Bulgaria, Croatia, Estonia, Finland, Georgia, Ireland, Kazakhstan, Kyrgyz Republic, Latvia, Lithuania, Moldova, Romania, Russia, Slovakia, Slovenia, Sweden, Switzerland, the former Yugoslav Republic of Macedonia, Turkmenistan, Ukraine, and Uzbekistan.

iv) Mediterranean Dialogue

In 1994, NATO initiated a dialogue with Egypt, Israel, Jordan, Mauritania, Morocco and Tunisia, with Algeria becoming a participant in March 2000. The Dialogue supports good relations and better mutual understanding throughout the Mediterranean, as well as promoting regional security and stability, based on the Alliance's recognition that security in the whole of Europe is closely linked to security and stability in the Mediterranean.

v) Dialogue with Russia

On 27 May 1997, NATO and Russia signed the "Founding Act on Mutual Relations, Cooperation and Security between NATO and the Russian Federation." In addition to agreeing on principles and designating specific areas for political and military cooperation, the Founding Act establishes the NATO-Russia Permanent Joint Council, an organ for consultation, cooperation and consensus-building.

vi) Organization for Security and Confidence in Europe

Formerly known as the Conference on Security and Cooperation in Europe (CSCE), the OSCE has the status of a "Regional Organisation" under Chapter VIII of the UN Charter. All the countries of Europe plus Canada and the US come under a common broad concept of security, including human rights and freedoms, democracy and the rule of law.

The OSCE has promoted dialogue and cooperation between its members and introduced confidence and security-building measures in military affairs. The 1992 Helsinki Summit expanded its role in peacekeeping, early warning and crisis management, which in turn led to close relations with NATO and other international organizations. OSCE-NATO relations are generally informal and ad hoc. The NATO Secretary General has participated in OSCE ministerial and Summit Meetings and NATO officials have contributed to OSCE seminars on peacekeeping, early warning and conflict prevention. The OSCE Chairman in Office routinely attends the North Atlantic Council, the Political Committee and other NATO bodies. In addition to their cooperation in Bosnia and Herzegovina, NATO and the OSCE have been working together since October 1998, to try to prevent further escalation of the conflict between Serbian military and ethnic Albanian forces in Kosovo.

IV. CONCLUSION

NATO's Strategic Concept reaffirms the defensive nature of the Alliance. It is based on dialogue, cooperation, and reinforcing instruments for preserving the peace. The flexible strategy can reflect further developments in the environment. It is the basis for the development of defense policy, operational concepts, conventional and nuclear force posture and collective defense planning arrangements.

As we shall see, both the new members and the aspiring member countries from central Europe will have values antithetical to NATO's. Materialism and individualism are not surprising given the state of the economies of the former Warsaw Pact countries after fifty years of enforced ideology. However, these values lead to national strategies with significant consequences for the mid- and long-term.

Table 2: The Strategy of NATO

Values	communitarianism, non-materialism
Strategy	indirect strategy of suasion
Goal	security of Europe
Tactics	cooperation and dialogue: ESDI, EAPC, PFP, Mediterranean dialogue, dialogues with x-USSR collective defence: conventional forces, nuclear forces
Style	defensive, indivisible, equitable

PART 3.
I. ROMANIA'S NATIONAL STRATEGY

Ukraine borders the former Socialist Republic of Romania to the north and east, Moldova to the northwest, Hungary to the northwest, Yugoslavia to the southwest and Bulgaria to the south. The Black Sea washes the southeast coast. The official language is Romanian with minority groups speaking Hungarian, German and other languages. Most inhabitants are Christians, with 84% professing Romanian Orthodox Catholicism. Formerly Part of Turkey's Ottoman Empire, Romania became an independent kingdom in 1881. It was an ally of Nazi Germany under the dictatorship of the fascist Iron Guard movement, and when the pro-German regime was overthrown, Soviet forces entered the country.

The Romania People's Republic was proclaimed in 1947. In 1952, the country adopted a Constitution similar to the Soviet model. Georghiu-Dej became the unchallenged leader, implementing large-scale plans for industrialization of the country, despite the Soviet preference for agricultural goods. Ceausescu succeeded Georghiu-Dej in 1954, and continued his predecessor's relatively independent foreign policy. His use of foreign loans for investment in industry and infrastructure led to serious indebtedness, and by the early 1980s Romania was experiencing severe economic problems. Ceausescu managed to maintain power by making frequent personnel changes in the party leadership and government. In October 1985, the country's long-running production difficulties in the energy sector led to an unprecedented crisis and a declaration of a state of emergency in the electric power industry.

Under the 1991 Constitution, the Parliament has a 343-seat Chamber of Deputies, the lower house, and a 143-seat Senate or upper house. Parliamentary representatives are elected by proportional representation every four years. The President of the Republic serves at most two 4-year terms and is elected directly. He appoints the Prime Minister, who in turn appoints the Council of Ministers.

II. EXPERIMENTAL VARIABLES

Information about the Romanian national strategy is limited. The fall of the Ceausescu regime was followed by a strong nationalist mobilization. The population witnessed these revolutionary events on television, and new rituals and myths overrode the old ones, but only the social order was changed.[67] These awkward realities, as well as the institutionalization of the Romanian parliament since 1990, have been analyzed using political culture by Roper and Crowther.[68]

A. National Value #1: The Rise of Individualism in the Sandpaper Revolution

In November 1989, President Nicolae Ceausescu told the Communist Party congress that Romania would continue to follow orthodox Communist policies. But in December 1989, President Nicolae Ceausescu criticized the Romanian Communist party and asked for improved consumer services. In Timisoara, security forces used water cannons, tear gas and gunfire, killing at least 2000, in a clash with thousands of demonstrators protesting the deportation of a dissident clergyman. Ceausescu blamed fascist elements for instigating the revolt and declared a state of emergency. Violent protests followed, with government troops again firing on demonstrators. In Timisoara, soldiers had joined the growing protest movement and army units fought with police. Army units joined protesters in Bucharest the following week, and forced Ceausescu from power. Fighting between the army and pro-Ceausescu security forces was heavy as the new government, the Council of National Salvation, arrested former government officials and took control of state-run television. Ceausescu and his wife fled as Romanian television reported finding mass graves in Timisoara, where security forces buried as many as 4,000 protesters. The new government captured the Ceausescus and, after a secret trial, executed them by firing squad on Christmas Day. Ion Iliescu was named interim President by the new government, and over seventeen countries immediately recognized the government. Pro-Ceausescu forces began to surrender, and the government started easing authoritarian restrictions on such things as abortion and the registration of typewriters (!). The Communist Party then dissolved itself.

As special military courts started trying members of Ceausescu's security forces for shooting civilians, various political parties debated the best date for national election, eventually scheduled for April 1990. The Council of National Salvation outlawed the Communist Party and held a referendum on the death penalty. In March 1990, demonstrators in Bucharest and Timisoara protested the continued domination of Communists and the Securitate in the new government. Ethnic tensions began to emerge, with 2,000 nationalists attacking 5,000 ethnic Hungarian protesters in Transylvania, eventually having to be separated by government tanks and troops.

In May 1990, anti-government protesters walked out of a meeting with President Iliescu and asked for his resignation. In the first free national elections in decades, the National Salvation Front (or NSF, composed of former Communists) won by a wide margin, a victory greeted by anti-government protests. In June, troops again shot anti-government demonstrators, killing at least four people, after protesters set fire to police headquarters and raided the state television offices. Thousands of miners from northern Romania travelled to

---

[67]Anneli Ute Gabanyi, "Romania: the Staged Revolution," *Sudost-Europe* 47:3-4 (1998), 163-183.
[68]Steven D. Roper and William Crowther, "The Institutionalization of the Romanian Parliament: A Case Study of the State-Building Process in Eastern Europe," *Southeastern Political Review* 26:2 (June 1998), 401-426.

Bucharest and attacked anti-government demonstrators, after President Iliescu asked them to rescue the country from a 'fascist rebellion.' The House of Deputies, where the National Salvation Front held a majority, voted to use force to end demonstrations.

In July, again in Timisoara, more than 10,000 protesters demanded the release of dissidents and the resignation of President Iliescu. For five nights in August, antigovernment demonstrators protesting Communist elements in the government clashed with police in Bucharest, the largest anti-government rallies since December 1989. In December 1990, more than 10,000 workers staged a three-day anti-government strike because of slow reforms. The anniversary of Ceausescu's overthrow saw massive rallies commemorating the people killed by security forces and a visit from King Michael, Romania's deposed monarch. In October 1992, President Iliescu won reelection and appointed Nicolae Vacaroiu, a departmental head in the Economy Ministry under the previous government, as prime minister.

At the fifth anniversary of Ceausescu's overthrow in 1994, more than 15,000 demonstrators marched on Prime Minister Nicolae Vacaroiu's offices in Bucharest, calling for the resignation of President Iliescu and the return of King Michael. In November 1996, Centrist Democratic Convention candidate Emil Constantinescu won the presidency with more than 53% of the vote.

Following extensive negotiations, a new coalition agreement was signed in February 1998 designed to stabilize the political situation and accelerate the economic reform program. A new cabinet was formed, including members of the center-right coalition which had won the November 1996 general election. A quarter of a million health workers withdrew from the work place in February 1998, in order to get better salaries. Several government officials and foreign diplomats accredited in Bucharest were implicated in the smuggling of contraband cigarettes in May 1998. Homosexuality was decriminalized following repeated criticism of existing legislation by international human rights organizations.

The Minister of Health resigned in June 1998 after it was made public that he had been a Securitate informant, but by July 1998, the rest of the cabinet was cleared of links. That September, the Finance Minister was dismissed after he opposed Cabinet amendments to the budget which cut the army's funding by 3%. In October, the Privatization Minister resigned just before the US credit agency Standard and Poor's downgraded Romania's credit rating. The Prime Minister had often complained that privatization was moving too slowly. Romania's Alternative Party left the ruling coalition because the country's economy was worsening and reforms were delayed, as did the ethnic Hungarian Democratic Union of Romania over the demand for a Hungarian language state university. In November 1998, the leaders of the ruling coalition parties agreed on a formula to restructure the government. The number of ministries was reduced from twenty-three to seventeen, with four new departments to report directly to the Prime Minister to increase the pace of reforms. Reforms have so far failed to win the confidence of investors and capital markets.

In April 1993, after forty-five years of exile in Switzerland, King Michael celebrated Romanian Orthodox Easter in Suceava. In October 1994, President Iliescu said King Michael's 'hope to return as king' was a threat to the constitutional order. As a result, the king was denied an entry visa in October but the government restored his citizenship and he returned in February 1997.

B. National Value #2 Materialism for an Economy in Disarray

The economic problems of Romania led to unrest and eventually the political revolution that was a feature of Christmas 1989. In October 1985, the long running production difficulties of the country's energy sector culminated in an unprecedented crisis and the declaration of a state of emergency in the electric power industry. Shortages of fuel and power led to strict energy rationing in early 1987. The situation was exacerbated by adverse weather conditions, and public discontent became evident: anti-government leaflets circulated and a number of strikes protested the food shortages and delays in payment of wages were organized in provincial factories. In March 1987, it was reported that certain vital factories and mines were placed under military supervision to forestall the threat of further labor unrest. In his May 1987 visit to Bucharest, Soviet leader Mikhail Gorbachev emphasized the desirability of economic reforms, a view he reiterated during Ceausescu's return visit to the USSR in October 1988. In November thousands of people marched through the city of Brasov and even stormed the local Romanian Communist Party (RCP) headquarters, over the decline in living standards and in working conditions. There were similar protests in Timisoara and other cities in December. President Ceausescu announced improvements in food supplies and increases in wages, but continued to oppose any reform of the economic system.

In March 1989, there was an open letter to the President from six retired Romanian Communist party (RCP) officials. The officials accused him of disregard for the Constitution, economic mismanagement, and discrimination using the rural urbanization program imposed on the ethnic Hungarians. The unrest spread (and a variety of other political events occurred, described above) until Ceausescu was captured while attempting to flee and was executed after a summary trial.

In October 1990, Prime Minister Petre Roman introduced laws to accelerate Romania's transition to a market economy. The new rules privatized state-owned enterprises and allowed free-market prices for nonessential goods. In November 1990, for a week, demonstrators throughout the country protested price increases on consumer goods. The increases were the result of the government's decision to lift price controls on November 1. Economic discontent remained the focus of the politics of the country to this day.

III. THE INDEPENDENT VARIABLE: NATIONAL STRATEGY

A. The Previous Strategy

Romania was a member of the Warsaw Pact until the organization's dissolution in 1991. However, Romania did not participate in military exercises, nor did it allow Warsaw Pact troops on its soil. With the values being individualism and materialism, Romania should choose a direct strategy of action.

B. Components of Strategy

1. The Goal

The goal of the successive governments since the end of the Ceausescu regime has been to develop the market economy in Romania.

2. The Style

During the communist era, numerous social and political constraints limited civic engagement in communities throughout Central and Eastern Europe. Such lingering effects have slowed the process of democratization in Romania, where people discuss politics less, engage in interactive forms of political participation at lower rates and know less about their neighbors than similarly situated communities in the US. They also fail to link the interests of people in the community to broader political judgments.[69] A study of elite attitudes carried out in 1998 showed that Romanians intellectuals held a neo-traditionalist discourse whereas the Magyar or Hungarian Romanians held a conservative, historicizing discourse, when looking beyond the official statements.[70] Moreover, Leninist and Byzantine traditions have coalesced in uniquely cynical and manipulative formation of authoritarian mentalities and practices in Romania, which may explain why the Romania path is a different one.[71]

3. The Tactics

(a) Economic Affairs

After Ceausescu's overthrow, a complete restructuring of the economy was planned, with emphasis on the market forces and private ownership. In late 1991, a unified exchange rate was introduced and the internal convertibility of the currency, the lei, was established. Foreign businesses were initially reluctant to invest in the country. In early 1993, the government announced a four-year economic reform program supported by the IMF. This plan included progressive elimination of price subsidies for staple goods and services, removal of controls on interest and exchange rates, trade liberalization, accelerated privatization and reduction in inflation.

Under the government's decollectivization program, 46% of the agricultural land was returned to original owners by early 1994. By 1995, 80% of the farmland had been privatized, but the agricultural GDP declined by an annual average of 1.4%. Industry in 1995 accounted for 42.5% of GDP and declined by an average of 2.1% between 1990-95. Manufacturing, a sector employing one-quarter of the labor force, was hampered by shortages of electricity and raw materials, and output increased by 3.3% between 1980 and 1990, but declined by 18.7% in 1990 and continued to fall through 1993. Recovery began in 1994-95.

Romania had a trade deficit of US $2.4 billion, with both the principal source of imports and market for exports being Germany and Italy. The overall budget deficit for 1994 was 2.9% of GDP, with an external debt of US $8.3 billion. The cost of servicing the debt was

---

[69]Jeffery Mondak and Adam Gearing, "Civic Engagement in a Post-Communist State," *Political Psychology* 19:3 (September 1998), 615-637.

[70]Antonela Capelle-Pogacean, "Les représentations de la nation chez les intellectuels hongrois, magyars de Roumanie et roumains après 1989," *Revue D'Études Comparatives Est-Ouest* 29:1 (March 1998), 5-33.

[71]Vladimir Rismaneanu, "Understanding National Stalinism: Reflections on Ceausescu's Socialism," *Communist and Post-Communist Studies* 32:2 (June 1999), 155-173.

13% of the income from exports of goods and services. The government implemented a price liberalization program which led to an average annual rate of inflation of 117% from 1991 to 1996. It was 256% in 1993, and 155% in 1997, with unemployment rates of 8-9%. The Finance Minister was dismissed because reforms were too slow and were not meeting the requirements for World Bank credits.

By late 1995, the situation appeared to have improved, despite austerity measures leading to considerable unrest. But in 1996 the economic performance deteriorated, with an increase in inflation, current account deficit and import expenditure as a result of currency devaluation. During the first half of 1997 the IMF and the World Bank achieved some economic reform, reducing the current account deficit and liberalizing most state controlled prices.

In 1996, the GNP was estimated at $US 36.2 billion, having increased at an average 0.1% annually. Over the same period the population decreased by an average 0.4%. The GDP increased by an average of 0.5% annually during 1980-90, but there was no appreciable increase from 1990 to 1996. In 1996 it grew by 4.5% but declined by 6.65% in 1997.

From mid-1997, though, increasing prices and plans for closure of unprofitable state-owned enterprises provoked social and labor unrest. By September 1997, though, there were over 40,000 state enterprises remaining to be sold. Disputes within the ruling coalition of political parties contributed the slowing pace of reform, and inflation had by the end of the year increase dramatically. Real GDP had declined by 7%. Escalating political instability stalled economic reform and delayed the budget in 1998. The Vasil government promised to encourage foreign investment in April 1998.

In December 1998, the legislature approved the government restructuring plan, and the first state-owned bank in Romania was privatized. The January 1999 strike by coal miners in Jiu escalated into Romania's worst incidence of civil disorder since protesting miners cause d the fall of the government in September 1991. The Interior Minister was forced to resign amid accusations of incompetence. The leader of the miners, having been sentenced to eighteen years in prison for his role in the riots, began a protest march on Bucharest with 2000 supporters on February 16, 1999. Four people died in the protest's clashes with police.

In January 2000, the government restarted talks with the IMF about conditions attached to the second installment of their slice of their standby credit agreement. Prime Minister Mugur Isarescu announced a major financial reform program to satisfy the stringent conditions and revive the struggling economy, cutting public expenditure and overhauling the tax system. Analysts agreed that unless Romania received financial assistance it would face difficulties in meeting external obligations. While there has been progress, obstacles to liberalizing the economy, foreign policy and politics are considerable when dismantling an economic and social system inherited from Communist.[72]

A leaked banking scandal threw Romanian investors into panic, resulting in the collapse of a national investment fund. The information leak - apparently politically motivated - was the first in a string of events aimed at weakening the current government. The scandal combined with success at the polls in recent elections strengthened the hand of the formerly Communist Social Democrats. Supporters of the ruling Christian Democratic Party largely boycotted local elections on May 4 and, along with low voter turnout, helped throw the

---

[72]Tom Gallagher, "Romania's Desire to be Normal," *Contemporary Politics* 4:2 (June 1998), 111-125, *passim*.

elections to the Social Democrats. In November, the country will hold parliamentary and presidential elections. The public's awareness of the corruption surrounding the banking sector suggests an imminent collapse of the Romanian administration. If the Social Democrats can continue to expose government corruption while influencing voters at the municipal level, they may be able to manipulate mass sentiment enough to position themselves for a win in November.

Poverty took its toll on national well-being. The health figures for this period were not reassuring: owing to persistent shortages of food, many Romanians were believed to be suffering from malnutrition. International attention focused on the orphanages of large numbers of unwanted and neglected children, many of whom suffer from AIDS, hepatitis and other serious illnesses.

(b) Ethnic Policy and the Extreme Right

In September 1992, in Bucharest, Germany and Romania signed a pact in which Romania agreed to accept back all its citizens who were there illegally. About 50,000 Romanians in Germany were affected, most of them Romany (i.e. Gypsies). Germany contributed $US 20 million to fund the deportations and job training in Romania for the returnees. In May 1993, Romany leaders from fourteen countries and government representatives from eleven countries met to address human rights and other issues that affect Romany communities. After more than thirty murders of Romany in Romania and the former Czechoslovakia, and after economic instability increased in the region, tens of thousands fled to wealthier nations.

The Social Democracy Party of Romania announced in November 1998 that it would boycott the legislature until the ruling coalition had pledged to respect the opposition's right to express its views in the legislature. The Senate had refused to discuss a motion against President Constatinescu about alleged abuses and illegal actions. Extreme right parties announced in November 1998 that they were merging.

(c) Political Instability

The Ciorbea government got notable results in economic stabilization and normalization of relations with neighboring countries. The chances of furthering the reconstruction of the country were lost by instability. The crisis in the governing coalition, because of differing views by various parties, the lack of political and technical experience and the rivalries for power, put these gains at risk. In 1997 and 1998, the political crises became institutional, where the new government found itself with the same heavy problems faced by its predecessors.[73] In March 1998, Prime Minister Victor Ciorbea resigned, then eighteen months later Prime Minister Vasile was dismissed because they could not control the five-party ruling coalition and have the government function properly. Ten government ministers resigned from their posts during the same period.

(d) Military Affairs

Military service is compulsory in Romania, lasting 12 months in the army and air force and 18 months in the navy. In August 1997, active forces totaled 226,950, including 127,000 conscripts, with the army at 129,000 (90,000 of them conscripts), navy at 17,000 and air force

---

[73] Anneli Ute Gabanyi, "Roumania: Government Policy in Times of Crisis," *Sudost-Europa* 47:9 (1998), 393-420.

at 47,000. There were also 22,0000 border guards, a gendarmerie of 10,0000 and a security guard of 47,000, all of which are under the control of the Minister of the Interior. The 1997 budget allocated 5.5 billion lei to defense.

The Romanian state no longer realized its claims to sovereignty based on historical territoriality and became oriented to trans-border as well as territorial constituencies. Globalization has stimulated greater involvement of international and regional agencies in governance. This rise of supraterritoriality has also encouraged some devolution and some privatization of regulatory authority in Romania, posing substantial challenges for democracy.[74]

In January 1994, Romania became the first former Warsaw pact state to join NATO's Partnership for Peace program. In August 1995, Romania peacekeeping troops were dispatched to Angola as the first Romanian forces to participate in an international UN military operation. The victory of pro-European forces in the 1996 elections brought to an end the post-communist regime.

After the 1996 victory, the new government embarked on a policy of reconciliation with Hungary and the Hungarian minority in Transylvania and concentrated its efforts on its bid to join NATO.[75] There was no popular backlash when NATO accepted Hungary's application but declined Romania in July 1997.[76] However, enthusiasm for post-nationalist initiatives waned. In all probability, NATO will not start enlargement negotiations with Romania in 2002. Early entry into NATO would do little to solve the basic structural difficulties in Romania, which have little to do with the West and its supposedly failed promises. Rather, the current government will probably not survive the 2000 elections and for the next government the economic reforms will matter far more than the issue of NATO enlargement.[77]

Table 3: The National Strategy of Romania

Values	individualism, materialism
Goals	economic development
Tactics	economic policy, ethnic policy, military affairs, efforts for stability
Style	historical, elitist

---

[74]Jan Art Scholte, "Globalization, Governance and Democracy in Post-Communist Romania," *Democratization* 5:4 (Winter 1998), 52-77, 55.

[75]Tom G. Gallagher, "The West and the Challenge to Ethnic Politics in Romania," *Security Dialogue* 30:3 (September 1999), 293-304, 293-4.

[76]Tom G. Gallagher, "The West and the Challenge to Ethnic Politics in Romania," *Security Dialogue* 30:3 (September 1999), 293-304, 293-4.

[77]Michael Mihalka, "Enlargement Deferred. More Political Instability for Romania? A Rejoinder." *Security Dialogue* 30:4 (December 1999), 497-502, *passim.*

PART 4.

I. ANALYSIS OF INTERACTIONS

NATO's expanded role and mandate now includes the political and the economic. Accordingly, this study has examined the political and economic dimensions of national strategy of all the participants involved. This allows for an analysis of the strategic interactions between each country and NATO, as well as interactions between each of the countries.

NATO has adopted a communitarian value while the states studied here have all become more individualist. This communitarianism is reflected in the decision to admit Poland, Hungary and the Czech Republic. Genuine integration, to say nothing of interoperability, will take at least a decade and relations will be uneasy for the foreseeable future.

Table 4: NATO-Romania Strategic Interactions

Components	NATO	Poland	Interaction
Values	communitarianism, non-materialism	individualism, materialism	antithetical
Goals	security of Europe	consolidation of state security and independence, optimal economic and social development, worthy political and social position in world	synergistic
Tactics	cooperation, dialogue, collective defense	National security foreign policy, economic interest	mixed; see below
Style	defensive, indivisible, equitable	comprehensive, lawful, principled, ideally defensive	compatible

Table 5: Czech-Romanian Strategic Interactions

Components	Czech Republic	Romania	Interaction
Values	individualism, materialism	individualism, materialism	identical
Goals	comprehensive security	economic development	neutral
Tactics	**foreign policy**: Slovak relations, Visegrad group, German relations, EU membership **military affairs**: NATO membership, reform of the ACR	economic policy, ethnic policy, military affairs, efforts for stability	neutral
Style	comprehensive and diverse	historical, elitist	antithetical

Table 6: Romanian-Bulgarian Strategic Interactions

Components	Romania	Bulgaria	Interaction
Values	individualism, materialism	individualism, materialism	identical
Strategy	--	National Salvation; Bulgaria 2001	--
Goals	economic development	agreements with international financial institutions; redistribution of social burden; restored land ownership; fight organized crime, corruption; declassifying police files of politicians and public servants; membership in NATO and EU	complementary
Tactics	economic policy, ethnic policy, military affairs, efforts for stability	foreign policy: EU membership, regional stability, fight against crime defense: armed forces reform, NATO membership	complementary
Style	historical, elitist	interwoven foreign/defense/domestic policies; European civilizational identity; national mobilization	antithetical

II. SOME LIMITATIONS OF THE METHOD

The development of any new theory (or part of a theory) is always speculative, and this theory is certainly no exception. Disproving theories, after all, is the very stuff of science: no theory ever lasts forever. This book ends, therefore, where theory of International Relations often begins, with a discussion of its own strengths and weaknesses. Having given a summary of the findings of the study, this closing discusses some implications of the study on a theoretical level.

This report has identified national values as the unknown half of the strategic equation. It argued in favor of the importance of national interest as an analytical concept, but it also declined to discuss the relationship between national values and national interest until more was known about national values. This exploration having taken place, it is now clear that it does not answer all the questions: a full study of the relationship could do that. Reconciling national interest and national values goes beyond International relations, it being "one of the central problems of all human experience and philosophical speculation."[78] The immediate problem is the tendency of the literature to confuse the two, for definitional reasons outlined in Part 1.

Having studied values in relation to strategy, however, it is clear there is another source for the trouble. Strategy is a difficult concept because it is both an idea and an action, tangible and intangible. National values share this tangibility and intangibility, as does national interests. The national interest is in most circumstances a set of national goals based on the state's ideal of welfare, as well as consideration for the practicalities of the situation. The solution to this problem probably lies in a fuller understanding of circumstances in the

---

[78]Robert E. Osgood, *Ideals and Self-Interest in America's Foreign Relations? The Great Transformation of the Twentieth Century*, (Chicago: University of Chicago Press, 1953), i.

phenomena of strategy, values and interest. The traditional triangle of strategic theory, therefore, needs to be expanded.

In essence, the theory is compatible with the existing scholarship about national interest. Although existing literature provides the basis for understanding this four-way relationship, it needs to match the theory's detail and degrees of abstraction before any more questions are to be answered. It is also possible that the theory will be found to be overly simplified by experts in areas I judged to be, if not peripheral, then certainly less central. If values and strategy are at the heart of the theory, then states, political will, national goals, and even national interest is less central. The empirical hypotheses are not exact predictions for several reasons. First, strategy is a tool for macro-analysis: it has the advantage of helping to analyze complex situations in the long term, but it has the disadvantage of not being worth the trouble in the short term, because it requires too much time and information. Until the theory is refined, it will be unsuccessful in predicting the outcome of a single decision. It cannot determine, explain or predict tactics.

In addition, the theory begs four questions.

Does the theory replace a simple and acceptable explanation, with a complicated one? That is one of theory's most common failings. Why takes the trouble of establishing a complex causal relationship when the dictum that circumstances dictate a state's strategy is commonly accepted? To do so implies that the relationship between national values and state behavior is important enough to warrant the exploration, a question of judgment on the scholar's part. In that case, the more obvious the cases study, the better: it can only serve its purpose as an illustration better.

Is the state being personalized? Because each step of theory-building builds on the previous, implications from this assumption naturally appear throughout the theory. These implications do not reach the state however: its functions and characteristics were specified right from the start, and are distinct from society, population and leaders.

What are the chances of this theory being policy-relevant? To gain acceptance with decision-makers, the theory has to clear several hurdles. It must avoid most of the traditional criticism of strategic studies, which it does.[79] For instance, strategists have behaved in a manner incompatible with the integrity of scholarship in that they have advised official agencies on a paid and privileged basis. There is not basis for a critique of a book along these lines.[80] Another complaint is that strategists transcend the bounds of scholarship in that they advocate particular policies. However, it is difficult to imagine anyone accusing a theory as abstract as this one of being too political. Third, strategists ignore ethical questions. Professional strategists are usually more concerned with attaining objectives than with questions of right and wrong, and the theorists who assist them inevitably do the same. This theory could be putting all ethical issues on the same footing. On the other hand, it does emphasize them by placing philosophical issues at the center of decision-making, which other strategic theorists or specialists of decision-making do not. Fourth, strategists are fascinated by violence. My decision to approach the problem theoretically was motivated by the desire to liberate strategy from its historical association not only with violence but also with conflict. Sixth, strategists ignore public opinion. This theory actually tries to liberate strategy not only

---

[79]Colin Gray, *Strategic Studies / A Critical Assessment* (Westport: Greenwood, 1982), 158.

[80]As Lucien Poirier puts it, "*Je ne me fais pas d'illusion: notre travail, çà n'intéresse personne.*" Interview with author, Paris, February 1992, personal notes.

from the battlefield, but from any association with violence. It also provides decision-makers with the means to consider how one strategic option or another will sit with public opinion, through the mechanism of appreciation, among others. Finally, strategists indulge in a differential morality in their appraisal of the behavior of states. This charge is not within the parameters of this study, since morality is an individual matter.

In addition, the theory has to be readily accessible to decision-makers. The plain fact of the matter is that unless decision-makers are convinced that the method is worth the time and effort, they are unlikely to go to much trouble. The method proposed here requires rigorous logic, but no calculus. The most strict requirement is the use of a new vocabulary. It is possible, however, that decision-makers resist this theory because of its implications. Leaders may wish to believe something else than the list of assumptions and conditions about the world. They may not wish to acknowledge their values, if they are different from what they profess publicly. Decision-makers may not want to foresee the consequences of their actions quite so clearly. If decision-makers are also elected leaders, they may find that insoluble problems are not popular with the electorate.

Is this chapter a trickle of content in a canyon of notes? Because so many issues needed to be clarified, it is inevitable that this chapter creates that first impression. The theoretical support is substantial, and this is the second regional study using this framework, although it is the first including a regional organization. This impression is probably inevitable, given the fact that this is the opening of a new chapter in strategic theory. A new method had to be developed in enough detail for other scholars to use it. All the methodological and theoretical problems also had to be solved up front and once and for all. That happens only once, but it has to happen at the start. As the general theory of strategy is developed, the impression of top-heaviness and excessively throat-clearing will fade.

So I argue that the theory is general enough and powerful enough to be applied to other cases and other actors. The only requirement is that the actor always be capable of cognition, evaluation and appreciation of information. To test this particular theory further, one could proceed empirically or theoretically. Empirical studies require generating predictions and investigating them. Theoretical studies require variations on conditions and assumptions, or using other propositions to contradict the findings of the current study.

One final thought: above and beyond these more immediate studies are applications of the template to non-state actors, particularly minorities. A sage once said that the problem of all strategy of minorities is the problem of waiting for circumstances to improve.[81] If the possibilities that this theory offers are realized, perhaps minorities can play something else but a waiting game.

---

[81]M. Courtès, interview with author, Montpellier, February 1992, personal notes.

Chapter 2

EU ACCESSION AGRICULTURAL POLICY OPTIONS FOR SLOVENIA

E. Erjavec[*] and S. Kavcic

University of Ljubljana
Biotechnical Faculty, Chair for Agricultural Economics
Policy and Law
Ljubljana, Slovenia

ABSTRACT

This paper's aim is an assessment of economic effects of Slovenia's accession to the EU in the field of agriculture and a discussion about some key dilemmas about the introduction of CAP in the new member states. For the purpose of assessing economic effects, a new sectoral model of Slovenian agriculture APAS-PAM has been compiled which allows assessment of market and income effects for ten key agricultural products with regard to various accession scenarios. The accession under the scenario of equal treatment of new member states would bring significant improvements in the aggregate income levels. On the other hand, discrimination of the candidate countries in the field of direct payments ("phasing in" process) would result in a fall of aggregate income level by an eighth. Moreover, non-competitive production structures in the food-processing sector would deteriorate the economic situation of agricultural production by up to further 40 %. The positive effects of different accession scenarios are expected in the sugar beet and - under assumption of eligibility for direct payments - also in coarse grains, beef and sheep meat production. The economic situation in milk production is not expected to change significantly. The negative accession effects can be expected in pork, cereal, egg and, potentially, poultry production. The results reveal a great significance of equal treatment and differentiation approach to negotiation process for the preservation of the economic situation of Slovenian agriculture after accession. This holds especially for cereal, beef and sheep meat production.

Keywords: CAP, EU enlargement, sectoral partial equilibrium models, accession effects

[*] Corresponding Author: Emil Erjavec, University of Ljubljana, Biotechnical Faculty, Groblje 3, SLO-1230 Domzale, Slovenia Tel.:+386 1 7217 852 E-mail: Emil.Erjavec@bfro.uni-lj.si. Author names are in alphabetical order.

1. INTRODUCTION

The June 2001 Göteborg European Council reaffirmed the time framework of the enlargement, according to which negotiations with the best prepared candidate countries should be completed by the end of 2002. This would enable enlargement to take place in 2004. The completion of negotiations with candidate countries is thus within sight and, like in previous enlargements, agriculture and the adoption of the CAP will have a crucial role in the final stage of negotiations. The conclusions of the Berlin Summit in March 1999 clearly defined the financial framework of EU enlargement in the area of agricultural policy. The figures reveal that the new-coming Member States will not be fully participating in the CAP mechanisms. Moreover, it can be expected that the candidate countries will have to agree with the transitional periods, particularly as regards direct payments. We can foresee the "phasing in" process for direct payments, which is to start at a relatively low level of payments (maybe 20 % of current member states) and last at least for a few years. The reason for this is lower current price levels as well as negative social and macroeconomic effects in the candidate countries. Higher prices are also expected to be a stimulus to growth of agricultural production in the new members, and this could consequently contribute to serious additional budget pressures on CAP. The reservations concerning implementation ineptitude could also affect the EU decisions. Regardless of how justified these reservations are, the issue of equal treatment puts to the test the basic principles of equality and equal competitive opportunities. Taking all this into account, the main arguments for excluding the candidate countries from direct payments are in fact political ones. It is thus clear that the issues concerning direct payments and equal treatment will be on the top of the political agenda in the negotiating process of the next EU enlargement.

In the negotiations on agriculture, the European Union uses a horizontal approach for all the candidate countries, which can, at least for some, pose an additional problem and further aggravate their accession to CAP. This is particularly the case for Slovenia, which has already made considerable progress in adapting its agriculture and agricultural policy to that in the EU and horizontal approach could, therefore, hinder its prospects and further development in agriculture. In contrast to other applicant countries, producer prices in Slovenia are almost at the EU level, and due to its natural and structural conditions, Slovenia is a net importer of food items, with a smaller potential for production growth (OECD, 2001). In addition, the Slovenian agricultural policy framework (objectives and measures) is rather close to that of the CAP. Furthermore, direct payments and intervention mechanisms (but not quotas) introduced by the 2000-2002 agricultural policy reform aim at harmonising domestic policy to such a degree that accession would not entail dramatic modifications for producers. The level of support to agriculture in Slovenia is moderate. PSE estimates[1] by OECD (2001) show that Slovenian producers were subsidised for the whole period of 1992-2000. It is apparent that market price support represents more than 80 % of total agricultural support. In 1995-1999, the average percentage PSE in Slovenia (41 %) was above the OECD level (35 %) and nearly the same as that in the EU (42 %). The level of support in Slovenia exceeded

---

[1] The PSE measures the money value of transfers from consumers and taxpayers to agricultural producers arising from government policies. The percentage PSE gives an indication of the proportion of total farm gross receipts originating from support, whether that includes, among others, subsidies paid directly on outputs and inputs, and per head and per hectare payments.

significantly that of any other Central and Eastern European country. The high PSE levels in Slovenia reflect substantial domestic price support and border protection for the most important agricultural commodities (milk products, beef, and pig meat), as well as steadily growing budgetary transfers to producers. In 2000 budgetary transfers in Slovenia already reached 70 % of the level of budgetary transfers provided for in the CAP.

The objective of this paper is, therefore, to contribute to the discussion on EU enlargement by an estimation of the accession effects (market trends, agricultural income and competitiveness) on the agricultural sector in Slovenia, by using relevant empirical tools. One of the main objectives of the paper is determining the policy dimension of the "equal treatment issue". For this purpose, we tested the degree of dependence of Slovenian agricultural sector on the level of EU direct aids after accession, and the importance of the differentiation approach for the "smooth landing" of the Slovenian agriculture to the single market.

The paper is structured as follows: first, the empirical framework and three policy scenarios within which Slovenia could evolve after accession are described; second, market projections and resulting trade flows start the presentation of the model results; and third, comparisons of different scenarios of accession concerning competitiveness and agricultural income are presented. The paper concludes with policy evaluation and some policy recommendations.

2. METHODOLOGY AND SCENARIOS

2.1. Methodology

The upgraded version of Agricultural Policy Analysis Simulator (APAS) combined with the Policy Analysis Matrix (PAM) models have been used for estimation of the accession effects. The data and methodology are described extensively in Stoforos et al., 2000 (some additional explanation can be found also in Mergos et al., 1999). The APAS is designed as a static, partial equilibrium, multi-commodity, national sector model, taking into account the specific features of Slovenian agro-industry and recent policy changes (Kavcic 2000). On the other hand, PAM has been used for analysing income, protection and competitive issues for the same policy scenarios. The newest version of APAS-PAM model provides the possibility for calculation both DRC and RBC (domestic resource cost ratio and rate of bilateral competitiveness) indicators of competitiveness. The later one refers to the ability of producers to be profitable when faced with policy scenario of assumed EU market and tradable input prices, with the costs of the factors of production measured in terms of their opportunity costs (for more detailed explanation see Gorton and Davidova, 2000).

The APAS model provides the possibility to simulate market effects of different policies, as well as time trends, in an easy and understandable way. A simplified approach was used, expanded mostly in the analysis by models of partial equilibrium based on the principle of Marshallian surplus (Scandizzo 1989). The changes were calculated by a simultaneous system of equations, with prices acting as exogenous variables. Elasticities, generally obtained by previous empirical research (Erjavec and Turk 1997, Erjavec et al. 1998, Turk et al. 1999, other sources, e.g. Gardiner et al. 1989), were adjusted during the process of model calibration.

The model is now amalgamated to include all commodities together - contrary to previous division into three sub-models. Currently, it includes all most important agricultural "PSE commodities" (arable crops: wheat and maize, barley and sugar beet as well as livestock products: milk, beef, pork and poultry, eggs and sheep meat). Together these commodities account for approx. 80 % of Slovenian gross agricultural output.

For each product four equations were constructed: total area or livestock number, production per hectare or per head, production/domestic supply as a product of the latter two, and demand. Any disequilibrium between supply and demand is brought back into balance through foreign trade. Special attention should be given to maize and barley as the main fodder components in the equations for livestock production; conversely, livestock production is taken into account as the main factor in the demand for fodder.

Results of APAS simulations are directly incorporated in PAM calculations both at individual producer as well as aggregate level, relaxing the static nature of the original PAM.

The model is designed to analyse the economic implications of policy changes that can have an important impact. A policy is usually represented in the model by a fixed price wedge: a wedge between the traded price and the domestic incentive price. The policy price wedge data are based on calculations of producer and consumer subsidy equivalents where a wide range of support policies was translated into a common measure. Policies can also be implicitly introduced into the model through price transmission parameters that regulate the transmission of world price changes to the domestic economy, and by shifting supply equations to capture production control policies. Along with market prices and budgetary payments, deviations in input costs (material costs and depreciation) have been used as correction factors for determination of policy scenarios' incentive prices. For this reason matrix of price elasticities in the earlier version of the model have been replaced by "quasi-income" elasticity matrix. Authors believe that this, although uncommon modelling procedure, leads to more reliable market projection results.

The relevant data for the analysis were provided by the Agricultural Institute of Slovenia (Volk 2001a and 2001b, Golez 2001) and various published or recalculated sources of the Statistical Office of the Republic of Slovenia (SORS).

2.2 Scenarios

The simulation was run using three policy scenarios:

- **Baseline scenario (BS).** It assumes continuation of agricultural policy from 1999/2000 and predominantly serves as a comparison tool.
- **"Equal treatment" scenario of Slovenia's EU accession (EU+++).** The scenario of full adoption of CAP and equal status as enjoyed by current Member States. This scenario assumes equal position of Slovenian producers with regard to drawing direct payments and eligibility for the whole package of structural and environmental payments from Agenda 2000. It also assumes no negative effects of (potentially) non-competitive food processing industry on producer prices.
- **Expected EU negotiating position scenario of Slovenia's EU accession (EU+-o).** The accession scenario for candidates (i.e. Slovenia). It assumes relatively high level of producer prices (probably questionable, at least in some markets), direct payments

amounting to 15 % of the current Member States' level, and two third the package of structural and environmental payments (comparable with EU+++).

- **"Non-competitive agro-food sector" scenario of Slovenia's EU accession (EU--o).** Reduced EU producer prices are the most significant characteristic of this scenario. This EU--o scenario assumes no EU or domestic direct payments and reduced structural and environmental payments (the same amount as in EU+-o). In fact, this scenario assesses the effects of non-competitive domestic food-processing industry. It differs from the EU+-o scenario in terms of the level of producer prices (differences for individual products are shown in Table 2.1) and direct payments.

Table 2.1: Scenario Assumptions - Producer Prices in Slovenia and in "Comparable" EU Markets, 2000 (EUR/t)

Scenario and year	Wheat	Maize	Barley	Sugar beet	Milk	Beef	Pork	Poultry	Eggs	Sheep meat
EU 2000	107	120	100	46	283	2546	1271	923	808	3341
SLO 2000	138	114	117	40	290	2507	1491	1048	1207	4045
Index SLO/EU	129	95	117	88	102	98	117	113	149	121
EU-.. deviation from EU+.. [%]	-15	-5	-5	-5	-15	-10	-10	-20	-35	-15

Sources: Statistical Office of the Republic of Slovenia, Agricultural Institute of Slovenia, Eurostat, model assumptions

Assumed as accession is the period from 2004 onwards, with the full absorption capacity for the CAP measures starting in the same year. 2004 is also the period observed in the model.

3. RESULTS

3.1 Agricultural Markets

Mainly due to price and budgetary revenue disparities, assumed by analysed accession scenarios, some significant changes on the supply (and less on the demand) side can be predicted even in the short-run (Figure 3.1). Wheat, pork and eggs production would be affected most by the price reduction on the supply side under EU+++ scenario. Milk and poultry production would also be reduced. Due to price and cross price effects, maize production is expected to increase in comparison with baseline. Beef and sugar beet production is also expected to increase or, under least favourable conditions, only slightly decrease. On the contrary, wheat and eggs production could be reduced by as much as a quarter.

Figure 3.1: Projected Supply and Demand under Various Policy Scenarios (BS = 100)

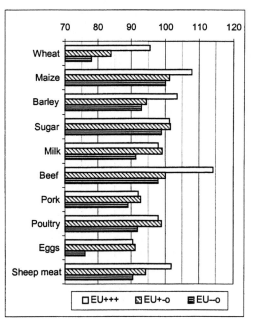 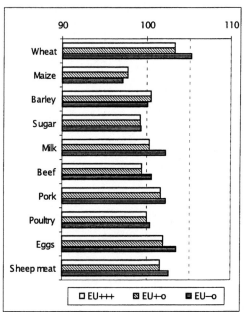

Lower protection of pork and poultry and lower prices of milk, sheep meat and barley would also result in a much lower production under the pessimistic accession scenario (EU -- o). Production of cereals, beef and sheep meat will be most sensitive to direct payments. Wheat production, if lower prices are not compensated for at least to the level provided for in the common market organisation, could decrease by almost 25 %. On the contrary, maize production is expected to increase. The extent of increase depends strongly on compensation eligibility. The importance of accession conditions is also observed in beef production. On the demand side, wheat is expected to increase the most, predominantly due to price reduction effect, resulting in its increasing competitiveness as a feed component. On the other hand, demand for maize will be reduced mainly due to higher prices and reduced livestock production (pork, eggs, but also milk and poultry).

In the sectors under investigation, Slovenia will not switch from a net importer to a net exporter or vice versa (the only probable exception is beef, Figure 3.2). However, important deviations caused by the EU accession will occur predominantly in wheat and pork (higher imports) and coarse grain (possibly lower imports) sectors. Due to long-term trends of (producer) price reduction, it is expected that Slovenia will become a net importer of poultry before the EU accession regardless of the scenario under consideration (also BS). Also milk and dairy products surpluses should decrease.

Figure 3.2: Expected Levels of Self-Sufficiency (%)

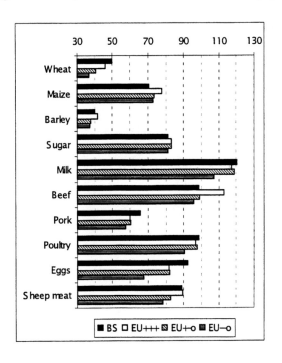

The results could confirm the hypothesis that inevitable changes will take place in trade flows due to the changes of economic conditions at the time of accession. Variations can be found in the field of price levels and budget support. A part of changes will also occur as a result of different food-processing industry' competitiveness. Authors expect that in the case of Slovenia, changes affected by low competitiveness could be even greater than presented in the analysis. It is important also to state that due to relatively low supply response assumed in the present model (see Stoforos *et al.* 2000), market effects are smaller in comparison with some previous estimates for Slovenian agriculture (e. g. Münch 2000).

3.2 Competitiveness

The rate of bilateral competitiveness (RBC) indicator was estimated for all products under consideration. Results obtained are presented in Figure 3.3. They show relatively favourable competitive position of Slovenian agriculture in the event of non-discriminative EU agricultural policy environment (EU+++), conditioned upon (competitive) domestic food industry. However, differences between various commodities are obvious. Arable and cattle (dairy and beef) production seems to be more competitive than pork, eggs and sheep meat production. The reason for this are mainly high direct payments and/or highly protected markets, resulting in high revenues in proportion to domestic opportunity costs. Cereal production with very small or no direct payments (EU +-o and EU --o) will not be competitive at all (with possible exemption of maize). The same holds also for beef production. Pork and eggs production is far from being competitive regardless of the scenario under consideration. It is important to stress that EU accession - even under most optimistic scenario - will not significantly improve the competitiveness of great majority of investigated commodities. In cases where RBC ratio increases under EU+-o in comparison with baseline, it is a consequence of still high discrepancy between domestic agricultural policy and the current CAP. Under the pessimistic scenario, only commodities with production quotas (milk and sugar beet) seem to remain/become competitive (within single EU market).

Figure 3.3: RBC Ratios for Products under Investigation

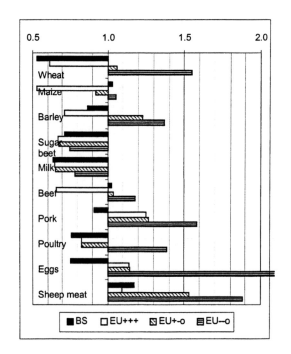

3.3 Agricultural Income

The results of the policies under the optimistic scenario point to a slight improvement in the income situation of dairy farmers and sugar beet producers (Figure 3.4). A significant improvement, but conditioned upon direct payments, is expected only in currently discriminated coarse grains and beef production. Situation is expected to be the worst in poultry and eggs sectors. In the case of low (EU+-o) or no direct payments (EU--o), a rapid stagnation of cereal production is expected. Income situation of pork production will be also deteriorated.

Unless Slovenia enjoys an equal treatment as the current member states, profitability of cereal and beef production will be deep below break even. Milk production is expected to remain most firmly attractive unless the CAP in milk market changes. On the other hand, production of many commodities will become/remain unprofitable, with revenues covering less than 80 % or even 70 % of (total) production costs. It must be mentioned that the results for both sugar and milk sectors are not constrained with quota regime, which is accounted for, but will not have effect on profitability when investigated in terms of per unit of production. For individual producer it means a threat of not allowing expansion of potentially attractive production and thus the necessary structural changes.

**Figure 3.4: Likely Agricultural Income Situation (In EUR/Ha Or Hd[2])
and Percentage Rate of Production Rentability**

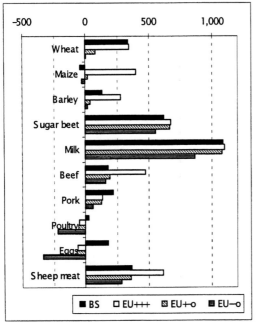
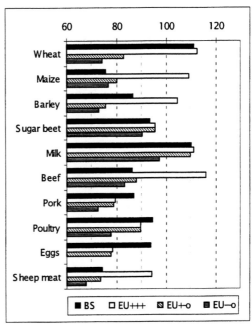

At the aggregate level, farmers' income will slightly increase in comparison with the baseline scenario if direct payments are granted (optimistic scenario), but it will decline dramatically without them and without a significant increase (to the EU average level) of competitiveness of the domestic food industry (pessimistic scenario) - Fig. 3.5. The difference between the mean policy accession scenario (EU+-o) and the baseline scenario is approximately 12%, and the difference between optimistic and pessimistic one is as much as 76 %. These results show the sensitivity of accession conditions. Accession, without direct and reduced structural payments and considering low competitiveness of the food industry, is far from being attractive for Slovenian producers. The general picture is even the opposite to the one that can be expected taking into account several general conclusions about EU enlargement effects. In the case of no eligibility for the whole amount (equal treatment as current member states) of direct payments, accession means a reduction of total agricultural income with enormous changes within some sectors (industrial livestock production and cereals).

---

[2] 10 pigs or sheep, 10,000 chickens or 100 layers.

Figure 3.5: Aggregate Level of Agricultural Income (BS = 100)

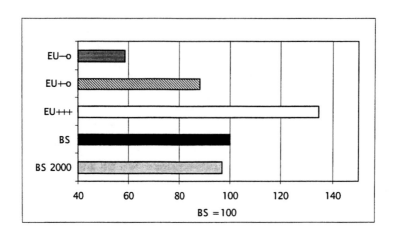

4. DISCUSSION AND CONCLUSIONS

The results obtained by this model reconfirmed the importance of equal treatment of new member states and differentiation approach to negotiations in the field of agriculture in the next EU enlargement. They clearly demonstrate that accession under the presented scenarios (which represent the full range of possible accession effects) will not significantly increase agricultural production in Slovenia. This is true for milk and sugar beet sectors, both with quota regime in the EU. Extensive reduction is expected in pork, poultry and egg sectors. Changes in the economic environment will affect also the pattern of trade flows. Differences will occur due to changes in (relative) prices and budget support. A part of the changes can be apportioned also to different degrees of food processing industry's competitiveness.

Compared with the baseline scenario the income situation of some sectors and at the aggregate level will improve only under the less realistic conditions of equal-treatment accession scenario. Regardless scenario under investigation income situation could improve in the maize and beef sectors, but this improvement should not bring any enthusiasm concerning the perspectives of these sectors, as competitiveness and actual income situation in these sectors is low. A better and more satisfactory situation under this unrealistic accession scenario can be expected only on a small number of well-organised and managed milk farms with already high milk production (quota will, therefore, not impose real production restriction). On the other hand, any marked deviation from the equal-treatment accession scenario means for majority of commodities as well as on the aggregate level a considerable deterioration of economic situation of Slovenian agriculture. Moreover, the whole dimension of negative economic changes will largely depend on the competitiveness of Slovenian food industry, whose potential deficits will also be felt in the agricultural sector in the form of the pressures for reducing the producer prices.

The model results also reveal the weaknesses of the use of horizontal approach for all the candidate countries. Without a serious differentiation among the candidates, enlargement cannot be economically and socially just. However, every enlargement negotiations are a political process and negotiating partners are often not in equal positions (which is undoubtedly the case of this enlargement), and talking politics and the predominance of partial interests are an unavoidable fact. To be able to solve the problem of equal, or better phrased, "quasi-realistic" treatment of Slovenian agriculture, original solutions should be sought within the framework of the *acquis* in force. Full direct payments are unlikely to be the final result of negotiations. However, a reasonable level of payments, for example the same as received in the pre-accession period, could be achieved by covering the missing funds from the state budget or in combination with the funds from CAP in the form of transitional payments. These additional payments would be - after the approved EU payments increase - gradually decreasing. The transitional payments proved to be an efficient measure for achieving the required price levels in the enlargement with Austria and Finland. To place too strong emphasis on the existing direct payments under CAP is - in view of the foreseen reforms - also a less rational solution. Various forms of lump-sum or flat-rate payments, like the ones used in the small-farmers scheme, are also worth consideration, as they could - especially in the case of predominantly small-farm structure in Slovenia, prove the most appropriate. Moreover, various forms of support provided for in the second pillar of CAP should also be examined. Different rural development measures, in particular agricultural environmental measures, are gaining importance as the negotiations proceed. They are becoming also more targeted, production de-coupled and in line with quite justified and still increasing expectations of consumers and taxpayers concerning the future role of agriculture and agricultural policy. Perhaps it could be by these measures that the principle of differentiation is most efficiently applied and Slovenian agriculture can most efficiently prepare for the single market after accession. However, agricultural support from the EU-funding is not important for Slovenia only as an argument of protection of domestic agriculture, but also from the viewpoint of a balanced budget account with the EU common purse.

Regardless of all the endeavours for equal treatment and the adherence to the principle of differentiation, Slovenian as well as other candidates' agricultural policy should not neglect the needs for restructuring of agriculture. In the long run, the increase in competitiveness is the key issue for Slovenian agriculture and the down-stream industry. This can be achieved efficiently also by measures such as faster trade liberalisation, support for factor mobility, more targeted budgetary policy in terms of externalities and, in the first place, a clear description of the actual and projected situation for domestic producers.

Slovenian agricultural policy is in the pre-accession period faced with very demanding tasks. Most importantly, negotiations have to be concluded as successfully as possible, although the model results as well as the reality of political process indicate that the positive results - i.e. preservation of agricultural incomes at the pre-accession levels - will be rather difficult to achieve. At the same time, Slovenia should step up the processes of restructuring of agriculture and increase the number of competitive farms, able to cope with the pressures and to further develop in the open and demanding EU single market.

ACKNOWLEDGEMENT

Authors would like to thank George Mergos and Chrisostomos Stoforos from the University of Athens for their help during initial model development, as well as Miroslav Rednak and Tina Volk for their valuable comments, assistance and provision of data.

REFERENCES

Erjavec, E., Rednak, M. and Volk, T. (1998) The European Union enlargement - the case of agriculture in Slovenia. *Food Policy, 23*: 395-409

Erjavec, E., Turk, J. (1997) Supply elasticities in Slovene agriculture. Zb. Biotehniške fak. Univ. v Ljubljani, Kmetijstvo, *Zootehnika, 70:* 85-98

Gardiner, H. W., Roningen, V. O., Liu, K. (1989) *Elasticities in the trade liberalisation database.* USDA, Agriculture and trade analysis division. Economic research service, Staff report No. AGES 89-20

Golez, M.. (2001) *Modelne kalkulacije 2000. Poljedelstvo.* (Model Calculations for 2000. Arable Farming.) Prikazi in informacije 219. Ljubljana, Kmetijski institut Slovenije

Gorton, M., Davidova, S. (2000) *The international competitiveness of CEEC agriculture.* Idara working paper series. Wye, Wye college, University of London

Kavcic, S. (2000) *Estimation of economic effects of possible agricultural policy options in Slovenian agriculture.* Unpublished PhD thesis. Domzale, University of Ljubljana

Mergos, G. J., Karadeloglou, P. and Stoforos, C. E. (1999) Exploring agricultural price and trade policy reform under transition in Albania. *Economics of Planning, 32:* 103-127

Münch, W. (2000) Effects of CEEC-EU accession on agricultural markets in the CEEC and on government expenditure. In Tangerman, S. and Banse, M. (eds.), *Central and Eastern European agriculture in an expanding European Union* Wallingford, CAB International, 113-132

OECD (2001) *Review of Agricultural Policy, Country Report: Slovenia.* Paris, OECD

Scandizzo, P. L. (1989) *Measures of protection: methodology, economic interpretation and policy relevance.* FAO economic and social development paper. Rome, FAO

Stoforos, C., Kavcic, S., Erjavec, E. and Mergos G. (2000) Agricultural policy analysis model for Slovenian agriculture. In Giannias, S. and Mergos, G. (eds.) *Selective readings on economies in transition.* Cahier Options Mediterraneennes, 44: 91-102

Turk, J., Erjavec, E., Gambelli, D. (1999) Supply trends in Slovenian agriculture under transition to the market. *East. Europ. Econ., 37:* 6-33

Volk, T. (2001a) *Modelne kalkulacije 2000. Zivinoreja.* (Model Calculations for 2000. Animal Farming.) Prikazi in informacije 218. Ljubljana, Kmetijski institut Slovenije

Volk, T. (2001b) *Modelne kalkulacije 2000. Domaca krma.* (Model Calculations for 2000. Feed.) Prikazi in informacije 221. Ljubljana, Kmetijski institut Slovenije

Chapter 3

Transitioning the Slovene Economy: An Information Technology Perspective

D. Lesjak
MIS and Management Institute

Overview

While Slovenia is now an independent country with a capitalistic economy, prior to 1990 its lands were part of socialist Yugoslavia. During the past ten years, as the country transitioned to capitalism, the number of small businesses increased almost six-fold (from nearly 6,500 to more than 35,000 in 1998). This development of new, small business is heart of this paper. Here, the focus is on IT as an enabler of new small business in Slovenia, particularly in strategic planning. The paper describes a study that identifies the degree to which information technology is used strategically in Slovene small firms. Its data also provide a baseline for future studies.

1. Introduction

1.1 Research Background

A belief commonly held in the popular literature is that information technology (IT) plays an increasingly critical role in the design and implementation of organizational strategy. IT has been described as facilitating the competitiveness, organizational transformation, increased market share, and heightened customer service (Callon 1996, Kettinger et al. 1994, Neumann 1994). Since IT provides information and communication channels among the various participants, many assume that adoption of IT must alter the basis for industry competition (Bhide 1994; Peppard 1993; Porter and Miller 1985).

Some but not all case studies support the idea that IT helps firms develop and implement strategy, and that through this route, IT yields direct economic benefit (Baura et al. 1995;

Taylor and Todd 1995). As IT becomes more affordable, IT plays a greater role in the design and evaluation of strategy (Bergeron et al. 1998).

Whether or not this is the case, the fact remains that less than two-thirds of the small and medium size enterprises use IT strategically (Taylor and Todd 1995; Lesjak 1993). Instead firms tend to design and implement strategy without the aid of the IT applications they may have, relegating IT to routine internal operations (Moreton 1995; Langley and Traux 1994).

The research discussed below introduces the concepts of IT Maturational models and research on IT use in developing nations.

1.2 IT Diffusion/Maturation Models

IT enables firms to change how they conduct business. There is wide belief that the process by which firms adopt IT in their business practices tends to follow a similar maturational pattern. One early model of this pattern, developed by Cooper and Zmud (1990), divides the process into six stages. A simpler model employs three stages of development: Awareness, Application Function, and Integration (Asian Productivity Organization, 1994). At the Awareness stage, IT users have low understanding of IT. IT expenditures are low to non-existent. At the Application Function stage, IT is implemented independently in first one, and then many separate functions. Firms at this level of development struggle with issues of integrating the various functions, training, and developing standards. The final stage of development is the Integration stage. Firms at this level strive to seamlessly integrate IT into all areas of the business, including strategy design and implementation.

1.3 Other Studies of IT Development in Developing Economies

The relationship between Information Technology (IT) investment and business performance in various countries has only recently been investigated in less developed business environments. These findings are not in concert with the common understanding of the use of IT in strategy found in studies conducted in industrialized nations.

Serafeimidis and Doukidis (1999) used the case study approach to investigate the impact of IT investment on business performance in Greece. They concluded that in their sample, IT investments could not be related to business financial success. They argue that part of the reason IT did not impact financial success in their sample was because managers did not have the education to make the best use of strategic information systems. This deficit kept the firms they studies at the Awareness and Application Growth levels of maturity.

Tam (1998) had a similar finding. He examined the impact of IT investment on firm performance in four newly industrialized economies (Hong Kong, Singapore, Malaysia, and Taiwan). His findings replicate those of studies in the US, finding no relationship between IT expenditures in large firms and stock market return. Tan did not directly study IT use in strategy.

Doukidis, Smithson, and Lybereas (1994) demonstrated the value of conducting repeated measurements over time. They report on a five-year follow-up of their earlier study of small business use of IT in Greece. One of their conclusions was that Greek small businesses do not follow the maturational stages seen in other studies.

1.4 Slovenia's Economic Transformation

The economy of Slovenia fits closest with a newly industrialized nation. Slovenia is a small country, with a population of fewer than two million. A decade ago, its economy, under Yugoslavian rule, was a form of Communism. The transition from Communism to Capitalism's market economy created new business opportunities, particularly in small businesses. The number of Slovene small businesses increased six-fold since 1990, when the transformation of Slovenia's economy began. In 1999, Slovenia had around 34,500 small businesses (almost all new businesses), compared to 887 large and fewer than 2,143 midsize firms (Ministry, 2000). Figure 1 shows this pattern of growth.

Figure 1. Number of Small Firms in Slovenia

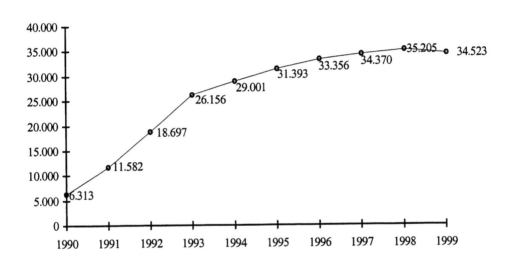

The growth in number of small business is large, small businesses themselves are disinclined to grow larger. It is expensive for business in Slovenia to hire workers. More than 30% of the small firms in Slovenia have no outside employees. Governmental regulations make it quite expensive for firms to fire or lay off employees and employer-paid employee taxes are high. The situation is worse in Slovenia than in the European Union. This situation keeps small business small.

Even so, collectively the many small businesses have a significant impact on the economy. In 1998, small firms accounted for nearly 21% of the total revenue, more than 36% of the total profit and 44% of the total loss in Slovenia. Since these figures include new start up firms, as expected, profits of small firms are much lower compared to other companies. Even so, profits from small firms are increasing and their losses are diminishing (Chamber of Commerce and Industry of Slovenia, 1999).

Structural differences between Slovenia's small business sectors and those of Western Europe as well as year-to-year indicators suggest that transition is still taking place among Slovene small businesses. The percent of employees employed by small firms ranges within Western Europe from Spain's high of 81% down to Belgium's low of 56% (Eurostat 1999).

All these figure are considerably higher than Slovenia's 24%. Therefore the time is ripe to collect baseline data.

2. RESEARCH MODEL

The purpose of this study is to identify whether Slovenian small business, particularly those established in the nineties, leverage IT for strategic advantage. It tests a new framework of strategic IT usage.

Based on existing literature (Cragg and King 1993, Grover 1993, Bergeron et al. 1998) we propose a framework for studying strategic IT usage in small firms. The framework is shown as Figure 2. These studies suggest at least two sets of influences that may impact the degree to which IT is used strategically: **firm characteristics** and **firm strategy**.

Figure 2. Framework of Strategic IT Usage

Firms' characteristics	*Firms' strategy*

⇓ ⇓

Firms' IT usage

⇓

Impacts of IT usage

⇓

Financial performance

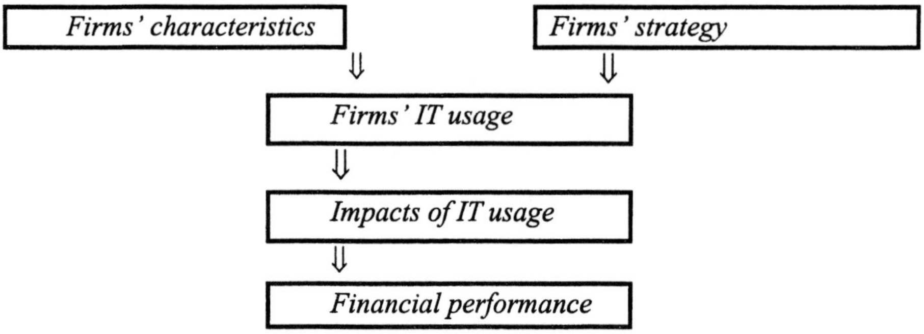

To test the framework in the context of Slovenia small business, we put forward the following hypotheses:

Firms' characteristics. As firms age, they tend to mature in their business practices. Thus, we see the firm's size and age as being positively associated with strategic IT usage. We hypothesize that:

H1: The older the firm, the greater the use of strategic IT applications.

Strategy. Research consistently shows that entrepreneurs and SME managers differ in their choice of competitive strategies (Covin et al. 1994; Kagar and Blumenthal 1994). Compared with large firms, small firms do not perform strategic planning as much or as formally (Bhide 1994; Rue and Ibrahim 1995). This may be due to the need for small firm employees to be generalists rather than specialist, as suggested by Matthews and Scott (1995), or because small firms are not always growth-oriented and thus have a variety of goals. These both impact the desirability of planning (Bhide 1994).

H2: Firms with well elaborated, formally written strategic plan, known by the employees, will tend to use IT strategically.

IT Usage. There is some evidence that the more IT is adopted among various business areas or functions and the deeper it is involved in different areas, the more familiar employees and management get with possible IT applications, and the more likely they will be to utilize IT strategically. Thus, we hypothesize that:

H3: The breadth of IT usage across various business areas and therefore the number of IT users (and IT experts) will positively correlate with strategic IT applications.

Impacts of IT usage. The impacts of IT usage can be classified into strategic and non-strategic ones, according to their contribution to enhancing the firm's competitiveness and co-operation. Therefore, we hypothesize that:

H4: The degree of strategic IT usage will positively correlate with the impacts of IT usage.

Financial performance. From the above framework, we expect that strategic IT usage will positively affect the firms' financial performance.

H5: The impacts of IT usage will positively correlate with the firms' financial performance.

3. METHODS

3.1 Measures/Variables

In operationalizing the variables, we rely on measurement instruments developed elsewhere wherever possible.

Strategy. Strategy is measured on using an 11-item scale devised Covin et al. (1994) and Kim and Choi (1994).

IT Usage. This study uses an 8-item measure of IT strategic usage. It is an enhancement of the 6-item measure developed by Cragg and King (1993).

Impacts of IT Usage. The impact of IT usage is measured by an 11-item scale designed specifically for the present study.

Financial Performance. Financial Performance is measured by 11-item scale designed for the present study that involves traditional economic criteria, such as sales, revenue, profit, and so on. We ask respondents to indicate how important a set of financial measures is in their firms and the degrees of satisfaction with firm performance on these outcomes. We also ask respondents to evaluate their relative standing on financial outcomes, compared to their competitors.

3.2 Research Sample

One of the problems in any study is in selecting the proper sample. For a study of small business, we want to make sure that they are both small enough to be considered small and large enough to have the maturation associated with strategic planning.

This study defines small business using the criteria adopted from the Agency for Payment System (APS) of Slovenia (Agency... 1998). A small business is defined as one that satisfied at least two of the following criteria:

1. It has 50 or fewer employees,
2. fixed assets should of US$0.5 Million or less, and
3. annual sales of US$1 Million or less.

Every country has its own legal definition of small business. The purpose here is to select small business as befits the local economy.

To ensure that our sample firms are large enough to have the potential for benefiting from strategic IS, we applied three additional criteria. First, we selected firms with annual revenue of more than $100,000. Likewise, we excluded micro firms having fewer than 10 employees. Firms with fewer employers may be disinclined to want to grow. Lastly, we excluded from the sample non-profit organizations, publicly owned businesses, and wholly owned subsidiaries of large businesses, as they do not within our working definition of small business.

The names and the addresses of small businesses that fulfill the above criteria were obtained from the APS of Slovenia. This yielded a population of 974 businesses, representing 2.84% of all small business in Slovenia.

Surveys were sent to all these 974 small firms in this population. Of these, 161 surveys were returned, yielding an initial response rate of 16.5%. Responses from 14 businesses with incomplete data were discarded, resulting in a final sample of 147 usable questionnaires, 15.1% of the population.

There is a danger that those firms that return surveys may be unrepresentative of the population as a whole. To test whether the respondents were similar in characteristics to the population, these final 147 firms were compared to the 974 in terms of the number of employees, income, and income per employee. (Data on all firms were obtained from the APS.) T-tests showed no significant differences on any of these measures (income: $t = 0.65$; $p = .52$; employees: $t = 0.30$; $p = .76$; income per employee: $t = 0.72$; $p = .47$). For this reason, we believe that the sample is representative of the population on the characteristics measured by the survey.

Table 1 presents the sample characteristics. On average, small businesses had 29 employees and mean annual sales per employee of $101,922. The average firm had 5.8 years of computer experience, and on average, about 50% of the firms' employees are computer literate.

Table 1. Characteristics of the Sample

Characteristic	Choices	Frequency	Percent
Sector	Manufacturing	68	46
	Trade	42	29
	Business Services	26	18
	Construction	11	7
Years in business	>8 years	25	17
	<8	122	83
Operating at a profit or loss	Profit	127	86
	Breakeven	1	1
	Loss	19	13
Number of full-time equivalent employees	10-20	80	55
	21-30	22	15
	31-40	16	11
	41-50	13	9
	51-	16	10
Computer usage in the firm	>8 years	44	30
	6-7	27	18
	4-5	43	30
	<3	33	22
Percent of employees who are IT users	86%-100%	40	27
	41%- 85%	33	22
	11%- 40%	38	26
	0%- 10%	36	25
Percent of employees who are responsible for IT	15%-100%	35	24
	6%- 14%	35	24
	1%- 5%	46	31
	0%	31	21

4. RESULTS AND DISCUSSION

4.1 Instrument Validation (Assessing Reliability)

Our first task was to assess whether our scales were reliable enough that they might be valid. We assessed for each composite variable the reliability (internal consistency) by calculating Cronbach's alpha coefficient, as suggested in Carmines and Zeller (1981). Non-performing items were dropped to create the final scales. Table 2 presents the results of reliability testing.

Since the reliability coefficients were higher than 0.7 (except strategy-low cost with an alpha = 0.67), we believe that the research variables are satisfactorily reliable (Nunnally 1978). The item-total correlation coefficients of items of research variables were also high, indicating reasonable reliability of the research variables.

Table 2. Reliability and Factor Analysis of Variables

Items	Item-total correlation	Factor loading
Differentiation Strategy:	.72[a]	55.0%[v]
1. Emphasizing product and/or service quality	.43	.67
2. Investing in research and development	.68	.86
3. Emphasizing education and training of employees	.48	.72
4. Developing new products or services	.48	.70
Low Cost Strategy:	.67[a]	50.9%[v]
1. Being a low-cost producer	.37	.62
2. Automating functions as much as possible	.60	.87
3. Maximizing efficiency of business activities	.44	.76
4. Maintaining very low-level inventories	.35	.57
Firm IT Usage:	.75[a]	37.3%[v]
1. Research and development	.43	.61
2. Purchasing/Procurement	.58	.72
3. Production	.62	.76
4. Marketing and Sales	.35	.50
5. Inventory (warehousing)	.38	.55
6. Transport	.50	.65
7. Personnel/Human Resources	.56	.63
8. Finance and Accounting	.27	.39
Impact of IT Usage:	.91[a]	52.2%[v]
1. The quality of products and/or services	.68	.75
2. Quality of producing products/services	.64	.71
3. Finding new business opportunities	.65	.72
4. Finding new markets	.64	.71
5. Business process redesign	.67	.74
6. Firm's capabilities to adjust to changes	.75	.81
7. Introducing new products and/or services	.68	.75
8. Introducing new production and business technology	.71	.77
9. Customer satisfaction	.62	.69
10. Employee satisfaction	.57	.64
11. Business risk	.56	.63
Financial performance:	.91[a]	54.6%[v]
1. Annual sales	.47	.56
2. Annual sales growth	.64	.71
3. Revenue	.66	.73
4. Revenue growth	.73	.78
5. Profit	.74	.82
6. Profit growth	.80	.86
7. Profitability	.76	.82
8. Return on investment (ROI)	.71	.78
9. Solvency	.58	.62
10. Ability to fund business growth from profits	.52	.57
11. Overall firm performance	.73	.77

[a]Cronbach Alpha (Standard), [v]Variance explained

To assess whether the item of the variables constituted different scales of variables, a principal component factor analysis was performed (Carmines and Zeller 1981). Table 2 indicates that almost all the factor loadings are greater than the recommended cut-off point of 0.5 (except the item Finance and Accounting in the Firm IT Usage column: 0.39) and all the items loaded on their hypothesized factors (Nunnally 1978). Hence, we are confident that construct validity was not violated. These results also provide confidence to combine various items under different variables into one construct.

However, the other scales could account for only 37.3% of the variance in the firm's IT usage variable, a value that we do not few as satisfactory. Further investigation, using factor analysis, revealed that the construct Firms IT Usage was composed of more than a single dimension. In fact, we found three dimensions to this construct. An Eigenvalue of 0.9 or above was used as a criterion to estimate the number of factors underlying the construct Firms IT Usage. The construct had 3 interpretable dimensions (which altogether explain 66.6% of the variance), and percent of explained variance was computed for each dimension, as shown in Table 3.

Table 3. Total Variance Explained for the Variable "Firm IT Usage"

| Components | Total | Initial Eigenvalues | |
		Percent of Variance	Cumulative Percent
C1	2.98	37.29	37.29
C2	1.41	17.58	54.88
C3	.94	11.71	66.59
...	...	....	....

For the first 3 components we performed Principle Component Analysis (using Varimax with the Kaiser Normalization rotation method) to identify any related forms of IT usage.

Table 4. Rotated Component Matrix

Firm IT Usage	Design and production activities	Trade and transport activities	Finance/account. And HRM activities
Research and development	.92		
Purchasing/Procurement	.35	.35	
Production	.72	.32	.29
Marketing and Sales	.20	.85	-.10
Inventory (warehousing)			.21
Transport		.80	.22
Personnel/Human Resources	.28	.11	.81
Finance and Accounting			.85

We interpret these components as representing different industries, as shown in Table 4:

- First component represents manufacturing firms because research/development and production functions have high coefficients,
- Second component represents trade, because marketing/sales and transportation functions have high coefficients, and
- Third component represents business services because personnel/human resources and finance/accounting have high coefficients in the contrast with marketing/sales.

4.2 Correlations

To test our framework, we employ correlation analysis. We show the Pearson correlation between the measures of strategic IT usage (i.e. Firms' Strategy, Firms' IT usage, Impacts of IT Usage and Financial performance) and sample "economic data" in Table 5.

Table 5. Correlations Between Strategic IT Usage Variables and Sample "Economic Data"

Variable	Strategy: differ.	low c.	IT usage in activities: R/D&P	T&T	F/A&HRM	Impact	Financial performance
Industry	.17*	.16*			.23**	.21*	
number of employees							
years in business							
Markets:							
Slovenia							
Ex Yugoslavia							
European Union							
Other	.17*						
Number of markets	.17*						.17*
Income/employee				.28**			.28**
Profit/loss							.26**
Profit/loss per employee							.36**

**p > .01 (2-tailed), *p > .05 (2-tailed)

Interestingly, there is no significant correlation between the number of employees and Strategic IT usage, nor between years in business and Strategic IT usage, so these data do not confirm Hypothesis 1.

There are some significant correlations among industries, number of markets, which will be investigated, and of course financial outcomes and financial performance as expected.

Interestingly, there is no significant correlation between years of IT usage, % of IT users and experts and strategic IT usage variables, so Hypothesis 3 is not confirmed. Perhaps the reason for this is the constriction in the years of IT usage variable as most all of these firms were established in the nineties.

In order to understand the relationship between the research variables, we performed partial correlations analysis, (controlling for "economic" (shown in Table 5) and "IT/IS" (shown in Table 6) data) to analyze the influence among the introduced measures/components of strategic IT usage, (i.e., introduced components for the following variables: Firm Strategy,

Firm IT Usage, Impact of IT Usage, and Financial Performance). The results are shown in Table 7.

Table 6. Correlations Between Strategic IT Usage Variables and Sample "IT/IS Data"

Variable	Strategy:		IT usage in activities:			Impact	Financial
	differ.	low c.	R/D&P	T&T	F/A&HRM		performance
Years of IT usage							
% of IT users							
% of IT experts							
Relation to IT						.27**	
Funds for IT		.17*		.19*			
IT vision	.31**					.23**	
IT usage/rivals	.36**		.23**	.21*		.40**	.37**
IT role					.19*	.18*	

**p > .01 (2-tailed), *p > .05 (2-tailed)

Table 7: Descriptive Statistics and Significant Partial Correlations between Variables

Variable	Mean	S.D.	Var.1.	Var.2.	Var.3.	Var.4.	Var.5.	Var.6.
1. Strategy: Differentiation	5.28	1.07						
2. Strategy: Low cost	5.49	1.02	.39**					
3. IT usage in manufacturing firms	4.78	1.63		.18*				
4. IT usage in trade firms	5.28	1.45		.36**				
5. IT usage in services firms	5.13	1.69						
6. Impact of IT usage	5.12	.87	.26**	.24**	.28**	.30**	.37**	
7. Financial Performance	5.00	.79	.31**	.23*		.19*		.18*

**p > .01 (2-tailed), *p > .05 (2-tailed)

Table 7 shows the following interesting significant correlations:

- Not surprisingly, low cost strategy correlates with the IT usage among manufacturing and especially trade firms. Interestingly enough there are no significant correlations among firms following differentiation strategy (such as business services firms) and IT usage. So we assert that hypothesis 2 is partially confirmed.
- IT usage in firms from all 3 industries significantly correlates with the impacts of IT usage, what is somehow anticipated, because if a firm uses IT heavily then impacts of that kind of usage are expected. So we assert that Hypothesis 4 is confirmed.
- Interestingly, there is a significant correlation only among IT usage and the financial performance of the firms from trade industry.
- Interestingly again, there exist a weak but significant correlation between impacts of IT usage and financial performance of firms. So, we could say that there is a certain influence of IT usage on financial performance of firm. This means that Hypothesis 5 is confirmed.
- Both strategies correlate significantly with the financial performance of the firms, but the question remains whether IT usage contributes to that performance?

Yet, despite these interesting findings, which partially confirm the Hypothesis, we want this research to explore in greater depth the relations among research variables from industries perspectives. The results of this investigation are shown as Table 7a, 7b and 7c.

Table 7a: Significant Partial Correlations between 7 Variables for Manufacturing Firms

Variable	Var.1.	Var.2.	Var.3.	Var.4.	Var.5.	Var.6.
1. Differentiation strategy						
2. Low cost strategy	.55**					
3. IT usage in R&D and P activities						
4. IT usage in T&T activities		-.28*				
5. IT usage in F&A and HRM activities						
6. Impact of IT usage						
7. Financial Performance	.35*	.30*				.42**

**p > .01 (2-tailed), *p > .05 (2-tailed)

Table 7a shows the following interesting significant correlations among manufacturing firms:

- Both Low Cost and Differentiation strategies correlate with financial performance. This finding supports the generally held view that both strategies are important even for small business.
- IT usage in "manufacturing" business activities negatively correlates with its usage in trade and transportation business activities. This is logical if we compare how these activities are supported with IT (means: R&D = 4.78, production = 5.12, trade = 4.40, transportation = 3.32).
- Correlation between Impacts of IT usage and financial performance provides additional support to Hypothesis 5.

Table 7b: Significant Partial Correlations between 7 Variables for Trade Firms

Variable	Var.1.	Var.2.	Var.3.	Var.4.	Var.5.	Var.6.
1. Differentiation strategy						
2. Low cost strategy						
3. IT usage in R&D and P activities						
4. IT usage in T & T activities		.52**				
5. IT usage in F&A and HRM activities	.40*					
6. Impact of IT usage						
7. Financial Performance	.50**					

**p > .01 (2-tailed), *p > .05 (2-tailed)

Table 7b shows the following interesting significant correlations among trade firms:

- As might be expected, low costs strategy is related to IT usage in "trade" business activities.
- On the other hand differentiation strategy is related to IT usage in "business service" activities even in trade sector.

**Table 7c: Significant Partial Correlations between
7 Variables for Business Services Firms**

Variable	Var.1	Var.2	Var.3	Var.4	Var.5	Var.6
1. Differentiation strategy						
2. Low cost strategy						
3. IT usage in R&D and P activities						
4. IT usage in T & T activities						
5. IT usage in F&A and HRM activities						
6. Impact of IT usage		.62*				
7. Financial Performance						

**p > .01 (2-tailed), *p > .05 (2-tailed)

Table 7c shows only one interesting significant correlation, which supports previous research and our current hypotheses that present and elaborated strategy has an influence.

4.3 Maturational Model

In the future, the data collected here will be compared with follow up data collected every five years on many of these same firms to determine whether the maturational models described earlier apply to the Slovenian small business environment.

5. CONCLUSION

The results show that Slovene small firms are using applications of IT strategically to a certain extend. The impact is strongest for manufacturing and trade firms that follow a low cost strategy. This is seen not only in various impacts of IT usage on firms, but also by the positive correlation between IT usage and firms' financial performance.

The findings can help small business narrow the gap regarding productivity and profitability between Slovenia and the European Union, in terms of competitive strategy and business areas in which IT usage could be used strategically. We note the following:

- In the near future, an additional 20% will be employed in the business sector and they will need additional IT. (Eurostat (1999)) This means that there will be a greater need for managers who understand how to use IT for strategic advantage.
- In more developed markets, business services firms are very strong IT users. This is not yet the case in Slovenia. This will change as small business matures in Slovenia.
- Global trends, such as usage of the Internet, e-commerce, and networked cooperation among firms, will have a big impact on small Slovene firms in near future. These changes definitely impact their attitude to IT and its usage.

There are a number of limitations in this study.

1. We assumed that the common utilization of IT applications in economic sectors was an indicator of areas of strategic importance. There may be some multicollinearity present, however, between the variables.
2. As is always the case, all our measures would benefit from further study. In light of our findings, our model for the adoption of IT strategic use needs to be refined.
3. Some of our measures rely on managers' opinions, which are subjective in nature.

In the next stage of this research, data will be collected and analyzed every two years to detect changes in the strategic use of IT in small Slovene firms. Future studies will be designed to enable additional appropriate analysis, such as structural equation modeling, to explore the underlying causes and effects of this complex situation.

REFERENCES

Agency of Payment System of Slovenia 1998. *Bulletin of the Business Result within the Economy of Slovenia*, Ljubljana

Asian Productivity Organization, 1994. Report on Conclusions and Recommendations: Symposium on Applications of Information Technology in National Development, November.

Baura, A., Kriebel, C. H., Mukhopadhyay, T. 1995. "Information Technologies and Business Value: An Analytic and Empirical Investigation". *Information Systems Research,* (6) pp. 3-23.

Bergeron, F., Raymond L., Gladu M., Leclerc C, 1998. "The Contribution of IT to the Performance of SMEs: Alignment of Critical Dimensions", In: Beats W.R.J. (editor), *Proceedings of the 6th European Conference on IS*, Aix-en-Provence, France, pp. 173-187.

Bhide, A. 1994. "How Entrepreneurs Craft Strategies that Work", *Harvard Business Review*, March-April, pp. 150-161.

Callon, J. (1996) *"Competitive Advantage through Information technology"*, New York, McGraw-Hill.

Carmines, E.G., Zeller, R.A. 1981. *Reliability and Validity Assessment*. Beverly Hills, CA: Sage.

Chamber of Commerce and Industry of Slovenia 1999. *Analysis of Business Results of Small Business in 1998*. Ljubljana, Chamber of Commerce and Industry of Slovenia.

Cooper, R.B. and Zmud, R.W. "Information Technology Implementation Research: A Technological Diffusion Approach," *Management Science* (36:2), 1990, pp. 123-139.

Covin, J.G., Slevin, D.P., Shultz, R.L. 1994 "Implementing Strategic Mission: Effective Strategic, Structural and Tactical Choices", *Journal of Management Studies,* 31, pp. 481-504.

Cragg, P.B., King, M. 1993. "Small-Firm Computing: Motivators and Inhibitors", *MIS Quarterly*, March, pp. 47-60.

Doukidis, G.I., Smithson, S. and Lybereas, T. "Trends in Information Technology in Small Businesses," *Journal of End User Computing* (6:4), 1994, pp. 15-25.

Eurostat 1999. *Enterprises in Europe*: SME Database Data, 1990-1995. Luxembourg: Eurostat.

Grover, V. 1993. "An Empirically Derived Model for the Adoption of Costumer-based Interorganizational Systems", *Decision Sciences*, 24(3), pp. 603-640.

Heikkila, J., Saarinen, T., Assksjavri, M. 1991. "Success of Software Packages in Small Business: An Exploratory Study". *European Journal of Information Systems* (1) pp. 159-167.

Kagar, J. and Blumenthal, R.A. 1994. "Successful Implementation of Strategic Decisions in Small Community Banks", *Journal of Small Business Management*, 32(2), pp. 10-22.

Kettinger, W., Grover, V., Guha, S., Segars, A. (1994) "Strategic Information Systems revised: A Study in Sustainability and Performance", *MIS Quarterly*, March.

Kim, Y., Choi, Y. 1994. "Strategic Types and Performances of Small Firms in Korea", *International Small Business Journal*, 13(1), pp. 13-25.

Langley, A., Traux, J. 1994. "A Process Study of New Technology Adoption in Smaller Manufacturing Firms". *Journal of Management Studies,* 31 pp. 621-652.

Lesjak, D. 1993. "Evaluating (Current and Future) Impacts of Information Technology Usage". In: *Advances in Management*. Windsor, Ontario, Canada: The International Institute for Advanced Studies in Systems Research and Cybernetics, pp. 143-148.

Matthews, C.H. and Scott, S.G. 1995. "Uncertainty and Planning in Small and Entrepreneurial Firms: An Empirical Assessment" *Journal of Small Business Management*, 33(4), pp. 34-41.

Ministry of Small Business and Tourism 2000. *Small Business in Slovenia*. Ljubljana: Ministry of Small Business and Tourism.

Moreton, R. 1995. "Transforming the Organisation: The Contribution of the IS Function". *Journal of Strategic Information Systems,* 4 pp. 149-163.

Neumann, S. (1994) *"Strategic Information Systems: Competition through Information Technologies"* New York; Macmillan College Publishing Co.

Nunnally, J.C. 1978. *Psychometric Theory*, New York Mc Graw-Hill Book Company Inc.

Peppard, J. 1993. "Using IS/IT to Gain Competitive Advantage". In Peppard, J. (ed.), *I.T. Strategy for Business*. London: Pitman Publishing, pp. 53-74.

Porter, M.E., Miller, V.E. 1985. "How Information Gives You a Competitive Advantage", *Harvard Business Review*, 4, pp. 149-160.

Rue, L. W., Ibrahim, N. A. 1995. "The Status of Planning in Smaller Family-Owned Business". *Family Business Review* 9(1) pp. 29-43.

Serafeimidis, V. and Doukidis, G.I. "Management of Information Technology Investments in Less Developed Environments: Experiences from Greece," *Journal of Global Information Technology Management* (2:4), 1999, pp. 4-22.

Tam, K.Y. "The Impact of Information Technology Investments on Firm Performance and Evaluation: Evidence from Newly Industrialized Economies," *Information Systems Research* (9:1), 1998, pp. 85-98.

Taylor, S., Todd, P. A. 1995. "Understanding Information Technology Usage: A Test of Competing Models". *Information Systems Research*, 6, pp. 144-152.

Žižmond, E. 1994. "Economic Development in Slovenia", *Eastern European Economics*, Nov-Dec., Vol. 32, No. 6, pp. 75-99.

Chapter 4

Waiting for Telecoms Consolidation in Central Europe: German, Italian, and Swiss Dilemmas

Robert C. Rickards
The Leipzig Graduate School of Management
Handelshochschule Leipzig
Leipzig, Germany
and
Harz University of Applied Sciences
Wernigerode, Germany
Email: rrickards@hs-harz.de

ABSTRACT

This chapter begins by contrasting the vision with the reality of third-generation telecommunication services. In doing so, it focuses on profitability, indebtedness, and industry consolidation issues. Next, the chapter reports where Germany, Italy, and Switzerland stand in the New Economy rankings. It also offers insights into why analysts are so skeptical about European telecoms' business models. The chapter then examines different dilemmas confronting Deutsche Telekom, Telecom Italia, and SwissCom. Finally, it closes with a few thoughts about the outlook for acquisitions and mergers in the European telecommunications industry.

VISION AND REALITY

A soccer star, dribbles, dodges a defender and drives the ball into the back of the net. Minutes later, cheers echo through a crowded subway, where a group of friends gather around a mobile phone to watch a video clip of the scoring play on its tiny screen. That is the colorful marketing vision for the long-hyped third-generation mobile-phone services in Europe.

Telecommunications companies there have lavished hundreds of billions of euros on the promise of untethering the Internet.

But now, like a bet whose odds grow longer after the gambler has put down his cash, that grand vision is slipping away. Third-generation telephony supposedly was going to be the next mass-market revolution in technology, putting the power of the Internet into a miniature gadget in the palm of a customer's hand, practically anywhere on the planet.

When governments throughout Europe reaped windfalls selling licenses for third-generation, or 3G, wireless services, they assumed that the requisite networks would be in place by now. Instead, technological glitches and the financial hangover from the telecom operators' spending binge are combining to delay commercial rollout of 3G-services.

To be sure, 3G will happen. Tests are under way at several European companies. A few promise to have limited networks up and running by the end of the year, like the one started in Tokyo by NTT DoCoMo in 2001.[1] But most analysts say viable commercial services – with acceptably broad network coverage, practical handsets, and coherent marketing – most likely will not be in place until 2004 or 2005.

Profitability may be even further down the road – if it ever comes. In the meantime, many money-losing operators will have to merge with others or fall by the wayside. At risk is the very existence of companies that bet on this revolution – some of which are the pillars of today's phone business – along with their workers' jobs and their investors' capital. Moreover, there is considerable uncertainty about both the business models involved and which players will survive.[2]

Some countries, such as Germany and Austria, individually sold as many as six licenses. However, analysts at Crédit Suisse First Boston (CSFB) estimate that eventually there will be no more than five or six major operators across all of Europe.[3] Pressure to combine likely will be greatest in those countries, whose license costs were highest, such as Germany and Britain.

The position in Germany of the Dutch phone company KPN illustrates that situation well. After describing KPN's position, this article examines in greater depth issues of profitability and indebtedness, together with the potential for industry consolidation. Next, it shows how European countries rank in the New Economy, explores the diversity of pricing models for GPRS-services, and discusses both skeptical and optimistic views on whether firms can make money offering those services. The chapter then analyzes the different dilemmas confronting three of Central Europe's largest telecoms before concluding with brief remarks on the current state of the industry's consolidation process.

SETTING THE STAGE FOR CONSOLIDATION

Recently, KPN announced it would take full control of a key asset, E-Plus Mobilfunk, the No. 3 German mobile operator, in a deal that could trigger consolidation in Europe's top telecommunications market. Stock in KPN tumbled after the heavily-indebted carrier said it

---

[1] Rickards, Robert C., "UMTS in Japan: Has the Future *Really* Begun?," *Current Politics and Economics of Asia*, (accepted for publication in 2002).

[2] Rickards, Robert C., "UMTS 2: A Game for Europe's Big Gorillas?," in Frank Columbus (ed.), *European Economic and Political Issues*, Vol. IV, (Nova Science, 2001; Chapter 7, pp. 105-140).

[3] Pfanner, Eric, "Next-Generation Cell Phones: Only the Fittest Firms Will Survive," *International Herald Tribune*, February 2-3, 2002, pp. 1,4.

would issue 234.7 million shares in exchange for the remaining 22.51 percent stake in E-Plus held by the U.S. carrier BellSouth.

BellSouth, which had an option to convert its stake in E-Plus into KPN stock or a stake in KPN's cell-phone business, KPN Mobile, will take a 9.4 percent stake in the parent company, becoming its second-largest shareholder. But analysts fear that BellSouth, which wants to refocus on its domestic markets, after exercising its option to switch out of E-Plus and into KPN, then will sell that stake on the open market. KPN's recently appointed chief executive, Ad Scheepbouwer, has complained that although BellSouth had agreed to inform KPN of any plans to sell its holding, the U.S. carrier subsequently has declined to discuss them.

The possible sale of BellSouth's stake in KPN thus likely will remain a threat to the latter's stock for the near future. Probably of greater interest to investors, though, would be the Dutch company's still unannounced plans for E-Plus, which is battling Deutsche Telekom and Britain's Vodafone for dominance in Germany's mobile phone sector. In this regard, many investors well may have the feeling that KPN is stuck with a bad investment.

Furthermore, KPN's net debt currently is about €16.5 billion. The company had said it planned to cut debt to €14 billion by the end of 2002. KPN now expects debt of around €14.9 billion following full consolidation of E-Plus.

At any rate, with KPN in full control of E-Plus, consolidation in the German market is beginning to appear more likely. At present, four of the six mobile phone operators in Germany are wholly owned. Given that the market is not big enough for so many competitors, if KPN continues to hold its German operator, it may decide to merge cash-intensive E-Plus with rival businesses, in which a telecommunications heavyweight such as France's Orange or Spain's Telefónica holds stakes.[4]

DISTANT PROFITABILITY

So, profitability in countries such as Germany and the U.K. could be a decade down the road, even for companies already having a strong presence in the market for existing services. For newcomers, it could be still more difficult.

Take, for instance, an established company such as Vodafone. With its low level of debt financing and broad reach – it has investments in most major European markets and over 100 million subscribers worldwide,[5] more than any other mobile phone company – Vodafone ought to thrive despite the massive investments it has made.

In contrast, a new entrant such as Hutchison 3G in the U.K., for example, has to carve out part of the British mobile market by offering video clips of soccer games as well as voice calls, text messages, Internet access, and maybe pornography. Supposedly, Hutchison is well along the road to building a viable network and lining up attractive services.

Though Hutchison 3G offloaded the nearly $7 billion cost of a British license to its majority owner, Hong Kong tycoon Li Ka-shing's Hutchison Whampoa, it took on £3.2 billion of debt to build the network. The parent company also has expensive investments in

---

[4] Reuters, "KPN to Take Over German Mobile Phone Operator," *International Herald Tribune*, January 31, 2002, p. 11.

[5] Reuters, "Vodafone Has 100 Million Subscribers," *International Herald Tribune*, January 23, 2002, p. 14.

several other European markets in addition to its Asian presence.[6] But assume that Hutchison collects, say, £10 ($14.11) a month from a customer for sending out video clips each time a soccer player scores a goal. In that case, Hutchison will have to sign up huge numbers of new service subscribers in a maturing market in order to cover its costs.

Like Hutchison and its parent, other big operators have taken on staggering amounts of debt. Most of the countries that held auctions of wireless spectrum for 3G – including Germany and Britain, which together reaped more than $80 billion of the more than $100 billion bid across Europe – required payment up front for the licenses.[7]

Not every country was so lucky. France, Spain, Portugal, Greece, and Ireland, which garnered only tiny fractions of the total, have had to adopt various alternative payment schemes. France, which was unable to sell two of the four licenses it offered a €4.95 billion each, has cut the price to €619 million in the hope of finding takers. Over and above that price, France also will collect 1 percent of future 3G-revenue.[8] Other countries, including Belgium, Greece, Liechtenstein, and Norway, simply have found themselves left with unwanted licenses.

Even the German government, which received $44 billion from the sale of its six advanced mobile-phone licenses in 2000, is facing growing pressure to let phone companies keep the licenses if they merge. Peter Erskine, the chief executive of BT's mobile subsidiary, mmO2, said he was in talks with the government to press for rule changes. He thereby joined France Télécom and Deutsche Telekom's T-Mobile International unit, which already had issued similar calls. The question of how much change Germany's regulatory agency will allow, though, remains unanswered.[9]

DEBILITATING DEBT

For their part, companies acquiring expensive licenses and then building networks often have incurred swelling debt. France Télécom and Deutsche Telekom are cases in point. Each plans a multicountry presence in 3G and each so far has amassed roughly $65 billion in debt.[10]

Moreover, debt at European phone companies may rise further because of agreements to buy and sell assets in the future that they have not recorded on their balance sheets. Called "contingent liabilities," these agreements are potential obligations that companies nevertheless must disclose. For instance, France Télécom has a contingent liability calling for it to buy back 49.7 million of its own shares from Vodafone on March 25, 2002. This liability is a legacy from the former company's acquisition of its wireless unit, Orange. France Télécom's current balance sheet nonetheless does not report that contingent liability because the purchase has not occurred yet. Still, investors can not afford to overlook off-balance-sheet

---

[6] Rickards, Robert C., "Asia-Pacific Telecoms: Technology, Turmoil, and Transition," *Current Politics and Economics of Asia*, Vol. 10, No. 4, pp. 277-301.

[7] Rickards, Robert C., "€140 Billion Out of Thin Air: Europe's UMTS-Auctions," in Frank Columbus (ed.), *European Economic and Political Issues*, Vol. III, (Nova Science, 2001; Chapter 2, pp. 19-42).

[8] Connell, James, "France Eases Terms on 3G," *International Herald Tribune*, October 17, 2001, p. 13.

[9] N.a., "Pressure Grows on Berlin to Ease License Rules," *International Herald Tribune*, February 6, 2002, p. 11.

[10] Bloomberg, "Phone Debt Watch," *International Herald Tribune*, February 6, 2002, p. 11.

items, even if (or rather, especially if) a company only discloses them at press conferences or in footnotes to its published financial reports.[11]

That is why concerns periodically resurface regarding the wireless carriers' ability to reduce their huge debt loads amid the slowdown in subscriber growth resulting from saturation of the big markets in Europe and North America. These concerns just have led the ratings agency Standard & Poor's to say France Télécom must shed at least €7 billion ($6.02 billion) of assets this year. In addition, to maintain its current debt rating, France Télécom also must avoid putting more money into its German affiliate MobilCom.

France Télécom therefore has pledged to cut its €65 billion in debt to between €37 billion and €47 billion by the end of 2003. As a result, S&P has left its "BBB-plus" rating on the long-term debt and its "negative" outlook unchanged. Another ratings agency, Moody's Investors Service, though, has changed its outlook on France Télécom's "Baa1" credit rating to negative.[12] By comparison, Deutsche Telekom's rating is A-.[13]

THE OBVIOUS ANSWER

Clearly the present situation in the European telecoms industry is untenable. Something must change. Yet the obvious answer, consolidation through acquisitions and mergers, is complicated too. Consortia of new market entrants, rather than individual companies, won many of the new 3G-licenses at the government auctions. Discussions about a possible merger agreement between two of these groups therefore easily could involve six or eight major corporate shareholders. Executives in any one of the companies might prove reluctant to admit having made a bad investment that now could force the write-off of huge sums.

Regulatory issues could stand in the way, too. In Germany, the government insists it will reclaim one of the licenses if two groups were to merge. Despite the abovementioned lobbying by operators for changes in the rules, regulators also continue to insist that the initial cost of both licenses would be nonrefundable.[14]

Moreover, even as the lineups get sorted out and the 3G-players move ahead with their network buildouts, technological stumbles continue to dog them. Because of the high cost of equipment to carry third-generation calls, most operators will start with 3G in dense urban areas. That means they will use existing second-generation networks for coverage in many other areas for at least a while. But new handsets capable of shifting from 2G, which uses the Global System for Mobile standard (GSM), to 3G cellphones have encountered numerous technical glitches. That is why NTT DoCoMo provided 3G-only handsets when it introduced the first new-generation network last year in Tokyo. Consequently, until March 2002, when NTT DoCoMo began to expand its new network nationwide, the phones were useless outside the city.[15]

Indeed, overall consumer response to 3G's precursors has been discouraging. In an effort to bridge the gap to 3G, European telecoms this year are rolling out a hybrid technology

---

[11] N.a., "Lurking Liabilities for Phone Firms," *International Herald Tribune*, February 7, 2002, p. 11.

[12] Bloomberg, "Phone Debt Watch," *International Herald Tribune*, February 6, 2002, p. 11.

[13] Stüwe, Heinz and Lukas Weber, "Telekom Needs New Cable Network Buyer," *Frankfurter Allgemeine Zeitung*, (English Edition) February 19, 2002, p. 5.

[14] N.a., "Pressure Grows," *op. cit.*

[15] AFP, "DoCoMo Seeks 3G Growth," *International Herald Tribune*, February 23-24, 2002, p. 10.

known as General Packet Radio Services (GPRS), or 2.5G. Some analysts expect 30 million sales of these phones by the end of the year, but so far the uptake has been slow. In Scandinavia, where there have been free trials, only 20 percent of customers buying the new phones actually have used them for GPRS-services.[16]

The main problem is the paucity of services currently available. That contrasts with Japan, where a competing 2.5G standard called i-mode has been hugely successful, with more than 30 million users. I-mode took off in part because its provider, NTT DoCoMo, created a pricing model that lets content providers share in the revenue generated by their services. In Europe, though, pricing models for GPRS and 3G still are under development.

NEW ECONOMY STANDINGS

Given that most European telecoms are betting they can profit from offering customers high-speed Internet access as well as downloadable data and services via cellphones, it may be useful here to review some numbers. Table 1 ranks the United States, Japan, and various European countries according to the relative contribution information technology makes to their respective economies. While Switzerland ranks fourth overall, neither Germany nor Italy is a heavyweight. They place eleventh and eighteenth respectively.

Table 1: New Economy Leaders

Country	Rank
United States	1
Great Britain	2
Sweden	3
Switzerland	4
Finland	5
Ireland	6
Netherlands	7
Denmark	8
Europe	9
Belgium	10
Germany	11
Japan	12
Austria	13
France	14
Greece	15
Spain	16
Portugal	17
Italy	18

Source: Merrill Lynch/*International Herald Tribune*

---

[16] Pfanner, *op. cit.*

Arranging the countries in keeping with their per capita expenditures on information technology and telecommunications produces similar rankings. As shown in Table 2, Switzerland then ranks first, followed by Germany (twelfth) and Italy (fifteenth).

Table 2: Expenditures for Information-Technology and Telecommunications in 2000

Country	Expenditure (in DM)/Capita
Switzerland	5292
USA	5090
Sweden	4028
Denmark	3915
Norway	3737
Japan	3406
Great Britain	3343
Netherlands	3241
Finland	3001
Austria	2898
France	2828
Germany	2737
Belgium/Luxemburg	2702
Ireland	2522
Italy	2083
Spain	1904
Portugal	1461
Greece	1352

Source: BITKOM/*Die Zeit*/Globus

Consequently, it is not surprising that both North America and the Asia/Pacific region are ahead of Europe in terms of mobile Internet usage. As reported in Table 3, each of the former regions has more than twice as many mobile Internet users as Europe does.

Table 3: USA Ahead

Region	Mobile Internet Users in the Year 2000 (in Millions)
North America	39.8
Asia/Pacific	36.1
Europe	16.7
Central and South America	1.3
Australia	0.8
Africa	0.2
Russia	0.2

Source: Zeit-Grafik, ResearchPortal.com, 2000

Within Europe, though, Germany, Italy, and Switzerland promise to be particularly dynamic markets for mobile Internet services in the near future. Ranked on the basis of revenues forecasted for 2005, Table 4 lists them first, fourth, and eighth, respectively.

Table 4: Dynamic Germany

Country	Forecasted Sales Revenues from Mobile Internet Services in Year 2005 (in € Billions)
Germany	17.2
Great Britain	13.5
France	13.2
Italy	9.6
Spain	5.4
The Netherlands	3.6
Sweden	2.1
Switzerland	2.0
Finland	1.8
Rest of Europe	8.0

Source: Zeit-Grafik, Durlacher Research

WHAT PRICE FOR GPRS?

But even as new GPRS-phones are becoming available and the requisite networks are coming online, European operators still really haven't figured out how to market new data services or how and how much to charge for them. Operators simply have no clue of what an optimal pricing strategy might be. That may be because many of them have yet to define the role GPRS will have in practice.

Thus, for now, most operators have chosen to charge according to the amount of data going into and out of their customers' mobile devices (not just cellphones, but also handheld computers, pagers and other end equipment). From the operators' standpoint, this choice produces a logical and technically relatively easy solution.

However, charging for kilobytes and megabytes may prove too arcane for the average user. Real people like simple models, such as flatrates for unlimited service. The problem with simple models, though, is that they don't reflect economic reality. Furthermore, an all-you-can-use monthly charge increases the potential for a clogged network. On the other hand, operators are nervous about introducing complex or usage-related charging that may put off many potential early GPRS adopters.

Hence, Mobilkom Austria is giving customers the option of sticking with the same pricing scheme used for voice calls – a per-minute charge for the time spent using data services – even though that makes little sense in the "always on" world of GPRS. Nevertheless, doing so has the clear advantage that people already are familiar with such pricing.

Alternatively, Telia Mobile was the first major operator to offer free GPRS. The Swedish company wanted to give its customers a chance to see what the new technology could do for them, especially following delays in handset deliveries. Telia Mobile therefore charged its Swedish customers nothing at all until mid-February 2002, when it reverted to charging per kilobyte. Telia's domestic competitors, as well as some Italian networks, have taken a similar approach.

West European telecommunications companies thus are all over the map when it comes to pricing GPRS services. While most have set charges based on volume, some companies have set low prices to lure consumers into trying the service, and others have set prices only businesses could afford. Below in Table 5 is a selection of current prices. (One megabyte is equivalent to about 500 WAP pages or 400 to 500 short e-mails.)

Table 5: Selected Current GPRS-Service Prices

Country	Monthly Fee	Data Charge per Kilobyte (KB) or Megabyte (MB)
Mobistar (Belgium)	€30	5 MB included, €12 per additional MB
	€90	50 MB included, €4 per additional MB
Sonera (Finland)	€16.65	Unlimited transmission of data
T-Mobil (Germany)	€10.2	Web access: 1 MB included, 3.6 cents per additional 10 KB WAP access: 1 MB included, 9.7 cents per additional 10 KB
VIAG Interkom (Germany)	Free	4.6 cents per 10 KB, 4.6 cents per WAP
Omnitel Vodafone (Italy)	Free	Up to 100 MB per month
Telefónica Moviles (Spain)	Free	From 2.4 cents per 10 KB up to 1 MB, to 3.2 cents per 100 KB for more than 10 KB
BT Cellnet (Britain)	€6.43	3.2 cents per KB
	€12.87	1 MB included, €6.43 per additional MB

Source: International Data Corp.

For their part, telecommunications executives and analysts say the ultimate goal is to be able to charge not just for bits and bytes, but also according to the quality of the content customers use. Operators then could sell time-sensitive information, for example, at a premium. If the information was, say, a 10-second video of a just-scored soccer goal, network operators would want to charge more than for a goal scored a week earlier. Of course, this type of billing becomes quite complicated for the networks because they need to know both how much data they are transferring and what content is inside the data packets.

Other challenges include managing the business relationship between content providers and networks, and allowing for alternative payment methods such as credit and debit cards or electronic wallets, as opposed to putting all charges on a phone bill. (Clearly, there is going to be an exploding market for billing services as the number of operators and content providers increases. Companies offering billing software therefore stand to benefit in the near term.)

Another important step – especially when it comes to attracting business customers – is roaming, or the ability to get seamless service from one country to the next. Most analysts say GPRS-roaming is at least a year away because operators need to come to billing agreements with foreign carriers. Mergers with or outright acquisitions of foreign carriers, of course, would obviate the need for such agreements.

WARRANTED SKEPTICISM?

Yet, over the next three years, an overwhelming number of European consumers have no intention of paying for high-speed Internet access services via cellphone or otherwise, a study by GartnerG2 says. The relatively high subscription price, the dearth of programming, and consumers' lack of awareness of broadband services are stifling demand in the United Kingdom, Germany, and France, Europe's three largest Internet markets. Unless prices drop dramatically, the firm predicts that just 10 percent of households in Britain, Germany, and France will have fast Internet access by 2005.[17]

In contrast, Kent Thexton, chief marketing and data officer at mmO2, predicts that the new crop of GPRS-enabled phones – with color screens, cameras, multimedia messaging services, and other features – will drive consumers to use the new data networks. The millions of Britons who pay 10 pence (14 U.S. cents) to send each short message on GSM networks now, Thexton says, probably will be willing to spend 20, 30 or even 50 pence to send a message that includes a picture, short video, or audio clip on GPRS. Thexton believes the applications are coming that will drive GPRS adoption. Indeed, he sees virtually all his customers moving toward that data world.[18]

Whether or not operators' prognoses warrant skepticism, at least one European Internet-access provider seems to be getting its operations under better control. In the third-quarter of 2001, Deutsche Telekom's T-Online unit, Europe's second-largest provider of Internet access, reported positive earnings before interest, taxes, depreciation, and amortization (Ebitda) for the first time. The financial director, Rainer Beaujean, also expects T-Online's Ebitda will remain positive for the whole year 2002. Furthermore, T-Online's foreign affiliates appear to be developing well. The subsidiaries in Austria and Switzerland, France (Club Internet) and Spain/Portugal (Ya.com) decreased their losses relative to the fourth-quarter of 2000 by half.

At a press conference, Thomas Holtrop, the board of directors chairman, explained the improved profit situation had resulted from cost optimization and expiration of the narrowband flatrate. Holtrop said strengthening synergy effects between the German parent and its foreign subsidiaries, for instance through joint procurement of prepaid services, could reduce costs by another 75 percent. In addition, all the companies now employ a unitary search engine. Holtrop emphasized T-Online currently plans neither further acquisitions nor larger investments abroad. Instead, his immediate goal is to make the firms profitable. The precondition for doing so, however, is that the market first attains a certain maturity.

Currently, Internet-access business comprises about 85 percent of sales revenue, while portal business (advertising and electronic commerce) has attained a 13.4 percent share. These figures reflect an increase of 77 percent relative to the prior year. The cause lies chiefly in T-Online's increased advertising rates due to the strong rise in user numbers. Although

---

[17] Reuters, "Broadband Blues," *International Herald Tribune*, January 5, 2002, p. 14.
[18] Connell, James, "Mobile Data: Networks Grope for the Right Price," *International Herald Tribune*, December 17, 2001, p. 9.

approximately half of the portal sales revenue comes through contracts with the parent company, Holtrop insisted that Deutsche Telekom was not cross-subsidizing T-Online in this way. By 2004 T-Online wants to increase the portal-business share of total sales revenue to 30 percent.[19]

DEUTSCHE TELEKOM'S DILEMMA

As for Deutsche Telekom, it is Europe's biggest telephone company. Another one of its units, T-Mobile, has 70% of the German wireless market, Europe's largest and richest.[20] Together with the success T-Online is beginning to have, that would seem to put Deutsche Telekom in an enviable starting position to profit from offering mobile Internet services. However, both Vodafone and France Télécom's wirefree subsidiary Orange have larger numbers of European mobile telephone customers, even though Telekom leads in the number of Internet subscribers.[21] Moreover, Vodafone's 2-year, $191 billion, worldwide takeover spree left it with just $9.5 billion in debt. That compares quite favorably with the $60 billion of debt accumulated by Deutsche Telekom for €61.5 billion of acquisitions during the same period.[22] In addition, while the other three firms have a presence in almost all of Western Europe's lucrative markets, and Vodafone is active even in China and Japan, T-Mobile finds itself shut out of France, Italy, Spain, and Sweden.[23]

Failure to make Deutsche Telekom a global player has brought its boss, Ron Sommer, harsh criticism. Announcements that Deutsche Telekom's 2000 annual report overstated the value of the firm's real estate holdings and its equipment have led to further criticism. These problems have contributed to a decline in Deutsche Telekom's share price from €104 in March 2000 to €15 in February 2002. Alleged overpayment to acquire U.S. mobile communications operator VoiceStream as well as sale of large blocks of shares by VoiceStream's former owners also have depressed the value of Deutsche Telekom's stock.

Yet Sommer so far has weathered these setbacks. In describing Deutsche Telekom's situation, he masterfully puts it in the best light. For example, he recently announced that preparations for T-Mobile's stock exchange listing in June or November of 2002 or 2003 are well underway.[24] Sommer plans to offer the public a 10-percent stake in T-Mobile, if the stock market situation is either extremely good or relatively bad. Deutsche Telekom will float more than 10 percent only at a "middle" share price. The objective is not to sell the company completely, but to generate tender for reduction of the parent company's debt.

Developments in customer numbers for 2001 appear encouraging too. T-Online currently is the choice of 10.7 million Internet surfers. It furthermore is the market leader with 2.2 million DSL-broadband connections. Worldwide, 66.9 million customers use cellphone

---

[19] Frühbrodt, Lutz, "T-Online schafft die Wende," *Die Welt*, 30. November 2001, p. 14.

[20] Youngblood, Robert, "Tech Brief: German Mobile Force," *International Herald Tribune*, March 22, 2001, p. 21.

[21] Pfaffner, Eric, *op. cit.*, p. 13, Bloomberg, "German Warning," *International Herald Tribune*, March 1, 2002, p. 13, and Stüwe, Heinz, "Cartel Office Keeps an Eye on T-Online," *Frankfurter Allgemeine Zeitung*, (English Edition), March 1, 2002, p. 5.

[22] Lütge, Gunhild and Gerti Schön, "Auf gleicher Welle," *Die Zeit*, 23. Mai 2001, p. 22.

[23] Zdf.msnbc.de, "Streit um UMTS in Schweden," 18. Dezember 2000.

[24] Bloomberg, "Telekom Plans on Hold," *International Herald Tribune*, February 23-24, 2002, p. 10.

networks belonging to Deutsche Telekom, including 23.1 million T-Mobile subscribers in Germany, 10.2 million One2One clients in the U.K., and 7 million VoiceStream patrons in the U.S.[25] Moreover, for 2002, Sommer forecasts VoiceStream will post positive earnings before interest, taxes, depreciation, and amortization.

However, the Telekom group was in the red in 2001 and will stay there for the next couple of years due to the high license fees paid for third-generation UMTS-mobile communications frequencies and acquisitions in the United States. Alone the interest payments on its huge debt reduced the group's Ebitda of €15 billion ($13 billion) by €4.5 billion. With investments financed from cash-flow of €10-11 billion and a dividend payout totaling €1.8 billion, the company posted a loss.

This negative cash-flow was a bad sign. Sommer expects a smaller loss in 2002, though, because Ebitda should grow at a double-digit rate, whereas the volume of investment will remain the same. In addition, interest payments will decrease slightly. With financial reserves of €25 billion to offset partially the outstanding debt of €65 billion, the losses in 2001 and 2002 should pose no danger to the firm. Given that it is not planning further acquisitions, Deutsche Telekom's cash-flow ought to be in the black again by 2003 at the latest.

In contrast, net profits, too, were negative in 2001. But due to goodwill write-offs worth a total of €16 billion, they will remain negative for years to come. In 2000, Telekom still had posted net profits of €5.9 billion. Although high, one-off effects influenced these results. Such effects also might have an impact on the numbers for the 2002 business year. Included among them could be Telekom's planned sale of its cable network for €5.5 billion as well as the IPO of T-Mobile mentioned earlier.

However that may be, Sommer has difficulties with Germany's regulatory authorities too. Despite having the world's most open telecommunications market and among the lowest prices for long-distance and overseas calls, they have criticized him harshly and repeatedly for uncompetitive practices. Hence, for example, since Jan. 1, 1998, Telekom has had to offer unbundled access to end consumers, unlike the former monopolists in Spain, Italy, or the United Kingdom. But Deutsche Telekom has done so so well (2.2 million customers vs. just 80,000 DSL subscribers for all competitors together) that the regulator now finds itself with a monopoly again.

Of course, Sommer denies that Deutsche Telekom is behaving monopolistically, achieving its prime market position through dumping prices. Instead, he insists his company invested to build its market position itself. Because the amount of investment required is much less than for mobile telecommunications, though, it quickly has become profitable. Any other firm could have done likewise. Sommer therefore cannot understand why the watchdogs recently ordered Telekom to increase prices for its end customers, while reducing line rental charges for competitors.[26]

Deutsche Telekom's dilemma thus consists of being the dominant provider in its home country, and thus subject to heightened competition as well as continuing regulatory scrutiny and directives, while at the same time failing to gain a foothold in many of Europe's most lucrative markets. The unsuccessful merger negotiations with Telecom Italia, discussed

---

[25] ZDFheute.t-online.de, "Deutsche Telekom erhöht Kundenzahl bei Mobilfunk und Internet," January 17, 2002.

[26] Winkelhage, Johannes and Heinz Stüwe, "Telekom Posts Further Losses in 2001," *Frankfurter Allgemeine Zeitung*, (English Edition), January 18, 2002, p. 5.

below, are a case in point. Yet, rather than management mistakes by Deutsche Telekom, Italian national sensitivities seem more to blame for the consolidation efforts' collapse.[27]

TELECOM ITALIA'S ATTRACTION

What made Telecom Italia, Europe's fifth-largest telecommunications company, an attractive takeover target in 2001 was its market dominance and profitability in a country, where UMTS-license distribution did not bleed the winners too badly. The last major West European sale of 3G UMTS-licenses ended with a whimper when Italy's auction of five permits raised only €12.2 billion. That was just half of what the government and most analysts had expected.

The license winners were Telecom Italia Mobile (TIM), Italy's biggest mobile operator; Omnitel Pronto Italia, which had backing from Vodafone; Wind, a joint venture of the state utility Enel and France Télécom; and IPSE 2000, which fronted for Telefónica of Spain and Andala, backed by Hutchison Whampoa of Hong Kong and Tiscali.

The Italian result underscored the wide variety of market conditions producing dramatically different auction results across Europe. In Italy, the high degree of market concentration held down prices. Together, Telecom Italia Mobile and Omnitel control nearly 90 percent of the cellphone market, making it especially difficult for competitors to gain a foothold. In addition, Italian mobile users spend less (a monthly average of €34) than their counterparts elsewhere in Western Europe (a monthly average of €40). That decreases further the opportunity for new entrants in Italy relative to other markets.[28]

Market dominance, together with such impediments facing new entrants, contributed to the high profitability of Telecom Italia's mobile division. In 2000, TIM said its profit rose 20 percent to €1.9 billion, while sales rose 6.4 percent to €7.9 billion.[29] For the first half of 2001, net profit rose another 31 percent to €1.15 billion as sales gained 19 percent to €4.93 billion. At the same time, Ebitda gained 11 percent to €2.38 billion. The company also said it expected "considerable improvement" in its full-year earnings.[30]

Thereafter, TIM announced plans to split into three separate units. The plan foresaw one unit each for Italy (where Telecom Italia Mobile has 22 million clients), the rest of Europe, and South America.[31] The intent behind this restructuring not only was to bring the firm's organization into line with its business segments. It also aimed at making it easier to sell off one or more of them. Robert Colaninno, whose holding companies at that time controlled both Olivetti and Telecom Italia, apparently intended to do just that. Deutsche Telekom was his most likely customer.[32]

---

[27] Lütge, Gunhild, "Schädliches Geraune," *Die Zeit*, 22. Februar 2001, p. 21.

[28] Buerkle, Tom "Hammer Lands with Dull Thud in European Phone Auctions," *International Herald Tribune*, October 24, 2000, p. 1.

[29] Connell, James, "Tech Brief: Roaming Europe," *International Herald Tribune*, Febuary 7, 2001, p. 13.

[30] Shannon, Victoria, "Telecom Italia Profit Rises," *International Herald Tribune*, September 6, 2001, p. 11.

[31] Connell, James, "Tech Brief: Italian Telecom Splits," *International Herald Tribune*, April 12, 2001, p. 13.

[32] Dixon, Hugo, Leslie de Quilacq, and John Paul Rathbone, "Breaking Views.com: Olivetti/Telecom Italia," *The Wall Street Journal Europe*, March 22, 2001, p. 7.

TIM'S FOREIGN EXPANSION

To make the company virtually irresistible to Germany's would-be global player, Colaninno forced the pace of TIM's expansion abroad. Brazil played a key role in his strategy.

In February 2001, Brazil sold three wireless phone licenses for 2.6 billion reals ($1.3 billion), raising more money than expected as companies paid a premium to expand in Latin America's biggest cellular phone market. Telecom Italia Mobile paid 1.5 billion reals for two licenses and Tele Norte Leste Participacoes, Brazil's biggest phone company, paid 1.1 billion reals for one license, lifting their wireless services ahead of market deregulation.

Brazil's government raised on average 20 percent more than the minimum asking price of 2.19 billion reals for the licenses, a surprising premium given the lackluster demand in recent European wireless auctions. TIM agreed to pay 997 million reals for a license to provide wireless service in Sao Paulo, Brazil's richest and most populous state. It also paid 543 million reals for a license covering nine states in Brazil's southern and western regions. Telecom Italia was the lone bidder for each license. This victory was important for TIM, whose strategic objective was to build a national wireless network.[33]

In a subsequent phase of the auction, Telemar, the country's largest phone company, offered 1.1 billion reals for a license to provide cellular services alongside its fixed-line area in 16 states in northern and eastern Brazil. In doing so, Telemar topped a 990 million reals bid from Telecom Italia.

However, Brazil was selling nine new licenses altogether in an effort to expand competition and increase investment in cellular services, opening a market expected almost to triple in the next five years. The government planned to raise more than $3.4 billion from these sales.

Brazil's auctions were not trouble free. Increasing competition, high finance costs, and money-losing cellular businesses worldwide reduced investor interest. Consequently, leading companies such as Vodafone simply withdrew from the auctions. Indeed, Brazil had to cancel a first round of sales scheduled for January 2001 due to a lack of bidders.

Nevertheless, Telecom Italia remained in the hunt for the additional licenses. In March, it became the first mobile-phone operator to secure national wireless coverage across Brazil, snapping up a license in the country's northeast region for 990 million reals ($482 million). Telecom Italia Mobile then went on to become the sole bidder for the last three of the nine licenses offered for sale.[34]

Telecom Italia also gained important footholds in European markets such as Austria (through a near 30 percent stake in Telekom Austria), France (by means of a participation in the third-largest French mobile phone company and UMTS-license holder Bouygues Télécom), Spain (thanks to a 27 percent stake in Auna Operadores de Telecommincaciones), and Turkey (via a holding in mobile operator Aria). On the other hand, its TIM unit showed little interest in taking over KPN's E-Plus in Germany.[35]

---

[33] Bloomberg News, "Brazil Wireless Auction Exceeds Expectations," *International Herald Tribune*, February 14, 2001, p. 13.

[34] Staszewski, Barbara, "Tech Brief: Telecom Italy Covers Brazil," *International Herald Tribune*, March 14, 2001, p. 11.

[35] Rickards, "Gorillas," *op.cit.*

Telecom Italia's reluctance to expand there may have been due to the possibility of cooperation between it and Deutsche Telekom. Although merger negotiations between the two enterprises failed in 1999, both telecoms remained in close contact with one another. In February 2001, their respective divisions, TIM and T-Mobile, concluded a roaming and price discount agreement for five countries (including Britain, Germany, and Italy) that lets them compete better against industry-leader Vodafone.[36] Through similar agreements with operators in other countries, Telecom Italia Mobile then introduced a fixed-price pan-European service in 30 countries, including Italy. The agreement enables clients to make calls between member networks for 65 euro cents (61 U.S. cents) a minute.

MORE RECENT TELECOM ITALIA ACQUISITIONS AND MERGERS

Following a court ruling in its favor at the end of a long legal battle, the Italian multimedia group Seat Pagine Gialle (Yellow Pages) received final approval to buy the broadcaster TeleMonteCarlo in May 2001.[37] Two months after that acquisition, Seat Pagine Gialle again made business news, this time with a merger deal involving Telecom Italia. The deal is noteworthy for two reasons. First, it is a classic example of how Italy Inc. works. Second, it provides background information essential for understanding how the subsequent hostile takeover of Telecom Italia took place.

The merger deal was between the Telecom-Internet corporation Tin.it and the Yellow Pages. In preparing for it, the international accounting and auditing firm KPMG had valued both Tin.it and Seat Pagine Gialle equally, despite objections on three separate occasions by a Turin court. Throughout the merger process, the judges questioned whether Tin.it's value really was equivalent to that of the Yellow Pages. The state attorney in Turin therefore suspected that irregularities might have occurred during the merger, which brought Telecom Italia control over the combined group. The investigation revealed that, while the merger was underway, Seat Pagine Gialle's chief executive, Lorenzo Pellicioli, exercised stock options earning him ItL168 billion (€85.9 million or $77.3 million).

Besides the KPMG auditor's questionable valuation and Pellicioli's clear-cut insider trading, the investigation also targeted Telecom Italia-president Colaninno. Together with a clique of entrepreneurs from Brescia, he at that point also was Telecom Italia's principal stockholder. The state attorney charged that Telecom Italia's managers and board of directors decided to accept a proposal from Colaninno to report large paper profits as income. Apparently, they did so without even exploring the potential for a conflict of interests between his dual roles as chief manager and major stockholder. By reporting anticipated profits from transactions that had not yet occurred, Colaninno allegedly received undeserved bonuses and stock options as well as increased dividends from the shares he already held. In addition, this action lent Telecom Italia the appearance of being a better credit risk for potential investors and lenders than it actually was.

---

[36] Connell, James, "Tech Brief: German-Italian Alliance," *International Herald Tribune*, January 31, 2001, p. 13, and "Roaming Europe," *op.cit.*

[37] Connell, James, "Tech Brief: Seat Gets the Go-Ahead," *International Herald Tribune*, May 31, 2001, p. 18.

Hence, the Turin state attorney ordered home searches of the Brescian entrepreneurs, including the house of Emilio Gnutti, one of the most important stockholders of the financial holding company Hopa, which indirectly controlled Telecom Italia. The stock price of Telecom Italia declined sharply when various reputable Italian newspapers reported that criminal investigations had begun against ten of its managers and stockholders.[38] Rumors about possible consolidation with a foreign telecom (Deutsche Telekom) circulated. Then came the sudden news of a takeover by two families of well-known Italian industrialists, the Pirellis and the Benettons.

THE TAKEOVER

The turnover in Telecom Italia's ownership might suggest that big changes are afoot in the way Italy Inc. operates. But a closer look finds less may be changing than meets the eye.

The old cliché says that in Italy, more than in most European countries, cozy shareholder agreements give effective control of large companies to small groups of insiders. These insiders then wield real corporate power with little regard for other stakeholders in the firm. Through complex networks of cross-shareholdings, families like the Agnellis of Fiat, the Pirellis, and the Benettons, together with their companies and banks, hold the reins on huge swaths of the economy. Moreover, behind them all lurks the influential investment bank, Mediobanca. Until his death in 2000 at the age of 92, Mediobanca's secretive chairman, Enrico Cuccia, masterminded this system of networks.

Even before Cuccia's death, though, there had been rumblings of change in the system. Curiously, few Italian business leaders were more aware of these rumblings than Colaninno. Just two years earlier, in 1999, Colaninno had startled the financial world when he tapped global capital markets to raise $30 billion. That war chest allowed Olivetti, once a typewriter manufacturer, to make a successful hostile bid for 54 percent of Telecom Italia.

Nevertheless, by 2001 Colaninno had to seek new financing to rescue Telecom Italia, which inherited $19 billion of debt due to his hostile takeover and subsequent actions. One could see the attraction for Colaninno in corralling a fan club of new investors to shore up his controlling position of 26% in Olivetti. But the terms he envisaged were unattractive to potential investors. They would have had to exchange liquid capital for shares in an unquoted private company (either Colaninno's Bell or his Bell 2 holding company, which also controlled the Telecom Italia empire through Tecnost, a holding company sitting just above Telecom Italia). So Colaninno clearly needed to offer his prospective new partners an irresistible inducement. It was pretty obvious what that could be: a profitable exit strategy.

One such strategy would have been to sell the whole group to Deutsche Telekom, whose attempt to merge with Telecom Italia in 2000 had failed. At the time, however, Telekom wasn't really in a position to undertake any more acquisitions due to investor disquiet over the expense of its VoiceStream acquisition (€30.7 billion) in the United States.[39]

Activist shareholders then blocked Colaninno's alternative proposal for $10 billion in share conversions and buybacks, arguing that it mainly would benefit Olivetti. That, in turn,

---

[38] Tp, "Ermittlungen in der Gruppe Telecom Italia?" *Frankfurter Allgemeine Zeitung*, 7. Juli 2001, p. 24.

[39] Dixon, Hugo, Leslie de Quilacq, and John Paul Rathbone, "Breaking Views.com: Olivetti/Telecom Italia," *The Wall Street Journal Europe*, March 22, 2001, p. 7.

led to the indirect takeover of Telecom Italia via Olivetti's controlling stake. Pirelli and Benetton offered an 80 percent premium to the owners of the 26 percent stake in Olivetti, who previously had backed Colaninno. Other Telecom Italia holders received nothing.

The chance to convert their investments into cash immediately for much more than they were worth apparently appealed to the Brescians and Colaninno, who resigned as chairman of Telecom Italia. Shut out altogether by the deal, the company's minority shareholders (including giant foreign interests like the American TIAA-CREF pension fund) protested its fundamental unfairness, despite its legality under Italian law. For their part, Pirelli's minority stockholders also appeared to reject the industrial strategy behind the takeover of Telecom Italia. They bid Pirelli's shares down 18 percent, to €2.55 ($2.23) following the deal's announcement.

Rather than aiming at giving minority shareholders a fair shake, the Telecom Italia tender apparently intended to keep foreign investors at bay. Maurizio Gasparri, Italy's industry minister, called the bid for Telecom Italia "satisfying" because a "group comprised entirely of Italian entrepreneurs" led it. That made the Pirelli-Benetton deal for Telecom Italia even more discouraging. Although the partners paid €7.6 billion ($7 billion) for their slice of Olivetti, they gained more than half of Telecom Italia, whose market capitalization at that point was roughly $65 billion! Gasparri said minority shareholders should "find satisfaction in an increase of the company's value," implicitly recognizing that the deal itself short-changed them.[40]

If the goal of keeping crucial Italian corporations in Italian hands was clear, it initially was less evident how the acquisition fit into the new owners' strategy. For Pirelli and its chairman, Marco Tronchetti Provera, the biggest challenge was how to reduce the debt resulting from the raid on Telecom Italia.[41] Because Pirelli and the Benettons agreed to pay Bell, Colaninno's Luxembourg holding company, the excessive price of €4.17 a share for Olivetti, the deal furthermore drained them of cash.[42] Consequently, between July and September 2001, shares in Telecom Italia, Olivetti's largest asset, declined more than 35 percent, while Pirelli's stock shed 45 percent of its value.

In the aftermath of the terrorist attacks in the United States on September 11, 2001, Olivetti's shares fell to €0.99. Provera therefore opportunistically seized on this development, announcing he wanted to renegotiate the agreement to take control of Olivetti.

At the same time, though, the 15-nation European Commission told Pirelli and the Benettons they would have to make concessions to gain its approval for the deal. "The companies are perfectly aware of the undertakings needed to receive first-phase clearance, to avoid an in-depth investigation," an EC spokeswoman, Amelia Torres, said. "As soon as the Commission has received those undertakings, the Commission will be in a position to take the decision." The Commission then set a Sept. 27 deadline.[43]

Brussels ordered the Benettons' subsidiary, Edizioni Holding, to sell its interest in Italy's smallest mobile-telephone company, Blu, in return for clearance. The European Commission also told Autostrade, in which the Benettons are the largest single shareholder, to sell a unit

---

[40] Tagliabue, John, "Italian Phone Deal Raises Some Old Insider Issues," *New York Times*, July 31, 2001, p. W1.

[41] *Ibid.*

[42] Shannon, Victoria, "Pirelli Backtracks," *International Herald Tribune*, September 19, 2001, p. 15.

[43] *Ibid.*

owning a 3,100-kilometer (1,900-mile) fiber-optic network in Italy. Those concessions overcame "serious concerns in the markets for transmission capacity and for mobile telephony in Italy," the European Commission said.[44]

Thus, Pirelli and the Benetton family ultimately won approval from European regulators for their purchase of a stake in Olivetti, allowing them to gain control of Italy's dominant telephone company. The original price of €7.6 billion, though, stuck. Olivetti shares consequently continued to fall on concern the company would issue new stock to cut debt.

CONSEQUENCES FOR TELECOM ITALIA

Additional pressure to begin dealing with the debt situation came when Telecom Italia announced its results for the first half-year. In September 2001, it reported net profit had fallen 51 percent as it paid more in interest on increased debt and had higher acquisition costs. Profit fell to €483 million ($437 million) from €979 million a year earlier. That was below analysts' average estimate of €794 million. Sales rose 10 percent to €15.59 billion. Ebitda also grew 9 percent to €7.05 billion, about what analysts had expected. The company furthermore said full-year net profit would fall by about the same percentage as it had in the first half. Rounding out the bad news, Telecom Italia's debt at the end of June had swollen to €24.5 billion.[45]

Taking aim at this debt burden, Telecom Italia's new owners unveiled plans to sell €6 billion ($5.5 billion) in assets and raise another €5 billion through a capital increase. The capital increase, slated for November, would offer existing investors the choice of buying convertible bonds or additional equity in the company. With these measures, Pirelli and the Benetton family hoped to begin regaining investors' confidence. Because shares in the controlling company had plunged more than 50 percent since the July takeover, Provera added that he wanted to slice Olivetti's debt too, from more than €17 billion to €13.5 billion.[46]

An Olivetti spokesman said it would focus on the group's core business of mobile and fixed-line telephony – a focus that would clear the way for this debt reduction through sale of some satellite and television activities. Telecom Italia and Olivetti respectively held €5 billion and €1 billion of the assets the group planned to sell. Investors gave cautious praise to the plans, viewing them as injecting needed liquidity into the group.

Three assets up for sale soon were in the news. Telecom Italia announced it planned to sell its stakes in the aforementioned mobile telephone operators Bouygues T l com and Aria. In addition, Provera said the company would sell its near 30 percent stake in Telekom Austria.[47] Over and above these steps, Provera promised to present early in 2002 a detailed industrial plan, including "difficult choices," to streamline its operations further by abandoning less profitable businesses.[48]

---

[44] Bloomberg News, "EC Clears Deal for Olivetti Stake," *International Herald Tribune*, September 21, 2001, p. 15.

[45] Shannon, Victoria, "Tech Woes in Italy," *International Herald Tribune*, September 13, 2001, p. 22.

[46] Reuters, "Italia's Debt Plan," *International Herald Tribune*, September 28, 2001, p. 13.

[47] Reuters, "Telecom Italia to Sell Stakes," *International Herald Tribune*, October 31, 2001, p. 13.

[48] Reuters, "'Difficult Choices' at Telecom Italia," *International Herald Tribune*, November 8, 2001, p. 13.

DOWNWARD TREND CONTINUES

Nevertheless, Telecom Italia's third-quarter numbers for 2001 were not good. It had a net loss of €811 million ($725.4 million) against a profit of €274 million a year earlier, even as it reduced the value of assets on its balance sheet. In its first results generated by the new Pirelli-Benetton management team, Telecom Italia also said that, for the first nine months of 2001, it had a net loss of €328 million compared with a profit of €1.25 billion a year earlier. Revenue rose 9.7 percent to €23.55 billion. At the same time, Olivetti reported a €1.1 billion third-quarter loss. Sales, more than 95 percent of which Telecom Italia generated, were €8.25 billion.[49]

So Provera continued with his asset sales. For example, Santander Central Hispano and three other companies agreed to buy Telecom Italia's 27 percent stake in Auna Operadores de Telecommincaciones for €2 billion ($1.8 billion) in cash. The transaction not only helped Telecom Italia, but also effectively paved the way for possible sale of Spain's second-biggest telecommunications company. Santander, Spain's biggest bank, and the power companies Union Fenosa and Endesa bought 17 percent of Auna from Italy's dominant phone company. The Dutch bank ING Groep purchased 10 percent.[50]

TELECOM ITALIA'S DILEMMA

Almost a quarter later, Telecom Italia said it expected to post its first full-year loss in two decades after writing down €3.8 billion ($3.3 billion) in assets. The write-downs had become necessary because Provera inherited businesses like the Brazilian Internet company Globo.com, whose value plunged after Colaninno bought them. Telecom Italia now puts no value on its 30 percent stake in Globo.com, acquired in June 2000 for $810 million. Provera did not specify the amount of the 2001 loss.

However, devaluing the assets will make them easier to sell, helping Provera reach his targeted asset sales to trim debt. Together with proceeds from other divestments, TIM's sale of its stake in Bouygues Télécom for €750 million already had put Telecom Italia three quarters of the way there. They allowed the Rome-based company to cut its net debt at the end of 2001 to €21.9 billion. No longer consolidating the debt of Telecom Argentina, in which Telecom Italia owns a 30 percent stake, also contributed to the debt reduction.

That cheered investors a bit, as did Telecom Italia's announcement it will pay a dividend this year equal to the 31 euro cents per common share paid in 2001. Provera then went on to present a three-year business plan to lift sales 4.5 percent a year through 2004. Telecom Italia shares gained 25 euro cents following the announcement, to close at €9.10.

Making the rest of the bad news public, Provera said more Telecom Italia assets needed revaluation. The company may have to write down €2.4 billion in shares of its Seat Pagine Gialle directory unit, for instance. J.P. Morgan Chase & Co. has an option to sell 711 million Yellow Pages shares to Telecom Italia by December 2005 for €3.40 each, more than five

---

[49] Reuters, Bloomberg, "Telecom Italia Turns in Loss," *International Herald Tribune*, November 14, 2001, p. 16.

[50] Bloomberg, "Telecom Italia Sells Stake," *International Herald Tribune*, December 20, 2001, p. 16.

times their current price. The chairman called it the company's last contingent liability not included on the balance sheet.[51]

But even assuming the plan represents a watershed for Telecom Italia's return to profitability, a serious dilemma remains for the firm and its new management. Under Colaninno, Telecom Italia had sought to become more profitable by growing to attain economies of scale. Doing so required foreign expansion and investment in new technologies. Ultimately, these efforts overtaxed the company's finances. The new management's foreign asset sales implicitly recognize this fact. The divestments likely will put Telecom Italia back on a more solid financial footing and thus prolong its existence as an independent entity. Yet the price of survival as a niche player probably will be reduced future profitability. If the Pirelli and Benetton families decide they need a higher return on their investment, they will have only two options. First, they could return to the failed strategy they just abandoned, which seems unlikely. Second, they could sell out to a stronger rival. This second alternative would leave both families wealthier, but the entrepreneurs owning the company might no longer be exclusively Italian.

SwissCom's Dilemma

The Swiss telecommunications company SwissCom is in trouble too. In itself, that is nothing extraordinary when one looks at other European firms in the industry. Unusual, however, is the type of problem SwissCom's management and its chairman, Jens Alder, currently have to tackle.

The former monopolist has a lot of money and does not know what to do with it. Alder recently told the press in Bern that the company's net liquidity amounts to almost Sfr3.0 billion ($1.8 billion). On top of that, more money is accumulating from year to year. With a free, operating cash flow (cash flow minus investment) of about Sfr1.5 billion, the management's problem becomes more acute every month. More and more money is left over and available for investment. For Alder, the last resort is a stock buyback, which would hand part of this capital back to the owners. According to him, the minimum volume for such an undertaking would be about Sfr1 billion. Analysts expect a decision during the first half of 2002.

Together with loans, though, SwissCom still would have just under Sfr10 billion at its disposal for an acquisition. Consequently, SwissCom has been looking for a sensible investment opportunity for some time now. Alder and his colleagues have set their sights high in terms of their investment criteria. The target of the investment would have to be in line with SwissCom strategically, they say. Moreover, good management would have to be in place with values similar to the ones SwissCom's board of directors holds. Of course, the price would have to be reasonable given the company's value too. Yet so far, on the basis of these criteria, the board of directors has been unable to find a suitable company despite intense searching. That is why SwissCom, which still accounts for 25 percent of the Swiss market, will remain a niche provider and look for further lucrative niches.

---

[51] Bloomberg News, "Write-offs Eat Telecom Italia Profit," *International Herald Tribune*, February 15, 2002, p. 15.

During the past three years, SwissCom's managers have asked themselves twice whether the firm wanted to move up to the first league of European telecommunication companies by means of acquisitions. Twice, a clear "no" was the answer to that question. The necessary level of indebtedness of the company, currently ranked seventh-largest in Europe, together with likely difficulties of integration would have posed too great a risk for the company and shareholders alike. Hence, management decided SwissCom should try to grow within its niche by, for example, increasing revenue through the sale of advanced data-transmission services. To do so, it began offering higher-speed GPRS mobile-phone services commercially on Feb. 1.[52]

According to Alder, the decision to remain a niche player also means SwissCom will not be able to take advantage of the economies of scale, which shape the industry in many of its business segments, as much as other companies. In the long run, that necessarily will call SwissCom's independence into question. Nevertheless, it is unlikely anyone will take over the company during the next three years. Swiss law stipulates the state must own the majority of SwissCom. For the time-being, then, a takeover of SwissCom is not legally possible.[53]

CONCLUSIONS

The gap between entrepreneurial visions of high-speed Internet access via cellphones and current European realities is large. The companies involved offer customers few services and themselves have no successful business or pricing models. Hoping to tap large, rich markets, debt-laden firms nonetheless limp along building their UMTS-networks. Consolidation through acquisitions and mergers no doubt would improve the industry's profitability and thus accelerate its progress.

At present, though, Central Europe's largest telecoms appear unable to avail themselves of either alternative. Deutsche Telekom exhausted itself financially during its recent buying spree, while Telecom Italia is recuperating from its failed attempts at foreign expansion. In contrast, cash-flush SwissCom can't find any smaller firms it wants to buy, but is itself too small to take over a giant like Deutsche Telekom or Telecom Italia.

Market forces, however, continue to work. As noted at the outset, teetering on the brink of bankruptcy, KPN desperately is seeking a partner to help shoulder losses suffered at its E-Plus unit. Moreover, recent reports say MobilCom, the fifth-biggest German mobile phone service provider, has fundamental differences with France Télécom, its UMTS business partner. Analysts expect MobilCom will go broke if the partnership falls apart.[54]

---

[52] Bloomberg, "SwissCom to Start GPRS," *International Herald Tribune*, January 17, 2002, p. 11.

[53] Winkelhage, Johannes, "SwissCom Has a Problem Spending Its Money," *Frankfurter Allgemeine Zeitung*, (English Edition), January 15, 2002, p. 5.

[54] Bloomberg News, "France Télécom Quarrels over Price," *International Herald Tribune*, February 19, 2002, p. 14; AFP, Bloomberg, "French Disconnection?," *International Herald Tribune*, February 21, 2002, p. 16; Winkelhage, Johannes, "France Télécom Threatens to Sue MobilCom," *Frankfurter Allgemeine Zeitung*, (English Edition), February 22, 2002, p. 5; Reuters, Bloomberg, "Stock Deal Strains MobilCom's Links," *International Herald Tribune*, February 22, 2002, p. 14; and Bloomberg, "MobilCom Responds," *International Herald Tribune*, February 23-24, 2002, p. 10.

It thus seems that a shakeout in Central Europe's telecommunications industry finally may be getting underway. If the competitors are unable to reduce their numbers sufficiently through acquisitions and mergers, then bankruptcies will do it for them.

Chapter 5

AFTER THE SHOCK: EAST GERMAN UNEMPLOYMENT, ACTIVE LABOR MARKET POLICY AND THE '*STANDORT*' DEBATE

*Corinne Nativel**

1.0 INTRODUCTION

Employment and welfare reforms lie at the heart of current debates on the politics and economics of Europe. Since the mid-1990s, governments have paid increased attention to Active Labor Market Policy (ALMP) as a strategic tool of intervention against contemporary forms of unemployment (see OECD 1994; European Commission 1995). This type of policy is traditionally associated with the social democratic regime of Sweden (Janoski 1994), although many liberal states such as the U.S. and Britain have also recently experienced with a variant known as welfare-to-work, which incorporates a much stronger compulsory element (Solow 1998). While a plurality of ALMP designs and delivery mechanisms is apparent both cross-nationally and locally (OECD 1999a), the decision to implement this policy is inevitably taken by national governments operating within the institutional framework of the political cycle and the constraints of voters' expectations.

This paper critically examines what active labor market policy can and cannot do in solving unemployment in the context of rapid and extreme forms of economic restructuring. It uses the case of East Germany, which provides the most recent European example of a massive governmental use of ALMP. The emphasis is on a historically-grounded and context-sensitive perspective, which in the case of the new East German states (*Länder*) explains the rationale for ALMP through the momentum of systemic transition and German unification.

The implications and outcomes of German Economic, Monetary and Social Union (GEMSU) are first briefly reviewed. Section Two defines ALMP and outlines the most common arguments both in favor and against this type of public intervention. The paper then illustrates the significance taken by ALMP to solve mass unemployment and questions its

---

* Research Fellow, University of Edinburgh, Scotland (UK)

medium to long-term validity. Finally, it comes to the conclusion that as a 'dependency economy', the eastern region of Germany is still ill-equipped to compete in the global environment. At the same time, the German Social Market Economy as a whole is confronted to the striking necessity of adapting to the new parameters of global competition.

1.1 BACKGROUND: THE SOCIO-ECONOMIC CONTEXT

The transition from a planned economy to the free market represented a radical form of systemic change described by evolutionary economists as a Schumpeterian process of 'creative destruction' (Müller 1991) and by sociologists as socio-structural change towards modernization (Zapf 1994). More generally, social scientists have emphasized its institutional dimension in terms of 'institutional transformation' (Wiesenthal 1996) or 'institutional change' (Lehmbruch 1994). Indeed, systemic transformation signifies a dynamic process of institutional change which wipes out past constraints and introduces a new mode of economic and social regulation. The command economy of the former German Democratic Republic (GDR) was abolished through German Economic, Monetary and Social Union on 1st July 1990, and through the extensive and rapid transfer of West German political, social and economic institutions.

The pace of the East German transition, of 'big bang' or 'shock therapy', has in retrospect led to a 'premature' form of integration (Stephan 1999). This premature integration of the East German into the West German economy poses concrete problems which are particularly visible in the labor market, referred to by Sesselmeier (1991, p.7) as the 'Kernstück', i.e. the core element of the transformation process. The transfer of western collective bargaining institutions forced East Germany into the trap of 'high tech high wage' economy (Sinn and Sinn 1994). On the positive side, this strategy has precluded a 'low tech' development path (Lange and Pugh 1998), but high labor costs have also prevented the East German workforce from competing with their East European counterparts on a level-playing field. The question as to whether mass unemployment could have been avoided through a more moderate wage strategy is beyond the concerns of this paper. Similarly, the paper does not engage with the contentious issue regarding the role played the *Treuhand*[1] and the Federal Labor Office in facilitating or precipitating this particular labor market strategy. In contrast, it is concerned with the role these state agencies played in helping those excluded from the labor market. Indeed, the nature of therapy and its adequacy must be analyzed on the following grounds: the asymmetric shock of systemic transition was the initial cause of high unemployment; this had disastrous social consequences for the indigenous population.

Like other command economies of former communist Europe, the GDR used to exhibit full employment levels which rested upon overmanning practices (or unemployment on-the-job). The constitution guaranteed the 'right to work' whilst employment conditions, wages and output were not set through competitive mechanisms but through central decision-making

---

[1] The *Treuhandanstalt* was an independent government agency established in March 1990 for the privatisation and use of former state-owned assets. Its mandate ended in December 1994. It was then replaced by the *Bundesanstalt für vereinigungsbedingte Sonderaufagaben* (BvS).

of the State.[2] As a result, the activity rate approximated 90 per cent and was one of the highest in the world (Rowell 1997). Unification made the former practices obsolete with unemployment as an inevitable consequence; this is why East Germany's unemployment problem has subsequently been termed 'transformation unemployment' (Hoose 1995).

Reported levels of labor participation in the former GDR differ widely according to the way data is calculated. Official GDR statistics for example did not account for the so-called x- area, which included officials from the secret police and other state agents. If this sector is also included, the aggregate employment level was 9.7 million workers. In 1992, the total level of employment had been reduced to 6.2 million, which indicates a drastic reduction of jobs by 40 per cent in a highly condensed period of 24 months.

This reduction of employment was linked to the massive de-industrialization of the GDR's economy, whose structures were lagging 20 years behind those of West Germany (Hoose 1995, p.18-19). Amongst the types of jobs which disappeared were the bureaucratic and administrative jobs which had to be rationalized. The same applies to agricultural employment. However it is the very core of the labor market, i.e. manufacturing jobs which was mostly hit (see table 1). In the absence of a large private sector able to absorb excess labor from the state sector, unemployment is an inevitable phenomenon.

Table 1: Changes in East German Employment Levels According to Sectors of Activity (1990-1998)

	1990	1991	1992	1993	1994	1995	1996	1997	1998
Active Population (9.7 million in 1989)	-9.5	-17.0	-12.8	-2.6	+1.8	+1.0	-2.0	-3.0	-0.4
Agriculture and Forestry (976,000 in 1989)	-20.0	-41.9	-37.9	-17.4	-2.6	-1.3	-4.9	0	+0.5
Manufacturing (4.3 million in 1989)	-10.1	-24.2	-23.6	-4.9	+1.7	+1.3	-3.9	-4.1	-2.0
Trade and Transport (1.5 million in 1989)	-7.1	-11.7	-7.7	-1.5	+0.5	-1.2	-2.1	-1.9	-1.0
Services (619,000 in 1989)	+10.5	+36.3	+8.5	+9.9	+10.1	+6.8	+2.7	-0.3	+4.1
State sector (2.2 million in 1989)	-11.0	-14.9	-2.4	-5.5	-2.3	-1.8	-2.7	-5.2	-1.9
Mining*						-6.1	-4.8	-4.2	+1.0
Construction industry*					+15.2	+6.5	-5.7	-7.4	-8.8

* For these two sectors, the data for the early 1990s is not available.
Source: Autorengemeinschaft (1999) *Aktuelle Daten Vom Arbeitsmarkt, Neue Bundesländer*, IAB Werstatt-bericht, Nuremberg, March 1999.

Unemployment counts drastically soared between early 1990 and 1992. In absolute figures, the total number of unemployed individuals has remained over one million ever since (see Chart below). In 2000 (ten years after Reunification), the official unemployment rate

---

[2] The 'right to work' was explicit in article 24 of the GDR constitution and in the law of April 1950 known as 'Gesetz der Arbeit zur Förderung und Pflege der Arbeitskräfte, zur Steigerung der Arbeitsproduktivität und zur weiteren Verbesserung der materiellen und kulturellen Lage'.

averages 18 per cent of the East German workforce. It is twice as high as the West German average and also above the average for most Post Socialist Economies (PSEs).[3]

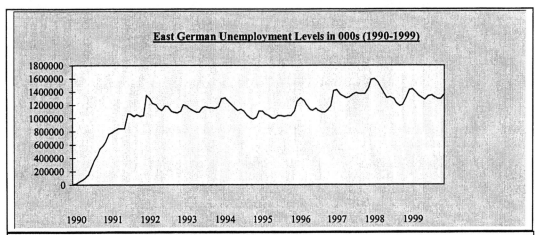

East German Unemployment Levels in 000s (1990-1999)

Source: Federal Labour Office, *Amtliche Nachrichten der Bundesantalt für Arbeit, Arbeitsstatistik* (various years) and IAB Materialen No.2/1991, p.7.

To summarize the impact on the East German economy, the shock therapy proved to be a simultaneous negative demand and positive supply shock (Hickel and Priewe 1994). Demand reduced drastically, on both external and domestic markets. First, the revaluation of the currency prevented former CMEA trade partners to paying for their imports in hard currency and made East German products too expensive for them. As a result, East Germany lost a huge market. Second, East German consumers who were eager to purchase sophisticated products shifted their demand towards West German goods which became easily available (Sinn and Sinn 1994). This represents a combination of classical and Keynesian features characterized by a situation of excess supply for many East German producers which occurred at a time when West German firms were already producing at a high degree of capacity utilization (Hagemann 1993).

There was a supply shock insofar that the East German production was suddenly exposed to national and international competition. This resulted in a sharp decline in output by two third of its initial level in just over a few months. The introduction of the common currency is often blamed for the extensive collapse of the East German industry. Yet, even with a more gradual revaluation of the currency and a more gradual elimination of tariff barriers, the end result may not have been much different. Given the productivity gap that existed between East and West German firms, East German industry could not have competed with western firms on price. Furthermore, eastern firms manufactured products that were essentially unwanted on Western markets.

It is against this background that the former Christian-democratic government of Helmut Kohl - who mistakenly believed that 'blossoming landscapes' would soon flourish in the Eastern states - decided to cushion the social consequences of systemic transition through a

---

[3] For more details on East Central Europe, the reader is advised to consult Eurostat or European Bank for Reconstruction and Development (EBRD) data.

massive implementation of active labor market schemes. Before examining the actual implementation of ALMP, the concept and its rationale must be clarified.

2. ACTIVE LABOR MARKET POLICY: SOME DEFINITIONS, JUSTIFICATIONS AND EFFECTS

Active labor market policy (ALMP) is a relatively recent term which should be used with caution as it is frequently ill-defined. ALMP measures are used by governments as an alternative to passive measures which solely consist of redistributing welfare payments, usual examples being the payment of unemployment benefits or the encouragement of early retirement which reduces the supply of labor. In contrast to unemployment insurance, ALMP is a discretionary policy. It includes various measures such as job placement (matching people to jobs), job training (teaching new skills to people to eliminate shortages of skills or production bottlenecks), and job creation (direct government efforts to create jobs either as individual employment subsidies to the private and public sector or as collective schemes in the form of public works).

Furthermore, three crucial features may be identified: ALMP is meant to be complementary, temporary and selective. It should be seen first as a *complementary* form of intervention, i.e. as a support to other policies relieving market failure. ALMP measures only make sense because they are not isolated policy instruments. Consequently they have a *temporary* dimension. They have been compared to a 'firebrigade policy' or 'policy of the first hour' (Brinkmann 1995).

In the literature the metaphor of a bridge is often used to illustrate the type of function endorsed by ALMP. This bridging function is only optimal if regular jobs are available. Indeed, it is not sufficient for a worker to improve his/her individual chances on the market (be it actually with state intervention or by individual effort), there also has to be a demand for this worker's output and the capital available to finance the workplace.

Table 2: Objectives of ALMP

Duration/Timescale	Level	
	Individual	Macro / labor market
Current unemployment reducing effects	Social security through wage compensation	Avoiding unemployment and easing pressure on the labor market
Improving prospects for the future	Bridging function: improving individual employment chances	Bridging function: developing new employment fields

Source: Brinkmann (1995), p.6

The above overview illustrates the dual approach of ALMP which results in outcomes at both the micro level (the individual) and the macro level (the labor market). The concept of *targeting* which is customary in public policy, indicates clearly that the recipients should be distinctive groups, the so-called 'hard-to place'. Despite some minor divergence from one country to another which do not allow for any conclusive generalization, empirical evidence has shown that the 'hard-to place' tend to be unskilled, younger or older workers, and more often female than male (see Schmid / O'Reilly / Schömann 1996). In other words, they tend to be those whose mobility will be constrained. Here not only occupational mobility must be taken into account, but also cross-geographical mobility to avoid regional and local polarization. Because ALMP addresses these specific impediments to labor market opportunities, it is thus also a *selective* policy.

However, one must also consider that this policy is not uncontroversial since public provision can spark off unintentional side effects such as *displacement, substitution, deadweight* and *dilution* effects.[4]

Displacement effects are directly related to output and reflect competition of labor market schemes within a given market segment. This takes place if the subsidized scheme takes away production which would have been carried out in the competitive sector. This could also be the case if a wage subsidy went to a private firm whose production or services would be favored at the expense of another. Jobs created can therefore endanger the existence of others, thus failing to lead to a net increase in employment or output. Within a given firm, a *substitution* effect arises if as a result of an employment measure workers subsidized under the scheme take the place of unsubsidized workers within a firm. Amongst labor market schemes, substitution can also occur when a project is privileged at the expense of another, which might turn out to be less cost-effective.

Deadweight reflects the fact that some of the subsidy of a labor market scheme goes to firms which would have increased their employment even in the absence of that expenditure. This is actually more likely to happen with individual wage subsidies or with on-the-job training schemes which large companies have to implement as part of their corporate human resource management policies. Deadweight effects can therefore be regarded as dangerous insofar that they divert public resources and impair the functioning of market-based resource allocation. Because of deadweight effects *creaming* effects can occur, as it can be the case with the most recently unemployed who are taken on because of the subsidy, but who had good chances of finding employment under normal conditions. The sum of the above adverse effects is referred to as *dilution* effect, which means that the net creation of jobs is lower than the number of subsidized ones.

The possibility of distortions within the East German labor market led a number of economists to warn against a massive implementation of active measures (see for example Sperling 1995).

3. ALMP IN EAST GERMANY: FROM 'POLICY OF THE FIRST HOUR' TO THE 'SECOND LABOUR MARKET'

In the early period of post-unification (approximately until 1992), ALMP was used as a strategic tool by policy-makers to maintain social peace as workers voiced their fear of becoming unemployed. Heinelt and Weck (1998) refer to this as the 'post-unification consensus' amongst policy-makers which preceded the period of 'dissonance and reflection'

---

[4] For a more detailed analysis of these effects, see G. Schmid (1996), "Process Evaluation: Policy Formation and implementation" in Schmid, G., O'Reilly, J. and Schömann, K. (eds.) (1996), International Handbook of Labour Market Policy and Evaluation, Cheltenham: Edward Elgar Publishing, pp. 198-231.

eventually leading to the '*Standort* debate'. During the year 1990, aggregate unemployment could be kept at a low level due to the government's decision to maintain a temporary export subsidy for the metalworking industry. But this had to be rapidly removed to make way for restructuring, a decision which was strategically accompanied by the introduction of two 'shocks absorbers', namely early retirement and short-time working schemes.

In fact, these represented the two first applications of ALMP in the new German *Länder*. Both provide earnings-substitution benefits not linked to maintaining qualifications or improving supply, although arguably, short-time work contributes to stabilizing employment. They are also convenient to implement since they do not necessitate a well-developed and established infrastructure of providers, as in the case of further training/retraining and job creation schemes.

Two special early retirement programs (*Vorruhestand and Altersübergangsgeld*) implemented until the end of 1992 allowed almost one million workers to leave the labor market. This represented approximately 7 per cent of the initial workforce (Hübler 1997, p.23); thereafter the impact of these measures declined significantly as participants entered the regular pension system. From an economic point of view, the rationale for the early retirement schemes can be discredited: while policy-makers emphasize the relief effect from lowering the supply of labor, especially with regards to the high participation levels inherited from the GDR, this strategy brings an increase in social insurance contributions. Moreover, many sociologists have pointed to the disastrous psychological effects of labor market exclusion on the individuals concerned (see Ernst 1996).

In contrast to early retirement, short-time work constituted a much more controversial measure. Indeed, this instrument can be regarded as useful in a period of recession, it is however doubtful whether it can efficiently accompany structural and systemic change. It soon became clear that with the de-industrialization process, short-time workers would eventually lose their jobs. The measure was therefore referred to as '*Kurzarbeit Null*' since employment was at zero hours. This also signified that the receipt of a short-time work allowance was akin to that of unemployment benefits. Short-time work was in fact used as a device to buy time until ALMP schemes could be implemented or until workers had reached the age of eligibility for early retirement.

Moreover, ALMP rapidly gained a new dimension: given the deteriorating situation on the east German labor market, job creation schemes came to the forefront as the major ALMP instrument. They were seen as conducive to the promotion of regional and local economic restructuring. The investment was not merely to be in human capital but also in mitigating the various locational deficits inherited from the GDR. The funds were hence used to directly promote and support the economic upswing and serve the community. For this purpose, large-scale public works were implemented which combined the traditional social objective of labor market policy with the redevelopment of industrial sites and plants owned by the *Treuhand*. By 1992, some 388,000 people participated in job-creation schemes and another 489,000 in training measures (Bach *et al.* 1998). But skepticism mounted about the effectiveness of ALMP and from 1993, measures were pared back for budgetary reasons. By January 1998 participation in work provision and training schemes in the new *Länder* had fallen to 177,000 and 125,000 respectively. However, unemployment remained intolerably high, at some 21 per cent of the labor force. Active labor market measures were thus ushered back in and given a favorable reappraisal. By November 1998 participation in eastern Germany had reached new highs of 442,000 for job schemes and 181,000 for training (Wurzel 1999).

Overall, ALMP in the East has delivered mixed results. Evaluations have highlighted various adverse effects such as deadweight and substitution. A recent employers' survey by the German Federal Labor Office (see bibliography) shows that almost a third of the companies interviewed in the east would have hired the same worker in the absence of the subsidy, while just over a fifth would have hired another person instead. Other studies have highlighted displacement effects caused by the presence of employment and training companies set up by the *Treuhand* to deliver active labor market schemes. The establishment of these companies represented a major institutional innovation. By the mid-1990s, some 400 employment and training companies (ETCs) had become predominant features of the East German economic landscape (Knuth 1996). As a result, many commentators criticized the emergence and institutionalization of a 'second' labor market sheltered from the competitive economy (see Nativel 1998). Recent debates have focused on the flaws inherent in the design of the schemes and the necessity for improved management (Wurzel 1999). ALMP has thus clearly revealed its limitations and the remaining high levels of unemployment cannot be addressed by this policy alone. Instead, obstacles and progress can be found within the broader framework of the unified German economy.

4.0 THE NEW GERMAN ECONOMY: PROBLEMS AND CHALLENGES

Notwithstanding the genuine and acute need for public measures in the post-transformation period, the East German labor market has been characterized, as demonstrated, by a strongly interventionist type of public policy. The long-term usefulness of such a strategy is discounted by the persistence of unemployment, which in the late 1990s had reached higher levels than in previous years. The average East German official unemployment rate of 17.4 per cent in 1999 was still well above the 9.1 per cent rate for the Western part of the country (German Council of Economic Experts 1999, see http://www.sachverstaendigenrat-wirtschaft.de). On the one hand, it could be argued that these figures merely reflect cutbacks in public expenditure on ALMP. On the other hand, and given the remaining high levels of participants in ALMP schemes (the rate of hidden unemployment[5] was at 27.7 per cent in 1999), it would be more accurate to argue that high East German unemployment actually reflects problems largely attributable to the structure of the unified German economy. This section examines the particular constraints on economic 'catching-up' inherent in the East German economy as well as the wider needs for social and economic reforms at the national level. Indeed, it can be argued that a number of institutional rigidities in national employment conditions and welfare provision exacerbate East Germany's economic problems. This raises the issue of institutional reform for the whole of Germany. In this connection, the recent reform agenda and policies of the Schröder administration will be briefly assessed.

---

[5] The hidden rate of unemployment accounts for both unemployment benefit claimants and ALMP recipients.

4.1 The Challenge of Moving beyond the Dependency Economy

The dramatic growth rates achieved in the first six years following German Reunification are attributable to considerable public investment in infrastructure, to exceptionally high levels of activity in the construction industry, and generally to the process of rationalization in the industrial sector. Fixed capital investment between 1991 and 1998 reached a level of DM 1.3 billion. The pace of investment has resulted in a considerable decrease in the average age of equipment and machinery from 32.6 years in 1991 to 25.3 years in 1994, according to calculations by the Federal Statistical Office. In comparison, the West German stock for the year 1994 was 21.3 years old (DIW / IfW / IWH, 1999).

Furthermore, labor productivity has considerably increased from its initial position, with the manufacturing industry catching up faster than other sectors, although the overall productivity level in 1999 remained just above 60 per cent of the Western equivalent (see table 3). The growth slowdown since 1997 indicates that the East German economy has entered a new phase of its transition which necessitates new indigenous strategies based on a downward adjustment of wages to match existing levels of productivity (Paqué 1997).

This would help in achieving greater autonomy as concerns have been expressed that the region has become a 'dependency economy' reliant on West German fiscal transfers (Nolte / Sitte 1995). Throughout the 1990s, a total of almost DM 1500 billion (approximately $690 billion) was transferred to the eastern *Länder* (DIW / IfW / IWH, *op.cit.*). Ten years on, the case for a substantial decrease in fiscal transfers cannot be made as it would jeopardize the development process set in motion. A drastic reduction will depend on the equalization of living standards based on East Germany's own capacity to sell its production.

This is why the development and regeneration of industrial networks is of prime importance. In the aftermath of systemic change, the situation in the East German economy was captured by the expression 'capitalism without capitalists' (Grabher 1993). That a private sector has emerged (particularly through the rapid privatization of state-owned assets by the *Treuhandanstalt*) is indeed undisputed. Yet industrial network patterns point to a number of obstacles towards the emergence of an East German entrepreneurial elite. Economic sociologists such as Windolf and Schief (1999) show that most large East German firms are owned by Westerns owners. The network of interlocking directorates is dominated by West German managers. This creates 'structural holes' in the network of East German companies which are bridged over by West German managers, exposing East German firms to structural external influence from the West. A further study of East German small-scale entrepreneurs indicates that self-employed persons had little in common with the idealized Schumpeterian entrepreneur (Thomas and Woderich 1997). The East German self-employed are not interested in expanding their companies through risk-taking activities, but choose instead survival strategies. The decision to become an 'entrepreneur' in the Eastern *Länder* largely reflects missing opportunities in the labor market.

A business-friendly *Standort* must thus be nurtured, in which indigenous risk-taking activity is facilitated and rewarded, principally through the access to finance. This should be applied to intangible investments in management, marketing and product/process innovation. At the same time, links with national sales and suppliers networks need to be improved.

Table 3: Key Data for East Germany's Economic 'Catching-Up' (1991 to 1999)

	1991	1992	1993	1994	1995	1996	1997	1998	1999
Population (in 000s)	15,910	15,730	15,648	15,564	15,505	15,451	15,407	15,380	15,360
Change from prev. year (%)	-	-1.1	-0.5	-0.5	-0.4	-0.3	-0.3	-0.2	-0.1
GDP in Billion DM 1)	206.0	222.1	242.8	266.2	280.1	285.5	290.2	295.6	302.9
Change from prev. year (%)	-	7.8	9.3	9.6	5.2	1.9	1.6	1.9	2.5
GDP Deflator (%) 2)	-	19.6	11.3	3.3	3.2	2.0	0.5	0.8	1.2
Active Population (in 000s)	7,321	6,387	6,219	6,330	6,396	6,259	6,053	5,965	5,965
Change from prev. year (%)	-	-12.8	-2.6	1.8	1.0	-2.1	-3.3	-1.5	0
per 1.000 inhabitants	460	406	397	407	413	405	393	388	388
Dependent workers (in 000s)	6.950	5.969	5.757	5.829	5.881	5.749	5.543	5.450	5.445
Change from prev. year (%)	-	-14.1	-3.6	1.3	0.9	-2.2	-3.6	-1.7	-0.1
Self-employed (in 000s)	371	418	462	501	515	510	510	515	520
Change from prev. year (%)	-	12.7	10.5	8.4	2.8	-1.0	0.0	1.0	1.0
Underemployment (in 000s) of which 3):	2,692	2,988	2,706	2,388	2,055	1,974	1,980	-	-
Registered unemployed	913	1,170	1,149	1,142	1,047	1,169	1,355	1,435	1,405
Workers in job creations schemes (JCSs)	183	388	260	280	312	278	235	245	305
Productivity (in 000s DM) 1)	28.1	34.8	39.0	42.1	43.8	45.6	47.9	49.6	50.8
Change from prev. year (%)	-	23.6	12.3	7.7	4.1	4.2	5.1	3.4	2.4
Unit Labour Costs	90.9	84.6	77.8	74.9	74.3	72.5	70.4	68.9	68.0
Change from prev. year (%)	-	-6.9	-8.0	-3.7	-0.9	-2.3	-2.9	-2.1	-1.3
Net fiscal transfers (bill. DM)	105.9	129.4	146.9	144.9	134.2	135.3	130.4	137.1	-
in % of GDP	51.4	48.7	45.5	39.6	33.8	32.7	30.9	31.6	-
West Germany = 100									
Productivity 4) 6)	31.0	43.5	53.1	56.0	57.8	59.4	60.4	61.0	61.2
Unit Labour Costs	150.6	139.4	128.0	126.0	125.6	123.9	123.1	122.7	122.2
Gross per capita income 7)	46.7	60.7	67.9	70.5	72.5	73.6	74.3	74.8	74.7

1) In 1991 Prices
2) Change of GDP deflator from previous year
3) Registered unemployed, participants in job creations schemes, in further training and retraining, short-time work, and early retirement schemes.
4) per capita GDP
5) Per capita gross income from dependent employment in relation to per capita GDP
6) In constant prices
7) Gross income from dependent employment
Source: German Statistical Office, Federal Labor Office and Ministry for Economic Affairs.

Of course, it proved convenient to resort to 'policy transfer' as a means of emergency treatment and to build East Germany in the image of its Western counterpart. Not only has this strategy placed particular strains on the West German economy, it may have actually prolonged the structural reforms which should enable Germany to adapt to the new economic parameters of global competition.

4.2 The Challenge of Reforming 'Modell Deutschland'

The need to reform the Social Market Economy which served West Germany well during the three post-war decades of the 'Golden Age' has been highlighted with regard to the country's deteriorated capacity to cope with new economic trends (see Funk 2000). Since its election in November 1998, the government of Gerhard Schröder has sought to portray itself as the one which will bring about much awaited change and reduce persistently high levels of unemployment across Germany. To date, key policy initiatives have addressed the areas of taxation, welfare and the labor market. Fiscal reforms are laid out in the government's *Zukunftsprogramm 2000* and *Steuerreform 2000*.[6] These include a consolidation of the federal budget 2000 through cuts in public expenditure by 7.5 per cent, medium-term public finance planning (aiming at a balanced budget), reform of the corporate and income tax systems (with a substantial lowering of the rates from 2001) and an ecological tax reform involving slightly increased levies on petrol and electricity over a four-year period. Additionally, the pension system is being reformed whereby the previous system linking pensions to net wages will be abolished. The usual index formula is to be dropped for pension increases in 2000 and 2001 when only minor adjustments for inflation will be made.

Moreover, reforms within the system of industrial relations and collective bargaining are also crucial. A move towards decentralized bargaining is increasingly perceived as a necessity for the German economy. According to Esche (1998, p.3), decentralized wage bargaining must:

- create a greater leeway for agreements at the plant level and encourage the adaptability of enterprises, business performance, and partnership structures;
- initiate solutions between the social partners at sectoral level, let individual aspects of negotiations become standard norms, maintain social peace, and consider the overall economic perspectives.

Departure from negotiated minimum wages have occurred in the East German context, although this has been more by necessity than by design. There has been speculation that the undermining of multi-employer bargaining which occurred in the Eastern *Länder* may be used as a strategic opportunity to deregulate collective bargaining in the whole of Germany (French 1998). Deregulatory practices in the East can undoubtedly be regarded as a catalyst for reform. Yet empirical evidence suggests that these are confined to small companies and will have limited impact in the West leading to a rejection of the 'normalization' thesis. In other words, the eastern practice cannot be expected to turn into a national norm. Failure to move in such a direction has been regarded as disappointing (see OECD 1999b).

Furthermore, changes in the system of wage determination also include the need for a medium-term consensual framework between the social partners and government which would come in the form of a tripartite employment pact. The time framework for the

---

[6] Programme for the Future 2000 and Tax Reform 2000.

negotiations is particularly crucial. The most important signal that could emerge from the negotiations relates to medium-term pay trends. If trade unions and employers could agree on the principle of orientating wage growth towards average, medium-term productivity growth, there would be a chance of creating employment without inflationary tension. A consensus on this issue could help avoid a destabilizing over, or undershooting of wages resulting from extreme positions in pay negotiations. While this imposes sacrifices in the short-term, the positive environment resulting from a sustained period of wage moderation would subsequently justify higher rewards.

Previous attempts to generate alliances for jobs and other employment pacts have failed (see Bastian 1997). The latest Alliance for Jobs (*Bündnis für Arbeit*) adopted by the government and the social partners in December 1998 and the various consultations held since have not led to any significant breakthrough in the wage bargaining practice.

Moreover, Streek and Heinze (1999) recommend that the transition to the service economy be actively promoted as part of the latest Alliance for Jobs. This would involve a policy explicitly aimed at increasing participation rates, in contrast the to traditional ALMP measures which have followed the opposite trend. Indeed lower unemployment, as exemplified by the United States, Canada or Denmark amongst others, has been correlated with higher participation rates than in countries such as Germany or France, which display high aggregate unemployment. For example, if a one per cent increase per year was set as a policy objective, by the year 2005, the active population in Germany would reach 76.1 per cent, which would be just below the current British rate. The advantage of a higher participation rate would be a reduction in the fiscal burden and an increase in domestic consumption. Creating jobs in the service sector would also involve an understanding that the supporting institutions must differ from those which apply to the manufacturing sector. In relation to this, Streeck and Heinze rightly consider different formal fiscal incentives but overlook the informal 'mental' and cultural constraints. The notion of 'service' carries a specific connotation in countries such as Britain, the Netherlands or Denmark, which have all to an important extent become service economies. Coincidentally, these countries have some of the most enduring parliamentary and hereditary monarchies in Western Europe, and 'serving' the crown still has a particular resonance. In connection with this, social structure (the historical significance of aristocracy) and access to education, particularly higher education, also explain the perceptions of services in the labor market, i.e. their relative appeal (or lack of appeal) to workers. These arguments are purely speculative, as echoed by Paqué's own assumptions that Germany is characterized by:

> a general distrust of the service sector [which] has always been looked upon as a kind of residual sphere of activity in which money is earned not as a result of hard production work, but rather by the workings of some odd properties of invisibles that are not really the core of a 'decent' and 'proper' economy (1996, p.15).

Overall, genuine reform attempts must be acknowledged. At the time of writing, it remains doubtful whether the present German government will indeed succeed in implementing far-reaching structural reforms, particularly concerning pensions. Funk (2000) rightly points to 'the abundance of chaos, confusion and contradictions' which have prevented the political move towards an 'improved middle way'. The difficulties confronting the German economy have been captured by terms such as '*Reformstau*' or '*Reformblokade*'.

This blockade is not solely attributed to consecutive governments' lack of stamina and coherence, but perhaps, more importantly, to the lack of support in German society. Esche (1998) for example pleads for a rupture with the '*Versorgungsmentalität*', i.e. the idea that individuals fear change and are over-reliant on welfare provision. In contrast, Gensicke (1998) rejects the claims that Germans are 'reform shy' as inaccurate. The notion of 'German Angst' he argues, is misconceived and only serves to discredit the German *Standort*.

These debates clearly illustrate the lack of a widespread perceived need to revamp the German 'model'. It is more plausible that given relative social stability (which has largely been promoted through ALMP in the eastern part of the country) will result in incremental as opposed to radical changes.

5. CONCLUSIONS

At the beginning of the 21st century, unemployment levels are still very high in East Germany. But without West German political commitment to social solidarity and inclusion of East German citizens in the wider German societal structures, official unemployment would be at least 10 points higher, unless of course, a more restrictive wage strategy had been pursued. Moreover, without West German commitment to the reconstruction of the East, the economic integration and development of the region would have stalled.

The OECD (1996) remarked in one of its studies that the extent to which ALMP measures were applied resembled the Swedish welfare policy traditions to a great extent. Using ALMP on such as large scale was clearly as strategic choice, which constitutes an integral part of the political economy of German Reunification.

This paper has sought to reconcile the opposite views which prevail in Germany. The one argues that greater state intervention and the extension of the 'second' or intermediate labor market is the sole possible way forward, whilst the other sees ALMP as a mere social therapy that cannot contribute to economic development. Yet ALMP can have significant employment effects and thus reduce politically and socially unacceptable aggregate levels of unemployment, and as such can be a legitimate tool in the occurrence of Schumpeterian transition. However, this form of public intervention is not without flaws since it can cause a number of adverse effects and labor market distortions. Considering the persistence of unemployment in the whole of Germany, it clearly does not represent the most adequate policy. Of course, curative policies cannot replace the more fundamental need for structural reforms which facilitate the functioning of labor markets. Policy emphasis should hence be placed on reforming labor law and the welfare system, a path upon which the current German government has embarked and must continue.

Finally, to effectively deal with unemployment and labor market restructuring, it is necessary to acknowledge the diversity of transitions an economy might be subjected to: there are asymmetric shocks, such as the ones experienced by former socialist economies, which require emergency costly treatment. Other transitions such as the move to a post-industrial knowledge-based economy may be more diffuse and require more complex treatment. The failure of central planning has demonstrated that when governments fail to implement the necessary political and economic reforms necessitated by social evolution, via democratization and the adoption of market mechanisms, the system cannot survive. By the same token, capitalist countries could fail to promote the welfare reforms which are required in an era of strong evolution in the economic sphere (characterized by globalization and the informational revolution) and in the political sphere (the retreat of the nation-state). In this sense, the fight against unemployment is not merely a task for governments, but for all economic agents and political actors.

REFERENCES

Bach, H.-U. *et al.* (1998) *Labour Market Trends and Active Labour Market Policy in the Eastern German Transformation Process 1990-1997*, IAB Labour Market Research Topics No.29, Nuremberg: Institute for Employment Research.

Bastian, J. (1997) *The institutional architecture of an alliance of Jobs in Germany*, IGS Discussion Paper No. 97/2, University of Birmingham.

Brinkmann, C. (1995) "Labour Market Policy in Eastern Germany: An evaluation Five Years after unification", European Commission, Employment Observatory East Germany, No.16/17, Brussels.

Deutsches Institut für Wirtschaftsforschung (DIW) / Institut für Weltwirtschaft (IfW) / Institut für Wirtschaftsforschung Halle (IWH) (1999) *Gesamtwirtschaftliche und unternehmerische Anpassungsfortschritte in Ostdeutschland*. 17th Report. Berlin; Kiel; Halle.

Esche, A. (1998) *"Ein neuer Ausgleich von Eigenverantwortung und Solidarität, Internationale Beispiele zur Sozial-und Tarifpolitik"*, Aus Politik und Zeitgeschichte No.11, pp.3-21.

Ernst, J. (1996) *"Alterserwerbstätigkeit und Ruhestand in Ostdeutschland"*, Arbeit No.2/1996, pp.201-222.

European Commission (1995) *Employment in Europe*, Brussels: DGV, the European Commission.

Federal Labor Office [Institut für Arbeitsmarkt- und Berufsforschung der Bundesanstalt für Arbeit] (1999), "Betriebliche Einstellungshilfen – Erste Ergebnisse zu Förderstrukturen und betrieblichen Rahmenbedingungen", *Werkstattbericht* No.6/1999, Nuremberg.

French, S. (1998) *Necessity or Opportunity? The undermining of multi-employer Bargaining in the New Länder*, IGS Discussion Paper No. 98/2, University of Birmingham.

Funk, L. (2000 forthcoming) "Economic Reform and Modell Deutschland" in R. Harding and W. Paterson (eds.) *The future of the German Economy: an end to a miracle?*, Manchester University Press.

Gensicke, T. (1998) *"Sind die Deutschen reformscheu? Potentiale der Eigenverantwortung in Deutschland"*, Aus Politik und Zeitgeschichte No.18, pp.19-30.

Grabher, G. (1993) *The embedded firm: on the socio-economics of industrial networks*, London: Routledge.

Hickel, R. and Priewe, J. (1994) *Nach dem Fehlstart; Ökonomische Perspektiven der deutschen Einigung*, Frankfurt/Main: Fischer Verlag.

Hoose, A. (1995) *Transformationsarbeitslosigkeit in den neuen Bundesländern: arbeitsmarkttheoretische und arbeitsmarktpolitische Analyse mit empirischen Daten*, Wiesbaden: Gabler.

Janoski, T. (1994) "Direct State Intervention in the Labour Market: the explanation of active labour market policy from 1950 to 1988 in social democratic, conservative and liberal regimes" in T. Janoski and A.M. Hicks (eds) *The Comparative Political Economy of the Welfare State*, Cambridge: Cambridge University Press, pp.54-92.

Hagemann, H. (1993) "On some Macroeconomic Consequences of German Unification" in H. D. Kurz (ed.), *United Germany and the New Europe*, Aldershot: Edward Elgar, pp.89-107.

Heinelt, H. and Weck, M. (1998) *Arbeitsmarktpolitik nach der Vereinigung. Vom Vereiningungskonsens zur Standortdebatte*, Opladen: Leske und Budrich.

Hoose, A. (1995) *Transformationsarbeitslosigkeit in den neuen Bundesländern: arbeitsmarkttheoretische und arbeitsmarktpolitische Analyse mit empirischen Daten*, Wiesbaden: Gabler.

Hübler, O. (1997) *"Evaluation beschäftigungspolitischer Maßnahmen in Ostdeutschland"*, *Jahrbuch für Nationalökonomie*, Vol.216, No.1, pp.21-44.

Knuth, M. (1996) *Drehscheiben im Strukturwandel*, Berlin: Ed. Sigma.

Kohaute, S. and Schnabel, C. (1998) *Flächentarifvertrag im Westen sehr viel weiter verbreitet als im Osten. Ergebnisse aus dem IAB-Betriebspanel*, *IABKurzberichte* No.19, Nuremberg: Institute for Employment Research.

Lange, T. and Pugh, G. (1998) *The Economics of German Unification: an Introduction*, Cheltemham: Edward Elgar.

Lembruch, G. (1994) "The process of regime change in Eastern Germany: an institutionalist scenario for German unification", *Journal for European Public Policy*, Vol.1, No.1, p.97.

Müller, K. (1991) *Joseph Alois Schumpeters ökonomische Lehre und die gegenwärtige Systemtransformation*, *Deutschland Archiv* No.5, pp.495-502.

Nativel, C. (1998) *The "Second Labour Market" in East Germany, a useful tool against Transformation Unemployment?*, IGS Discussion Paper 98/13, University of Birmingham.

Nativel, C. (2000) *Unemployment, Economic Transition and Active Labour Market Policy: Lessons and Perspectives from the East German Bundesländer*, Doctoral thesis submitted to the Faculty of Social Sciences of the University of Birmingham (UK).

Nolte, D. and Sitte, R. (1995) *Ostdeutschland als Dependenzökonomie*, *WSI Mitteilungen*, No.5, pp.300-306.

OECD (1994) *The OECD Jobs Study: Facts, Analysis, Strategies*, Paris: OECD.

OECD (1996) *The Public Employment Service: Austria, Germany, Sweden*, Paris: OECD.

OECD (1999a) *The Local Dimension of Welfare to Work: An international survey*, Paris: OECD.

OECD (1999b) Country Reports: Germany, Paris: OECD.

Paqué, K.-H. (1996) *From Miracle to Crisis? The German Economy at the End of the Twenthieth Century*, IGS Discussion Paper Series Number 96/2, The University of Birmingham.

Paqué, K.-H. (1997) *"Neue Wege der Neuen Länder"* in *Frankfurter Allgemeine Zeitung*, No.171 (26 July 1997), pp.13-15.

Rowell, J. (1997) *"Les femmes sacrifiées de l'ex-RDA"*, *Le Monde Diplomatique*, May 1997, p.9.

Schmid, G., O'Reilly, J. and Schömann, K. (eds) (1996) *International Handbook of Labour Market Policy and Evaluation*, Cheltenham: Edward Elgar Publishing.

Sesselmeier, W. (1991) *Der Arbeitsmarkt: Probleme, Analysen, Optionen*, Marburg: Metropolis.

Sinn, G. and Sinn, H.-W. (1994) *Jumpstart: the economic unification of Germany*, Cambridge Massachussets: MIT Press.

Solow, R. M. (1998) *Work and Welfare* (Ed. Gutman, A.) Princeton, N.J.: Princeton University Press.

Sperling, I. (1995) *"Aktive Arbeitsmarktpolitik. Möglichkeiten und Grenzen von Qualifizierungsmaßnahmen"* in Arbeitsgemeinschaft Deutscher Wirtschaftswissenschaftler Forschungsinstitute (ed.), *Wege aus der Arbeitslosigkeit*, Berlin: Duncker und Humblot, pp.231-244.

Stephan, J. (1999) *Systemic transformation and the Conditions of Economic Development in Hungary with particular reference to the Experience from the East German case*, London: Macmillan; New York: St Martin's Press.

Streek, W. and Heinze, (1999) *"An Arbeit fehlt es nicht"*, Der Spiegel No.19/1999, pp.38-45.

Thomas, M. and Woderich, R. (1997) *"Berufliche Selbständigkeit-ein innovatives Erwerbmuster im strukturellen Wandel?"*, Berliner Debatte Initial No.8, pp.49-71

Wiesenthal, H. (1996) *"Die neuen Bundesländer als Sonderfall der Transformation in den Ländern Osteuropas"*, Aus Politik und Zeitgeschichte No.40, pp.46-54.

Windolf, P. and Schief, S. (1999) *"Untermehmensverflechtung in Ostdeutschland"*, Kölner Zeitschrift für Soziologie und Sozialpsychologie No.51, pp.260-282.

Wurzel, E. (1999) "Getting Germany back to work", *OECD Observer* No. 219 (December), Paris: OECD.

Zapf, W. (1994) *Modernisierung, Wohlfartsentwicklung und Transformation: Soziologische Aufsätze 1987 bis 1994*, Berlin: Ed. Sigma.

Chapter 6

HOW DOES FOREIGN DIRECT INVESTMENT INFLUENCE POLAND'S EXPORTS TO THE EU

Marzenna Anna Weresa[1]

ABSTRACT

The favorable climate for inward investment in Poland resulted in a dynamic growth of foreign capital flows in terms of both quantity and value. The number of firms with a foreign capital stake reached nearly 45 thousand, rising six-fold during the nineties. The total value of foreign direct investment (FDI) stock amounted to $36.475 billion at the end of 2000, and was nearly 350 times larger than in 1990.

The objective of this paper is to examine the links between foreign direct investment in Poland and trade performance with the European Union, and, in particular, to find out how the activity of firms with foreign capital influences the competitiveness of Polish exports to the EU. The problem seems to be important, as the EU predominates in Poland's foreign trade, as well as in exports and imports of foreign investment enterprises (FIEs).

The importance of FDI in shaping the pattern of Poland's foreign trade with the EU has been growing in the 1990s, as FDI companies accounted for more than half of Poland's overall trade turnover in 2000, compared with one-fourth in 1995.

The inflow of FDI does not substitute for Poland's trade with the EU. On the contrary, it creates trade flows, as foreign investment is made mainly in sectors where Poland already has a comparative advantage in trade. Export creation, through the multiplier, has a positive effect on the pace of economic growth.

On the other hand however, the quality level of Polish exports is still lagging substantially behind that of the EU countries. In the short run the Polish trade pattern seems to be relatively stable. There are no significant shifts in Poland's export specialization towards the EU. Poland is increasingly specializing in traditional, price sensitive sectors, and this process is, to some extent, supported by inward FDI. The

[1] World Economy Research Institute, Warsaw School of Economics, Al. Niepodległosci 162, 02-521 Warsaw, Poland, tel./fax +48 22 848 91 32, e-mail: mweres@sgh.waw.pl

Polish trade pattern will probably be changing in the long run. Externalities created by trade and FDI inflow will cause gradual upgrading of local production and influence specialization patterns. There have already been some positive shifts in high-tech trade competitiveness, which may result in changes of Poland's specialization pattern.

Keywords: foreign direct investment, foreign trade, Poland

INTRODUCTION

Foreign capital is acknowledged as essential to the development and modernisation of the Polish economy (see for instance: Olesiński, 1998; Sadowski, 2000; Weresa, 2000). Since 1989, successive Polish governments have sought to attract and maintain foreign capital. Despite some debate about the appropriate level of foreign ownership in certain strategic sectors, all mainstream political parties and social groups generally welcome foreign direct investment (FDI). One exception is foreign ownership of agricultural land, which remains a sensitive issue subject to strict control.

The favourable climate for inward investment in Poland resulted in a dynamic growth of foreign capital flows in terms of both quantity and value. The number of firms with a foreign capital stake reached over 40 thousand, rising six-fold during the nineties. The total value of FDI stock amounted to $36.475 billion at the end of 2000, and was over 300 times larger than in 1990[2].

It has been widely discussed that foreign direct investment has a significant impact on a country's foreign trade performance (for the theory see: Mundell, 1968; Puvis, 1972; Kojima, 1978; Bhaghwati & Brecher, 1980). At least two aspects of this interrelationship have to be taken into account. One is FDI influence on the volume and value of trade, and the other is connected with qualitative parameters of trade reflected in the competitiveness of tradables.

The objective of this paper is to examine the links between foreign direct investment in Poland and trade performance with the European Union, and, in particular, to find out how the activity of firms with foreign capital influences the competitiveness of Polish exports to the EU. The problem seems to be important, as the EU predominates in Poland's foreign trade, as well as in exports and imports of foreign investment enterprises (FIEs).

FDI AND EXPORT PROPENSITY: FOREIGN INVESTMENT ENTERPRISES (FIES) AND DOMESTIC FIRMS COMPARED

The different theoretical studies on the impact of FDI on country's trade volume suggest that there can be either substitution or complementation between these two phenomena. Furthermore, it is expected that with the opening of the economy for capital some quality or technology caching –up will occur (for the review of different theoretical approaches to FDI and trade links see for instance Weresa, 2001). The interrelationship depends mainly on the motives of international production and on the relevant type of FDI (Stern, 1997). Thus, the impact of foreign capital inflow on exports and imports can not be determined *a priori*. It

---

[2] This data related to FDI in Poland is based on National Bank of Poland balance of payments statistics.

must be determined empirically on the case-by-case basis. Table 1 summarizes possible impacts of FDI on export performance.

Table 1. Main FDI Motives and their Impacts on Export Performance

Main FDI Motives	Type of investment	Channels of FDI impact on trade	Possible improvements in the export sector
Local market penetration	Market – oriented investment	Spill over of technology from FIEs to local Polish exporters Competition effect	Quality upgrading of exports Increasing quality competition
Cost reduction	Resource seeking investment Or Component-outsourcing investment	Demonstration effect "Learning by doing" effects Technological upgrading of exports created by firms with foreign capital	Productivity gains in the export sector Inter-industry or intra-company trade creation
Improvement of investor's global competitiveness (including export expansion)	Efficiency-seeking investment	Spill over of technology & imitation Direct technological and quality improvements in the exporting FIEs	Creation of intra-industry trade

The Polish case confirms that the relationship between FDI and foreign trade cannot be reduced to a dichotomy of substitution and complementation. FDI has both direct and indirect effects on trade. The indirect impact of FDI on foreign trade embraces a wide variety of effects, both micro and macroeconomic, which are associated with the use and diffusion of technology, the extent and direction of knowledge-transfer regarding production, management or distribution.

As a rule however, firms with foreign stakes are more export –oriented than "pure" Polish companies. Throughout the whole transition period export propensity, measured, as a share of export sales in the total sales, has been nearly two times higher for companies with foreign participation than for domestic firms. The companies with foreign participation seem to be more export oriented, although export propensity has been declining for both groups of enterprises since 1994. They have become relatively more oriented towards the internal market, which is to some extent a result of growing domestic absorption in 1996 and 1997. The picture changed in 1998, when FIEs improved the export performance in terms of its value related to the value of total sales, and after a slight swing in 1999 export propensity rose again, reaching 16.2% in 2000 (table 2).

Table 2. Export Propensity of FIEs in Poland
(Export Sales/Total Sales in %), 1994-2000

	1994	1995	1996	1997	1998	1999	2000
FIEs	15.6	15.3	13.9	13.8	14.1	13.2	16.2
Domestic firms	9.0	9.5	8.8	8.0	7.1	6.4	6.2

Source: Author's calculations from Poland's Main Statistical Office (GUS) data.

Moreover, FIEs are more effective in their export activity. In 1995-2000 export per employee has been continuously increasing, while it has been rather stable for domestic firms. In 1995 export per employee in FIEs amounted to 24,715 zlotys, compared with 8,557 zlotys in domestic enterprises. In 2000 these results were 71,024 zlotys and 12,926 zlotys respectively, so the gap widened in real and relative terms.

There is also a growing difference in productivity of both groups of enterprises, measured by income per employee. Figure 1 illustrates the statistical findings.

Figure 1

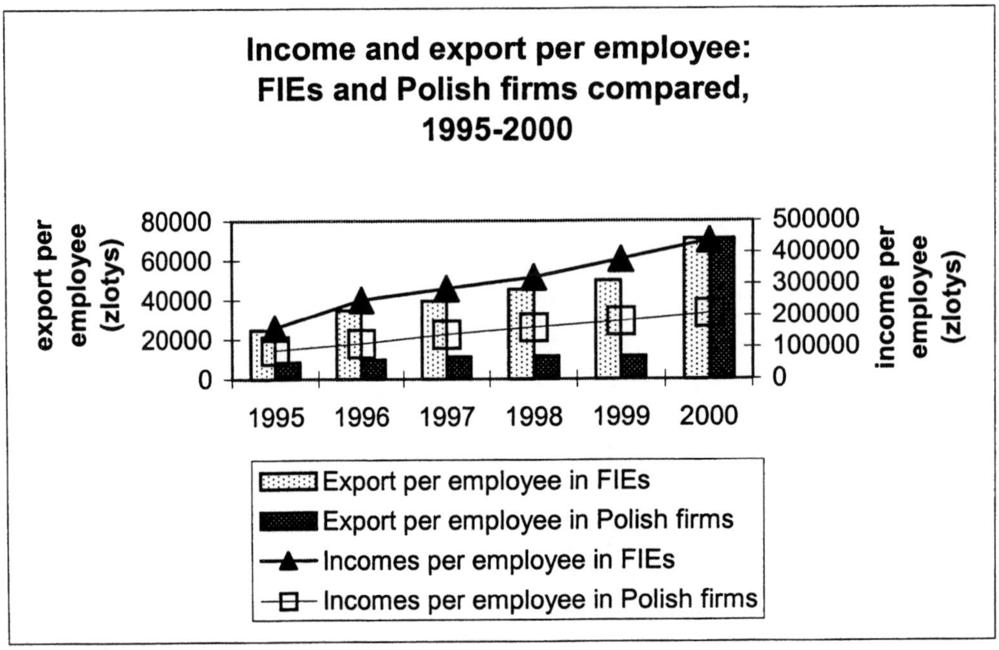

Source: Author's calculations based on GUS data.

The influence of FIEs on the volume of Poland's total exports, as well as on Polish exports to the EU is relatively large. Since 1994, both the exports and the imports of FIEs have been increasing at a higher pace than Poland's total exports and imports. Their share in Poland's foreign trade has been constantly growing. In 1995 FIEs exported to the EU $6,130.1 million, creating 32.8% of Poland's exports, while in 2000 their export to the EU reached $13,468.2 million, which is 60.8% of the total. Import from the EU has been developing even more rapidly. In 1995 FIEs imported $9,140.7 million worth of goods (48.7% of Poland's imports from the EU), while in 2000 their imports rose to $18,890.8 million, constituting 63.1% of Poland's total imports from the EU countries. During the whole transition period exports to the EU created by the companies with foreign participation have doubled, while exports of "pure" Polish firms have decreased (Figure 2).

Figure 2

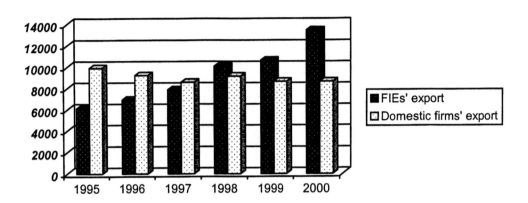

Polish Exports to the EU: FIEs and Polish firms compared (in \$m), 1995-2000

Source: Tabulated from GUS and IKiCHZ data.

FDI and Geography of Polish Exports to the EU

There is some similarity between the structure of the FDI stock in Poland by individual EU countries and the geographical composition of Poland's foreign trade with the EU.

In terms of value, Germany predominates in Poland's foreign trade with the EU, while in terms of capital stock value it is the second biggest investor in the Polish market. In respect to exports and imports, Italy places behind Germany, although its investment position in the Polish market measured by FDI stock is relatively lower. For both Germany and Italy, the absolute value of trade (exports as well as imports) considerably exceeded the value of capital invested by companies from these countries. The same applies to their relative value. Their shares in the total export of FIEs are higher than the percentage of their total FDI stock in Poland. In 2000 export to Germany constituted 35.8% of total export of FIEs, while the stock of German capital invested in Poland reached only 12.8% of the total FDI stock. The gap between share in export compared with the share in total capital stock is even wider for Italy: export of FIEs to Italy constituted 11.3%, while Italian FDI stock was 7.5% of the total.

The biggest investor in the Polish market in terms of capital stock value is France, but it is not the leader in terms of exports. French capital share in total capital stock in Poland originated amounted to 17.3%, while France's share in FIEs' export reached in 2000 only 6.4%.

There is no statistical evidence that a country's share in FDI stock is correlated with its share in exports to the home country.

On the other hand, however, in case of four EU countries, namely Italy, Belgium, France and UK, the share of FIEs in total Poland's export to these countries was relatively high, exceeding the average for all EU countries. In case of Italy, for example, nearly 80% of total Polish export is created by FIEs (figure3).

Figure 3

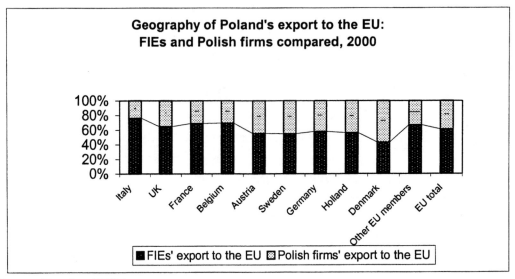

Source: Based on GUS data.

Measuring Export Competitiveness

Some quality or technology catching up is expected to follow the opening of an economy for goods, capital and technology. A catching up process, in relation to foreign trade, can be seen in some improvements in competitiveness of exports. How far has this process progressed in the case of Poland's export and what role has FDI played there?

There are some indicators, which may reflect the impact of foreign capital inflow on competitiveness of exported products. Theoretically, the growth of competitiveness could be expected, where foreign investors possess the ownership advantages, which sooner or later are acquired by domestic firms. Ownership advantages can be defined as managerial or technological know-how, patents, trading expertise, trademarks or other intangible assets (Dunning, 1993). As long as FDI leads to the diffusion of these advantages in the host country's economy, it affects indirectly the structural competitiveness of domestic enterprises and their products (Lall, 1998). Moreover, the presence of foreign investors increases competition and forces domestic firms to modernize their production processes and products. These indirect effects are stronger in the case of investment in technologically advanced goods. FDI in these sectors causes an increase in productivity of capital and stimulates innovation activity. The upgrading of technology and the transfer of technical know-how may alter the pattern of competitiveness. Some econometric evidence, as well as case studies for some countries show that the technological externalities of FDI (like knowledge spillovers or demonstration effect), influence factor productivity of local firms and their propensity to export (Aitken, Hansen & Harrison, 1994; Markusen & Venables, 1997). More efficient production processes and introduction of new goods and services are expected to have an impact on export performance.

There are at least two methods, which can be used for measuring changes in export competitiveness. One is the unit value concept and the other is revealed comparative advantage (RCA) index.

A study by Nielsen (1999) based on the unit value proved that in case of Poland's export to the EU there is no significant catch up. In the 1990s Poland's competitiveness has been increasing slightly in price elastic product groups, and decreasing in the intermediate range with no improvement in quality competition (Nielsen, 1999).

A stability of Poland's export specialization is also proved by the analyses based on RCA index (Weresa, 2000).

The statistical data show that the commodity structure of Poland's trade with the EU has also been relatively stable since 1995 (table 3). The main export items during the whole period are machinery and plant, textiles, transportation equipment, and base metals and products.

Table 3. Commodity Structure of Poland's Foreign Trade with the EU, 1995 and 2000 Compared

Commodity group	Poland's Export to the EU		Share in total		Poland's Import from the EU		Share in total	
	1995	2000	1995	2000	1995	2000	1995	2000
TOTAL	16036	22144	100.0%	100.0%	18781	29951	100.0%	100.0%
Livestock and animal products	533	402	3.3%	1.8%	255	200	1.4%	0.7%
Crop products	463	456	2.9%	2.1%	291	568	1.5%	1.9%
Fats and oils	160	5	1.0%	0.0%	139	111	0.7%	0.4%
Food products	355	423	2.2%	1.9%	773	743	4.1%	2.5%
Mineral products	1359	1240	8.5%	5.6%	653	719	3.5%	2.4%
Chemical products	780	788	4.9%	3.6%	2162	3575	11.5%	11.9%
Plastics and products	491	901	3.1%	4.1%	1488	2599	7.9%	8.7%
Leather and products	180	219	1.1%	1.0%	184	324	1.0%	1.1%
Wood and wood products	876	958	5.5%	4.3%	96	227	0.5%	0.8%
Pulp, paper, board and products	324	551	2.0%	2.5%	1096	1430	5.8%	4.8%
Textiles and products	2515	2374	15.7%	10.7%	2083	2235	11.1%	7.5%
Footwear and headgear	196	164	1.2%	0.7%	75	124	0.4%	0.4%
Stone and ceramic products, glass	292	429	1.8%	1.9%	469	756	2.5%	2.5%
Base metals and products	2684	2786	16.7%	12.6%	1550	2805	8.3%	9.4%
Machinery and plant, electrical and electronic equipment	1632	4911	10.2%	22.2%	5173	8810	27.5%	29.4%
Transportation equipment	1844	3241	11.5%	14.6%	1371	3451	7.3%	11.5%
Optical. Photographic. Measuring and control instruments	75	129	0.5%	0.6%	490	573	2.6%	1.9%
Miscellaneous finished good, furniture, building elements, toys	1245	1959	7.8%	8.8%	377	615	2.0%	2.1%
Other goods	32	208	0.2%	0.9%	56	86	0.3%	0.3%

Source: Tabulated from GUS data.

The trade structure in 1995 is strongly correlated with the trade structure in 1999. The correlation coefficient for export is 0.81, while for import is 0.98. Despite acceleration of FDI inflow since 1995 there have been no crucial changes in the commodity structure of Poland's foreign trade with the EU.

The reasons for this stability are related to the role of technology in shaping country's international specialization pattern. In the short run country's technological capabilities, as well as the resource allocation are relatively stable (Amendola, Guerrieri & Padoan, 1998). They shape country's trade specialization and constitute a basis for FDI flows.

Inward investment and foreign trade patterns can be explained using Vernon's product cycle model (Vernon, 1966) or technological gap theory (Posner, 1961; Krugman, 1979). Both theories predict that countries, which are leaders in terms of technology, will maintain their leading position in the future. The crucial element of these theories is timing. Either time lag in technology diffusion decides about innovator's advantage (technological gap theory) or changes of product characteristic over time influences optimal location of production (product cycle concept).

These elements have been further developed in the concept of technological accumulation, where innovation is seen as a cumulative process. This cumulative nature of innovation explains the existence of technology gaps, which allow firms, sectors and countries to create specific competitive advantages. It is difficult however, to move from an established competitive advantage in one industry to another. Technological accumulation theory assumes that for each country technological accumulation is comparatively high in some sectors and low in others. The process of catching-up is faster in sectors where country has comparative advantage in innovative activity (Cantwell, 1989). It has been proved that countries hold technological advantages in particular industries for rather long period of time. This implies that the process of "catching up" would start as a revitalization of traditionally strong sectors, rather than the development of new industries (Cantwell, 1989). The technological accumulation has been often used as an argument for explaining the stabilization of a country's trade pattern. The innovation history and experience can "lock up" country's specialization pattern (Arthur, 1989). The alternative way predicts that a country moves along trajectories of technological accumulations (Pavitt, 1988), which means developing comparative advantage in fields strictly related to traditionally advantageous sectors.

The interdependence between technological and trade advantages has been tested empirically for some OECD countries (Soete, 1987; Amendola, Guerrieri & Padoan, 1998). The results confirm the links between the two patterns and their relative stability. The same conclusions were drawn earlier by Pavitt and Cantwell, who proved that the technological specialization (and thus trade specialization) was stable in the short and medium term, but in the long run (more than 50 years) these patterns tended to change. This change is connected with the development of new technologies and new industries, which can revolutionize established international specialization patterns. Thus, changes in trade pattern are significant only in the long run. They might result from break-through inventions, but they might also be an effect of gradual upgrading of local production. FDI might speed up the process of technology imitation and diffusion, but the significant impact can be noticed over the longer period.

This theoretical explanation seems to be appropriate for Poland, as the empirical results show the stable commodity structure of Poland's trade with the EU during the 1990s. Moreover, Poland has been developing a comparative advantage in trade mainly in fields strictly related to traditionally advantageous sectors, such as textiles and wood processing (table 4).

Table 4. Poland's Specialization in Trade with the EU, 1995 and 2000 Compared

Commodity group	RCA in Poland's trade with the EU		RCA in FIEs' trade	
	1995	2000	1995	2000
Livestock and animal products	0.90	1.00	1.21	0.95
Crop products	0.62	0.08	-0.12	-0.23
Fats and oils	0.30	-2.80	-2.47	-1.34
Food products	-0.62	-0.26	-0.13	0.34
Mineral products	0.89	0.85	0.45	-1.04
Chemical products	-0.86	-1.21	-1.72	-1.39
Plastics and products	-0.95	-0.76	-0.42	-0.39
Leather and products	0.14	-0.09	0.23	-0.30
Wood and wood products	2.37	1.74	1.16	1.02
Pulp, paper, board and products	-1.06	-0.65	0.08	0.14
Textiles and products	0.35	0.36	0.57	0.31
Footwear and headgear	1.12	0.58	0.58	0.33
Stone and ceramic products, glass	-0.32	-0.26	0.07	0.14
Base metals and products	0.71	0.30	0.31	0.29
Machinery and plant, electrical and electronic equipment	-1.00	-0.28	-0.38	-0.21
Transportation equipment	0.45	0.24	0.26	0.40
Optical, photographic, measuring and control instruments	-1.72	-1.19	-1.11	-1.09
Miscellaneous finished goods, furniture, building elements, toys	1.35	1.46	1.37	1.34

RCA is calculated here using the following formula: $RCA_i = \ln [X_{ij}/ M_{ij}: X_j/ M_j]$, where X_{ij} is export of commodity i by country j, and M_{ij} is import of commodity i by country j. X_j and M_j are total country's j exports and imports. When RCA>0 a country is relatively specialized in this group of goods.

Poland maintained a traditional comparative advantage in trade of livestock and animal products, crop products, minerals, wood, textiles, footwear and headgear, base metals and products, transportation equipment, and furniture. The commodity groups where Poland lost its comparative advantage in trade with the EU were fats & oils and leather products, which might be connected with FDI inflow to these sectors, as RCA indices were negative for companies with foreign capital.

Furthermore, FDI is undertaken mainly in industries where Poland has a comparative advantage in total foreign trade, although these sectors are sometimes disadvantageous in trade with the EU. The food industry, for example, attracted the largest foreign capital flows (nearly 10% of the total FDI in Poland). The RCA index for food products is positive for all of both Poland's trade and the trade of FIEs, but it is negative for Poland's trade with the EU. This means that FDI in the food sector was motivated by the potential export to non-EU countries.

Although, there is no significant statistical evidence that the activity of FIEs caused restructuring of Polish exports to the EU, empirical findings confirmed the positive impact of FDI on the production processes, which over the longer period might result in upgrading the quality of manufacturing export. The results of the survey of a random sample of enterprises (foreign and Polish owned) showed that 46% of FIEs and 40% of domestic firms introduced crucial changes in production process during 1995-2000.

Table 5. Share of Firms having Introduced on the Market any New or Technologically Improved Product or Process, 1995-2000

	FIEs	Domestic firms
Percentage of firms, where products or production process were improved in 1995-2000	46.0%	40.0%
Changes in the field of:		
• Technology	93.1%	60.6%
• Product characteristics	96.6%	74.2%
• Distribution channels	24.1%	33.3%
• Organization of work	32.8%	25.3%

Note: The percentages do not add up to 100 since some of the subjects indicated several replies
The survey used a sample of 291 companies (126 FIEs and 165 domestic firms) and was carried out by the author in November 2000.
Source: Calculations based on the results of the author's survey.

In 1995-2000 over 90% of FIEs surveyed, improved quality of their products. Some changes in product characteristics were also reported by 74% of domestic firms. Technological upgrading of the production process was noted in 93.1% of FIEs and 60.6% of domestic enterprises. The results of the survey were better for domestic firms than for FIEs in the field of distribution channels, where improvements were introduced by 24.1% of FIEs and 33.3% of domestic firms.

Apart from technology, FDI might influence the competitiveness by improvements in organization of work, management and marketing. The survey confirmed that FIEs were more flexible in changing the organization of work: in 1995-2000 32.8% of FIEs compared with 25.3% of domestic firms implemented some changes in the organization of the production process.

As FDI is a method of transferring technology to the Polish market and improving the competitiveness of products, to what extent this has been reflected in the foreign trade of high-tech products with the EU?

During 1995-1999, Poland's export and import of high technological products were growing. The same tendency can be seen in Poland's high-tech trade with the EU. There is however, a strong asymmetry in high-tech trade with the EU as well as in Poland's total foreign trade of this group. In 1999 Poland's total import of high-tech goods was over 6-fold higher than total export, while its import of high-tech goods from the EU exceeded export to the EU 5-fold, and the gap has grown since 1995 (table 6).

Table 6. Poland's Foreign Trade with the EU in High-Tech Products, 1995-99 (US$ Million)

	1995	1996	1997	1998	1999
Poland's export of high-tech products	529.5	709.4	675.6	872.4	793.7
Poland's export of high-tech products to the EU (million US$)	294.9	372.8	382.6	517.4	489.7
As a percentage of total Poland's exports to the EU	1.8%	2.3%	2.3%	2.7%	2.5%
Poland's import of high-tech products	2551.4	3556.0	4384.3	4801.7	5071.4
Poland's import of high-tech products from the EU (million US$)	1523.4	1971.0	2338.4	2591.9	2784.9
As a percentage of total Poland's imports from the EU	8.1%	8.3%	8.7%	8.4%	9.3%

Source: Calculated from GUS data.

Although foreign trade in high-tech goods has been increasing in terms of value (except export in 1999), there have been upward and downward swings in the annual growth rate of high-tech export since 1995. Nevertheless, the growth rate was higher for export to the EU than for total Poland's high-tech export (figure 4). This result along with the growing share of high-tech goods in Poland's exports to the EU (1.8% in 1995 compared to 2.5% in 1999) indicates a slight improvement in Poland's position in high-tech export to the EU.

Figure 4

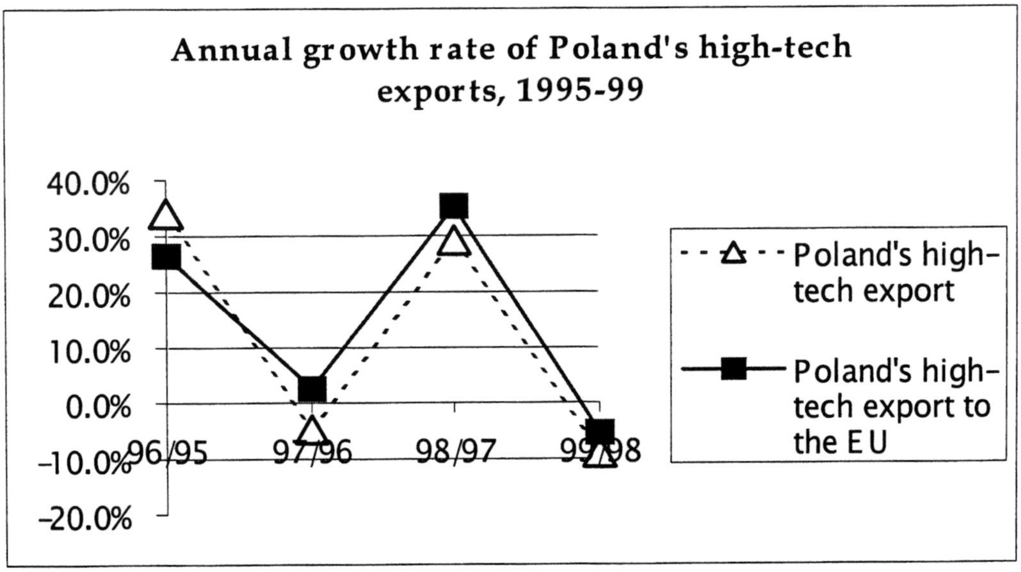

Source: Calculated from GUS data.

However, there were no significant changes in Poland's high-tech specialization in trade with the EU. In 1999 the products comparatively advantageous for Poland in trade with the EU were the same as in 1995. They included non-electrical machinery, aircraft, radio & TV components. In 1995 as well as in 1999 trade in computers, R&D equipment, drugs and chemicals was comparatively disadvantageous (table 7).

**Table 7. Poland's Specialization in High-Tech
Trade with the EU: 1995 and 1999 Compared.**

High-tech product groups	RCA index	
	1995	1999
Non-electrical machinery	2.63	2.27
Electrical machinery	1.55	1.85
Aircraft	2.45	0.29
Radio, TV & communication equipment	0.26	0.19
R&D equipment	-0.40	-0.05
Computers	-1.22	-0.51
Drugs	-0.50	-1.53
Chemicals	-0.75	-1.65

Source: Own calculations based on GUS data.

As Poland's high-tech export specialization towards the EU was not changed in 1995-99, so there is no statistical evidence that FIEs activity improved the competitiveness of Poland's export of high-tech products.

POLICY IMPLICATIONS

Since the beginning of transition Poland has significantly increased its openness to FDI and foreign trade. As these two phenomena are interrelated policy measures addressed to one usually affect both of them.

Empirical evidence assessing FDI impact on trade competitiveness indicates the following:

- Although the export propensity of FIEs is higher than that of domestic firms, there is no significant statistical evidence that the activity of FIEs caused restructuring of Polish exports to the EU
- The quality level of Polish exports is still lagging substantially behind that of the EU countries;
- There are no significant shifts in Poland's export specialization towards the EU. Poland is increasingly specializing in traditional, price sensitive sectors, and this process is, to some extent, supported by inward FDI;
- The changes in Poland's high-tech export to the EU are very slow, so FIEs have not yet contributed to the competitiveness of Poland's export of high-tech products.

These conclusions based on empirical results should be reflected in Poland's trade and FDI policy.

The main features of Poland's trade and FDI policy towards the EU in the 1990s are to a great extent a result of the Uruguay Round and WTO membership, the Europe Agreement (which provides for the adoption of the *acuis communautaire*).

The obligations tied with WTO membership include tariff bindings, the dismantling of quotas and other quantitative restrictions, the acceptance of disciplines in the field of export subsidies, agriculture, services, trade-related aspects of intellectual property rights (TRIPs), trade-related investment measures (TRIMs), health and safety regulations.

Apart form these general obligations connected with WTO membership Poland's policy towards the EU is shaped by the regulations of the Europe Agreement. Priority areas for the adaptation of laws include customs law (including elimination of tariffs and quantitative restrictions on imports), company law (and gradual facilitation of foreign investor's activity), intellectual property, financial services, competition policy, state aids, technical standards and environmental protection.

Within the framework of these international obligations Polish government has to identify priority objectives for the FDI and trade policy. From the trade competitiveness perspective they should include:

- more emphasis on attracting export-oriented investment,
- efforts not only to attract FDI, but also to divert it to selected sectors,
- targeted incentives promoting R&D related investment,
- wider promotion the development of linkages between foreign - owned and Polish firms[3].

It is also increasingly important to ensure the coherence between foreign investment policy, trade policy and other domestic policies and regulatory regimes. This includes domestic capacity building and efforts to reduce of several structural barriers, which might distort markets, as for example state aids, taxation policy, telecommunication regimes or anti-competitive business practice.

REFERENCES

Aitken B., Hanson G., Harrison A., (1994), *Spillovers, Foreign Investment, and Export Behavior*, NBER Working Paper 4967.

Amendola, G., Guerrieri, P., Padoan, P.C., (1998), "International patterns of technological accumulation and trade" in: D.Archibugi and J.Michie (eds.) *Trade, Growth and Technical Change*, Cambridge University Press, Cambridge, pp.141-168.

Arthur, W.B.,(1989), "Competing technologies, increasing returns and lock-in by historical events", *Economic Journal*, 99, 1989, pp.116-31.

Bhagwati J.N., Brecher R.A., (1980),"National Welfare in an Open Economy in the Presence of Foreign-Owned Factors of Production", *Journal of International Economics*, Vol. 10, pp. 103-115.

Cantwell, J., (1989), *Technological Innovation and Multinational Corporations*, Basil Blackwell, Oxford.

---

[3] Here, for example, the Hungarian experience can be used. In 1997 Hungarian government developed "Targeted Programme for Subcontractors", which was aimed at creating a network of domestic suppliers enjoying improved credibility with foreign - owned firms (OECD, 1999).

Dunning J.H., (1993), *Multinational Enterprises and the Global Economy*, Addison-Wesley Publishing Company, Wokingham.

Kojima K., (1978), *Direct Foreign Investment,* Croom Helm, London.

Krugman P., (1979), "A Model of Innovation, Technology Transfer and the World Distribution of Income", *Journal of Political Economy, 87.*

Lall S., (1998), "Changing perception of Foreign Investment in Development", in: P.K.M. Tharakan and D Van Den Bulcke (eds), *International Trade, Foreign Direct Investment and Economic Environment,* London, MacMillan Press Ltd.

Markusen J.R., Venables A.J., (1997), *Foreign Direct Investment as a Catalyst for Industrial Development,* NBER Working Paper 6241.

Mundell R.A., (1968), *International Economics,* Macmillan.

Nielsen Uff-Møller J., (1999), "Foreign Direct Investment in Poland and Quality Catch-up of Polish Foreign Trade".

Olesiński Z., (ed.), (1998), *Bezpośrednie inwestycje zagraniczne w Polsce*, PWE, Warszawa.

OECD (1999), *Background Report on Enhancing Market Openness through Regulatory Reform*, OECD, Paris.

Pavitt, K., (1988), "International patterns of technological accumulation", in: N.Hood and J.E.Vahlne (eds) *Strategies in Global Competition,* Croom Helm, London.

Posner, M., (1961), "Technical change and international trade", *Oxford Economic Papers,* vol.13.

Purvis D.D., (1972), "Technology, Trade and Factor Mobility", *Economic Journal*, September, pp. 991-999.

Sadowski Z., (ed.), (2000), *Kapital zagraniczny w Polsce – warunki działania*, PTE Warszawa

Soete, L. (1987), "The impact of technological innovation on international trade patterns: the evidence reconsidered", *Research Policy,* 16(2-4), pp.101-30.

Stern R.E., (1997), "Foreign Direct Investment, Exports and East-West Integration: Theory and Practice" in: Cooper R.N. Gacs J. (eds), *Trade Growth in Transition Economies Export Impediments for Central and Eastern Europe",* Elgar, Chelternham pp.329-357.

Weresa M.A., (ed.), (2000), *Foreign Direct Investment in a Transition Economy. The Polish Case*, SSEES UCL, London.

Weresa M.A., (2001), "The Impact of FDI on Poland's Trade with the EU", *Post-Communist Economies,* Vol.13, No.1, 2001.

Chapter 7

THE POST-SOCIALIST TRANSFORMATION OF AGRICULTURE IN CENTRAL AND EASTERN EUROPE

Dirk J. Bezemer[*]

Imperial College at Wye, University of London

ABSTRACT

In this chapter the reform packages applied to the agricultural sectors during the post-socialist transformations in Central and Eastern Europe in the early 1990s are interpreted in the context of the general theories of the transition to the market. The main economic goal of the reforms was an increase in technical efficiency, which was to be realised through the replacement of socialist-era wage-labour farms by individually operated, family farms. This structural change was assumed to follow land reforms. It is demonstrated that, in contrast to the expectations, 'individualization' of farming was limited and farm land fragmentation often extreme. This undermined the market viability of most family farms. Other problematic consequences of reforms include exploitation of farms by downstream industry and rural development problems due to labour shedding. An evaluation of the reform theories, their implementation, and their effects concludes the chapter.

INTRODUCTION

This chapter provides an overview of theories, policies and outcomes in the post-socialist transformation of the agricultural sectors in Central and Eastern Europe. The emphasis is on a discussion of the main ideas and general trends, rather than on reproduction of detailed

---

[*] Department of Agricultural Economics and Business Management, Imperial College at Wye, University of London, Wye, Kent TN25 5AH (d.bezemer@ic.ac.uk). I thank Michael Ellman for comments on earlier version. All errors and opinions are mine.

institutional descriptions or time series for economic and agricultural variables. These are readily available in other sources[1].

The aim of the chapter is to explain agricultural reform packages applied in the early 1990s in relation to their connection with more general theories of transition; and to show the relations, and the divergences, between theoretical expectations and empirical outcomes. In particular, the survival of wage-labour farms and the limited emergence of family farming is analysed.

THE PRE-REFORM ERA

Agriculture was an important sector in the socialist economies of Central and Eastern Europe. This is evident from four key indicators. In terms of its share in *employment* in 1989, it was just over 10 % in Czechoslovakia and Yugoslavia, 12-18 % in the Baltic states, about 18 % in Hungary and Bulgaria, close to 30 % in Poland and Romania, and nearly half in Albania. In comparison, Western European figures were mostly below 5 %. The pattern of shares in *GDP* was similar, ranging from 7 % in Czechoslovakia to 32 % in Albania[2]. Also *food trade* generally accounted for considerable shares of total trade, though with large differences. The share of *food outlays* in household expenditures was likewise high and more equal over countries – in 1989 roughly a third on average (but a quarter in Yugoslavia and Hungary, and half in Romania and Albania). In sum, the agricultural sector, its efficiency and the prices of its produce were important factors for the national economies as well as for consumer welfare in socialist Central and Eastern Europe (OECD 1996).

Although there was considerable diversity in the features of national agrifood systems in Central and Eastern Europe during the socialist era, they (except Poland and former Yugoslavia) shared five key characteristics: the corporate organisation of production; the scale of production; the integration of the sector; the bias in product mix; and the parallel private sectors. These are sector-specific manifestations of particularities of the centrally planned economy in general[3].

Wage-Labour Production Structures

Socialist farms were either collective or state farms. Collective farms in the central planning era were formally identical to co-operative farms, which are units of primary production in which both ownership and management of all fixed inputs are in the hands of a number of people, whose co-operation may or may not be defined in a formal contract. In practice however, property rights and management discretion were firmly in the hands of the

---

[1] For general economic trends during the transformation, see the annual "Transition Reports" published by the EBRD. For trends in agricultural sectors in post-socialist countries, see the annual publication "Agricultural Polices, Markets and Trade" by the OECD. For institutional details of the reforms and structural developments in agriculture in the region, see the volumes edited by Swinnen (1994 1997).

[2] Note that these figures are estimates based on Net Material Products, the socialist equivalent of GNP figures.

[3] See on the nature of centrally planned economies e.g. Ellman (1979), Nove (1987), and Lavigne (1995). See on socialist agricultural systems and policies Pryor (1992), Wädekin (1982) and Francesco et al. (1980).

state-appointed farm management and monitoring bureaucrats of the local and national government, as was the case on state farms. State farms were fully state owned and the official position of both management and workers was that of state employee. Although in practice functioning identically to collective farms, state farms were generally larger. Also they were more often used for realising specific tasks within the framework of agricultural policy, such as production in rough or newly cultivated areas, agricultural experiments, agricultural education, or production of particular crops in monoculture. In both cases, farms were *corporate* organisations. There was a separation between farm ownership, control over the production process and implementation of production tasks.

Scale of Production

Socialist primary producers operated on a large scale, by any standard. Farms in the socialist economies were the largest of their type in the world and, indeed, in history. Nowhere else would one find mixed (crop and livestock) farms of several thousands of hectares employing hundreds of workers. The preference for large farms was ideologically determined by the socialist, and particularly Soviet, enchantment with centralisation and industrialisation of the economy. Also the convenience of administering few large farms rather than many small farms appears to have been a factor (Pryor 1992, 145).

Farm size increased shortly after the installation of socialist regimes, when peasant and family farms were amalgamated into state and collective farms during the collectivisation drives in the late 1940s and 1950s. A wave of further concentration occurred in the 1960s. In the late 1970s and 1980s, farm size in many countries declined again. Within Central and Eastern Europe, average farm size (in number of hectares) in the 1980s was largest in Bulgaria (9,692 ha), followed by Hungary (4,356), Czechoslovakia (2,605), Romania (2,439), Albania (1,322) and East Germany (1,247). In Poland and Yugoslavia, where socialized farming was less important, the average size of such socialized farms as operated was much smaller (167 and 215 ha, respectively). These figures are collective farm sizes (except for Bulgaria); state farms were generally larger, but a ranking of countries would produce the same order. This is not true for a ranking of average farm sizes as measured by labour force; the land-to-labour ratio varied considerably over countries, from 0.8 and 4.5 hectares per worker in Albania and Romania to 8.2, 8.8 and 11.0 in East Germany, Hungary, and Yugoslavia, respectively[4].

---

[4] Data are for 1987, except Yugoslavia (1981), Albania (1983), and Czechoslovakia and Romania (1985). Numbers given here are indicative, not precise, for various reasons. First, the unit here classified as 'farm' is sometimes more than a food production enterprise, as in Bulgaria where vertical integration resulted in 'agro-industrial complexes'. Second, it is often unclear whether the data refer to total farm area, arable area, or area actually farmed. Moreover, not all collective farm area was always actually farmed collectively. Third, also definitions of the labour force vary, with data for 'total workers', 'full-time workers', and 'members' (often including pensioners). Also a large part of labour (up to 40 % in East Germany) was involved in work other than crop or animal production, e.g. in repair shops, cafeterias, administrative units, kindergartens, or building crews. Finally, hours worked per person per year were generally lower than in the west, e.g. roughly 2,500 in East Germany as compared to 3,000 in West Germany at the time of measurement (Pryor 1992, 141,142,145).

Vertical Integration and Diversification

Another shared feature of socialized agricultural sectors was diversification of economic activities and the high degree of vertical integration in any sub sector of agriculture – high, again, by any standard. *Vertical integration* "includes all the ways of harmonising the successive vertical stages of production and marketing" (Mighell and Jones 1962, 1). The extremes in market economies are, on the one hand, spot markets, where price is the sole co-ordination mechanism, and, on the other, ownership integration, where within-firm managerial orders move products between various stages of the production-processing-distribution path. That latter extreme is of course closest to the situation in central planning, were there also was a single owner (the state) for the entire chain. Indeed, vertical integration is almost by definition implied in having a command economy. The need to anticipate all quantities of inputs, semi-finished products, and outputs requires intensive co-ordination between all links in the chain.

This meant two things, which are best explained by employing the metaphor of the socialist system as a series of parallel chains. First, food availability depended on the entire food chain functioning as a unit. The demands on co-ordination were thus high, and small shortcomings could have important implications. Second, chains for a particular product or in a particular region hardly interacted with chains for other products of in other regions. Both consequences rendered food chains vulnerable and caused them to malfunction, given the defective chain maintenance that the central planning economy could provide. The image of the chain is helpful in understanding the chronic food shortages that characterized command economies (Hobbs et al 1997, 22).

Diversification refers to both agricultural and non-agricultural activities. Within the agricultural field of activities, socialist (particularly collective) farms often produced a wide variety of both crops and animals (in contrast, Western farms are most often either crop or animal oriented). From an economic point of view, collective farms were often over-diversified in the sense that the inclusion of so many products was one factor in sub-optimal overall technical efficiency. One reasons for this feature is that socialist farms often aimed to satisfy food demands for its workers or for a region, which necessitated producing a range of products rather than specialist production.

Diversification usually went beyond the agricultural domain. Non-farm activities were often included in the set of tasks that were performed by the farm organisation, such as machinery repair, building, and processing and transport of farm produce. (In addition, the farm, as most socialist enterprises, typically performed a number of social functions also not directly connected to food production.) Diversification into non-agricultural fields in socialist agriculture is also best explained by the defective operation of enterprises that were supposed to service farms in these areas. Farm management wishing to realise their production targets, or even simply to continue farm operations, would typically find it necessary to produce supporting goods and services themselves. Non-agricultural diversification and vertical integration went furthest in the Bulgarian *agro-industrial complexes* and the Romanian *integrator* model, and was least developed in Poland and Yugoslavia.

Product Mix

Throughout the socialist bloc, annual caloric intake *per capita* was at levels similar to those in the Western capitalist countries (at around 3,500 calories in 1984-1986), even though *per capita* income was considerably lower. Especially meat and dairy consumption were high in comparison with market economies of similar *per capita* income levels. This consumption pattern was induced by the price structure. It was preferred on ideological grounds by the socialist leaderships who wished to demonstrate that socialist citizens lived in an economic system that fed them well. It was also partly a result of the belief that the way to end food shortages was to increase production. In some countries, retail prices of food had not changed for decades at the end of the socialist era, even though real income had increased.

The costs of this policy during socialism included a high level of subsidies, particularly for dairy and livestock, and – since markets did not clear at these official prices - queues at shops and the development of black markets. After the collapse of the system, another cost became apparent: socialist agriculture had invested in a production structure that bore little relation to world market prices. This aggravated the restructuring challenge (Swinnen 1994, 5).

Parallel Private Sectors

A fifth feature of socialized agriculture were parallel private sectors, which were the sector-specific manifestation of the shadow economies pervasive in the centrally planned systems (Lavigne 1995, 41). Private plots, or gardens, existed in symbiotic relationship with the collective system throughout Central and Eastern Europe, their sizes fluctuating with shifts in ideological preferences regarding the centralisation of production. Private production was indispensable for an adequate food supply, especially of labour intensive products. In Hungary, for instance, in 1987 more than half of the grapes, potatoes, fruit, and vegetables were produced in private farms or gardens. Private production was insignificant in Albania and most important in Poland and Yugoslavia, were it accounted for the bulk of production and occurred on genuine farms rather than small plots (Swinnen 1994, 7).

REFORM INTENTIONS: ECONOMIC THEORY

Following the liberal revolutions in 1989-1991, the centrally planned systems throughout Central and Eastern Europe were abolished and the economies reformed. The theoretical ideas about post-socialist *agricultural* reforms are best understood in the context of the *general* economic theory of transition. That contemporary body of theories and policy implications known as 'the economics of transition' was, in turn, an application of the liberal variety of neo-classical, mainstream economic theory, certainly in its early and most decisive form.

Transition and Transformation

This theory concerned transition, not transformation. The wording implies the idea that the reform period would be limited in time and characterized by conceptually clear stages. One could argue, in this view, about the sequencing of stages and the nature of measures to be taken, but it was to be a transition from one economic system to another, not a gradual change with an uncertain outcome, as would be reflected in the term transformation. The latter term was more popular with economists that would label themselves as institutionalist, Post-Keynesian, or generally heterodox.

In recent years the differences between both views have become less pronounced. The importance of institutions, notably of the state, the analytical importance of socio-economic as distinct from 'purely' economic factors, and the viability or even necessity of more gradual change in some areas have become more broadly accepted. In the beginning of the 1990's, neo-liberal politics and economics still enjoyed intellectual hegemony, certainly in the economics profession. The introduction of market relations in (nearly) the entire economy and society as well as the merits of a minimalist state were prominent features of the professional economics literature. In consequence, the transition 'packages' proposed by economists to a large extent reflected the neo-liberal view on reforms[5] - a view that had already been put into practice in deregulation operations in many economies during the 1980s.

Liberalisation, Privatisation, Stabilisation

Traditional transition theory posed four 'pillars of transition' – policy measures that would mark the introduction of a market economy: price and trade liberalisation; privatisation; and stabilisation. *Prices* should be liberalized: price controls should be (largely) removed so that prices would come to reflect relative scarcities of resources, goods and services, in line with mainstream economic theory. Also subsidies, which distort market prices, should be abolished or decreased. *Trade* should also be liberalized. The efficiency gains of correct prices would only be effected if there would be transacting on the basis of these prices. Trade bans and the state trade monopoly should be abolished, and trade restrictions removed or decreased so as to cause minimal market distortion.

Moreover, the theory emphasized that, even with free trade and pricing, market-compatible pricing (and trade based on it) will not occur if economic agents have no effective ownership titles to goods, to labour or to firms. Therefore most enterprises should be *privatized*. Also competition, the force driving 'correct' price formation, would only develop in the context of private ownership structures.

Finally, a *stable monetary environment* is also a precondition for economic growth in a market economy. Price instability was expected to be the result of 'freeing' the considerable imbalances accumulated under socialism (forced savings and the monetary overhang) and also of the problematic budgetary positions of the newly post-socialist governments (resulting from large spending needs, reduced revenues from state owned enterprises, and no modern

---

[5] A concise presentation of these views is Blanchard et al (1991). A lucid textbook presentation of them is provided in Gros and Steinherr (1995).

system of direct and indirect taxes). The threat of inflation was a major concern, and monetary stabilisation programmes a vital part of transition packages.

Complementary Notes to the Orthodox View

As noted, this view of transition, while important to understand the reform plans, is now somewhat dated. Looking back, the points made by the early transition theorists – liberalisation, privatisation, and stabilisation - would seem to be correct but incomplete, in several respects. Theoretically, they took no or little account of the time dimension - it takes time for policies to mature and have their effect, and meanwhile the conditions on the basis of which policies are formulated change. Sequencing proved to be far more important than initially assumed. Furthermore, the theories were compatible with a wide spectrum of practical applications and institutional set-ups. Yet it developed that precisely this set-up controlled success to a very large extent. In addition, they paid little attention to initial conditions, such as location and income levels. Thus attention has shifted away from theoretical ideas and towards their actual implementation.

Moreover, the theories emphasized the destruction of the old system – central directives, price controls, subsidies, state ownership – more than the construction of new institutions. This view had harmful implications in three areas.

First and generally, it is now clear that creation of an institutional vacuum does not imply that efficient markets will spring up to fill the gaps (e.g. Schmieding 1993). Other, inefficient economic phenomena (such as economic cronyism, criminalisation, barter, looting of state assets, kleptocracy, etc.) might equally well come to dominate such an environment.

Second, the quality of the state suffered severely from the wish to dispose of the old regime without adequate attention to building a new political-economic system. The early consensus over-emphasized the stifling effect of state intervention in the economic process and neglected the constructive role that the state must have in both the creation and the regulation of markets and their institutions. Post-socialist economies typically operated under conditions of 'state collapse' or 'state desertion' (Ellman 1997; Abel and Bonin 1993). Later in the transformation, it became broadly accepted that healthy economies need a state that is both strong and limited (as already noted by Ellman 1994).

Third, also the importance of developing new enterprises, as opposed to merely disposing of state ownership, became apparent. State-owned enterprises that were formally privatized did not generally change their organisation or strategy, nor did they typically increase their efficiency and profitability. Moreover, the growth of the number of *de novo* enterprises was frequently more important for economic development and growth than the performance of privatized enterprises.

In consequence of their incomplete theoretical basis, the policies based on the traditional ideas led to the introduction of market economies more slowly, with many unforeseen drawbacks, and at larger economic and social costs, than anticipated.

REFORM INTENTIONS: AGRICULTURAL TRANSITION

Agriculture promised to be a suitable field for applying theories of transition. With its collectivized production mode, high degree of concentration of production, and intensive state intervention, it was heavily shaped by the socialist system. If reforms were designed to replace that system and improve economic structures, the agricultural sector would be most in need of their application and could most clearly demonstrate their beneficial effects.

Moreover, the potential for improvement of sector performance through the market mechanism appeared large. Apart from financial markets, agriculture is the most *competitive* sector in the Western economies with regard to its structure. Farmers usually are the price takers of the perfect competition model, and examples given in general economic textbooks to illustrate the working of the market often relate to foodstuffs and agricultural production. If the market was to work anywhere, it stood a good chance of demonstrating its efficiency in this sector.[6]

Policy Measures

Application of the principles of the theory of economic transition led agricultural policy advisors to the following recommendations (cf. Swinnen 1994, xvi; Tracy 1993, 264-271). *Property rights* over land and assets should be defined on an individual basis rather than collectively or as state ownership, as part of the privatisation process. *State intervention* should be changed qualitatively and quantitatively. Its nature should cease to take the form of bureaucratic directives with regard to input purchase, employment, the level and product mix of output, and quantities traded. Instead, agricultural programmes similar to those prevailing in the advanced market economies should be installed (import tariffs, export subsidies, credit programmes, and targeted support). Moreover, the extent of intervention should be drastically reduced: the level of domestic and trade subsidies as well as trade barriers should be decreased. Thus, what state intervention would remain would have to be compatible with the operation of market prices and the development of trade in line with comparative advantages.

A last component of reform concerned the agrifood sector rather than primary production only. Here *monopolies should be broken* – more precisely, the excessive concentration of businesses, either buyers (oligopsonies) or sellers (oligopolies), that was an inheritance from the central planning era, was not to be maintained under market conditions. The efficiency losses of imperfect competition are well-known theoretically, and post-socialist agriculture was a textbook example. Downstream industry, including businesses in food and fibre processing and wholesale trade, typically consisted of a few large firms in the entire country which were *de facto* monopsonies regionally. Hundreds of farms would deliver to a single processing or trade enterprise, with no alternative outlet option. The market power of these firms was further strengthened by the perishability of much agricultural produce and the specific investments made by farmers in, for example, milk production. There was a clear case for introducing competition, either by breaking down or regulating these firms or

---

[6] Interestingly, in another respect agriculture in the Western world is also most unlike the perfect competition model, namely with regard to state intervention. This is extensive in all developed countries except New Zealand.

through the entry of foreign businesses on the market (Hobbs et al 1997, 79; Brooks et al 1991, 155).

Policy Goals

As a result of the above measures, i.e. individually defined property rights, freer trade, farm-based decision making, the abolition or decrease of subsidies, and the introduction of competition, two developments were expected to occur. First, *relative prices* would come to reflect the scarcity of resources, goods, and services, and thus facilitate an increase in allocative efficiency. Second, and related, *farm structures* were supposed to change, leading to an increase in production (or technical) efficiency. If agents would have the legal possibility to dispose of farm land and assets while the structure of state intervention, such as it would be, would provide a 'level playing field' between alternative farm structures, these owners of the factors of production, pursuing their individual income maximisation, could then be expected to seek the most efficient use of their resources. This was expected to lead to the replacement of *traditional*, wage-labour farms (which where collective and state farms) by family farms, or *individual* farms.

Arguments for the view that privatisation of ownership would lead to de-collectivisation (in the restrictive sense of the replacement of traditional farms by individual farms) are mostly found in an applied transaction costs based theory, as promoted by Schmitt (1993) and others[7]. Here it is argued that the *raison d'être* for collective, large-scale production is the existence of economies of scale or scope. However, in most of the socialist economies, farms had a number of workers far exceeding the size of farms on which generalisations about scale and scope economies are based (Pryor 1992, 147). In addition, in much of agriculture, technical economies of scale and scope are argued to be soon outweighed by diseconomies in the *organisation* of production, and particularly of labour (Ferenczi 1994, 403).

The source of these diseconomies is thought to be primarily the rapid increase in transaction costs[8] with number of employees. The reason is an information asymmetry problem. Because of the specificity of agricultural work, the workers actually carrying out operations have considerably better information than the supervisors about such vital aspects of farm operation as the state of the land, crop, and animals and the amount of labour input required and actually applied. This information is costly to transmit, and communicating it is often against worker interests. Without it, it is difficult and costly for management to set up an incentive scheme that would induce the right amount of labour at the right time.

The alternative for correct incentives would be adequate supervision; but this is also costly given the nature of food production processes. Jobs in the production of a given product are sequential and the final result depends on the quality of any of the jobs. Attention to details that are hard to monitor at the time of implementation is often essential for the final

---

[7] Schmitt's paper, originally written in 1990, represented the dominant approach in the early transformation years. It was an application to post-communist farming of theoretical work on household production by Pollak (1985). For contemporary expositions of it, see Sarris *et al.* (1999, 315-317) or Mathijs *et al.* (1999, 4-8).

[8] Transaction costs are here defined as 'costs of defining, protecting and enforcing the property rights to goods' (as in North 1990, 28), notably including costs arising from asymmetrically distributed information (such as monitoring employees) as in Alchian & Demsetz (1972).

product. Work is seasonal and there are large peaks in the labour needed over the year, which either necessitates the use of temporary labour (generating experience, co-ordination and supervision problems) or implies underemployment of the permanent labour force. Finally, production is often dispersed spatially, which rules out efficient team supervision.

For these reasons, the farm size (in number of employees) that is regarded as optimal with regard to the production process is not expected to exceed family-farm size. In this mode of farming (here referred to as the individual farm), organisational diseconomies are argued to be largely excluded. Wage labour is not used and shirking or free-riding is supposedly difficult because of the small size, the hierarchical structure and the externally enforced continuation of relations within the household 'labour force' (Deininger 1995).

Based on these considerations and observations, the common perception of socialist-style farm structures in the early transformation years was that "the evident weakness of this organisational form provides the argument for full scale privatisation" (IMF *et al.* 1991, 157-158). The expectation was that "the private sector will be more productive than the collective" (Petit and Brooks 1994, 483). Significantly, 'private' was then equated to 'individually owned' and contrasted to 'collective'. This led to the generally accepted view that "privatization in ... agriculture mainly concerns the breaking up of large units..." (World Bank 1995, 2).

The expected structural change in agriculture resulting from reform policies was de-collectivisation in its narrow sense: the formation of family farms as successors of collective and state farms (Machness and Schnytzer 1993, 162; Mathijs 1998, 33). Such individualisation was not seen as optional, but as fundamental since "restructuring of large-scale farms (is) in line with the new ownership patterns and the principles of a market-based economy". Analysts claimed that "large-scale socialized farms are not suited for efficient operation under market conditions" (Csaki and Lerman 1994, 560,564). The conviction that individualisation was the main goal of reforms was by no means limited to the early transformation years, although the reasons given for it changed. Lerman (2000, 10) regards 'individualization of former socialist agriculture as a valid goal, ... since individual farms are the dominant organizational forms in market economies."

In sum, the view was that given its inherent inefficiency, collective farming had needed constant socialist government support to survive. Once this assistance was removed - as it was in Central and Eastern Europe - individual farming could be expected to replace collective farming more or less spontaneously. New, or newly effective owners would search for the most efficient and profitable use of their assets, and use them in (or rent them to) individual farms. Thus de-collectivisation was characterized as a market outcome rather than as part of a policy package.

And yet, it was also explicitly considered a policy goal. In many writings, the rise of individualized agriculture in a particular transition country was equated to reform progress in the agricultural sector. "Consequently, ... the new law [on land and farm structure reforms, DJB] may bring about a reversal in farm structure..." (Davidova on Bulgaria in Swinnen 1994, 42). "The present reform induces rapid structural change based on the new economic fundamentals: private property, free initiative and liberalized prices. ... The basic process of agriculture's transition toward a market economy is the establishment of private ownership and of the family peasant farm" (Gavrilescu on Romania in Swinnen 1994, 178).

Two reasons might be suggested for policy makers' and analysts' acceptance of this criterion for success in reforms. First, the long-standing tradition in the economics profession that ascribes efficiency and innovation to individually owned and worked farms, which are then contrasted to wage-labour farms[9]. Second, as was the case for the transition policies in general, the Western system was the (mostly implicit) model for reforms[10]. Perhaps it was only natural to anticipate the emergence of a Western-type structure of agricultural production (as recently advocated explicitly by Lerman, 2000, 10) following the introduction of the Western-type economic system in general.

REFORM IMPLEMENTATION

The theoretical rationales for reforms described above were identical over the Central and Eastern European countries where production had previously been centrally planned and agriculture was socialized. Naturally, the implementation, both in terms of concrete measures and timing, was not identical over countries.

Price Liberalisation

Off-farm prices for agricultural produce were liberalized and, although rising nominally, they dropped compared to input prices in the first reform years. Poland liberalized food prices immediately in October 1989; Hungary did the same in January 1990; Czechoslovakia, Bulgaria and Romania followed in July 1990, February 1991, and September 1992, respectively. The Czechoslovak and Romanian food prices were freed gradually over a half year period; the other prices were liberalized in full within weeks. (In practice partial price controls often remained in place for years, sometimes covering most food produced, as in Romania till 1997.) Price reform, including tax increases and subsidy decreases, was such that in some countries, such as Bulgaria and the Baltics, net farm subsidisation was replaced by net taxation (Swinnen 1994, 2,169).

Trade Policies

Soon after the liberal revolutions, all Central and Eastern European countries moved towards convertible currencies and away from trade monopolized by state trading agencies. Most barriers to trade dating from the CMEA era were lifted and replaced by arrangements in the frameworks of the Central European Free Trade Area, the Europe Agreements, the Czech-Slovak customs union, and a number of bilateral trade agreements that each country concluded with a number of other Central and Eastern European countries.

On the whole, the initial trade polices of particularly Central European countries were very liberal, for instance compared to those of their main new trading partner, the European

---

[9] For expositions of this view in seminal works in political economy and economics, see e.g. Smith (1976 ed, 386-9), Mill (1965 ed, 283-301), Marx (1965 ed, 601-2), and Marshall (1930 ed, 645-653).

[10] In Tracy (1993), an introductory text on food and agriculture in a market economy, written to "take particular account of the readers in Central and Eastern Europe", the description of the Western agricultural and food system was assumed to "be of special interest to countries seeking to transform their own systems" (Tracy 1993, 4).

Union. One indication of their dedication to freer trade as a means of economic integration is that all applied for (and in some cases, have already been given) membership of the General Agreement on Tariffs and Trade and the World Trade Organization - Albania was the last to apply in 1994 (OECD 1996).

Starting 1993, policy reversals occurred, often in connection with the replacement of liberal by nationalist, neo-communist or social democrat political parties in power. These changes, together with the increasing influence of producer interests, throughout the region induced higher levels of domestic support and more protectionist trade policies, both though variable and fixed tariffs and through qualitative trade barriers. Policy changes were often substantial, sudden, and haphazard. While increasing protection for producers, they also appear to have contributed to producer and consumer uncertainty over prices (see e.g. Hobbs et al 1997, 227-346 for more details and analysis).

Land Ownership and Farm Structure Reforms

The legal reforms of organisational options for farms and of land ownership patterns were closely related, and implemented simultaneously throughout Central and Eastern Europe in 1991-1992. They included four elements in each country, which however differed substantially in details of implementation:

1. Land ownership titles were defined on an individual basis. Most often the pre-socialism property pattern was restored, with a benchmark for land ownership somewhere in the late 1940s[11]. Land ownership by foreigners was often legally limited.

2. Collective farms in Central and Eastern Europe were most often re-defined as genuine co-operatives with real entry and exit options. (In Albania, Bulgaria, and Romania collectives were simply liquidated.) Members of the new co-operatives were the nominal socialist-era collectives members, while new owners of the land worked by it could also become members. Members owned a share of farmland and other assets. Co-operatives generally could be, and frequently were, transformed into corporate companies, on the initiative of their members.

3. State farms, other than those for educational or experimental purposes, were privatized into farming companies and sold if possible, either as units or asset by asset. The same procedure was applied to supporting organisations in primary production (mostly in construction and mechanisation, after the Soviet Machine and Tractor Station model) where these existed, as in Albania, Romania and Bulgaria.

4. Landowners were stimulated to start up their own, individual farm (rather than leave farm land and assets in the existing farm structures) by tax holidays, subsidized credit, and a variety of other subsidies. They were often prohibited from using their land for non-agricultural purposes for a number of years (e.g. 5 in Hungary, 7 in Czechoslovakia).

---

[11] Interestingly, selection of these dates reversed expropriations by the socialist leaderships, but did not return land to Jewish and German individuals expropriated in and after the Second World War.

As a concrete example, consider the Czechoslovak restitution and de-collectivisation processes, the legislation for which was enacted in 1991-1992. Ownership titles to land and assets were redistributed in the restitution process. *Restitution* refers to the restoring to private hands of state property acquired by state coercion (either through donation or sale) in the communist era after February 1948. Heirs to Czechoslovak citizens so treated could claim the ownership of these assets until August 1993, and restitution procedures were immediately started. Of all restitution claims made, 90 % were resolved by 1998, resulting in the transfer of 29 % of all Czech agricultural land.

Another 50 % had always been formally (though not effectively) owned by groups of individuals (collectives) throughout the communist era and had been used in the collective farming sector (Csaki et al. 1999, 27). These property rights were not restituted, but were made explicitly individual (rather than collective) again after 1992 in the formal *de-collectivisation* process. These newly effective owners could subsequently select their preferred use from a set of three options (OECD 1995, 78):

- to remain or become a member of the new co-operative farm (or other legal entity that was the successor of the collective), putting their land and assets at the management's disposal on a rental basis
- to cancel or refrain from membership, taking out any land and assets (or assets' pecuniary value) *provided* the aim was to take up farming outside the co-operative, either individually or in a new form of co-operation with other starters;
- to choose neither co-operative farm membership nor any other farming status. In this case the individual had the right to take out land and assets only after a seven-year adjustment period (i.e. in 1999), and was meanwhile entitled to an annual rent from the property.

The original objective of this policy is clear. On the one hand, reallocation of resources between the traditional and individual farming mode should increase efficiency. On the other hand, the outflow of land and assets should start only after farms have had time to adjust to market conditions and increase efficiency through individualisation. These twin developments should have ensured optimal resource reallocation initially and prevent excessive outflow afterwards[12].

TRANSFORMATION: MACROECONOMIC DEVELOPMENTS

We now turn from the reform measures to their effects, both in the economy at large and in agriculture. Five general macroeconomic trends, of relevance to the developments in the agricultural sector, were observable in the reform period.

---

[12] For detailed accounts of the Czech restitution process, see e.g. Lindemans (1997); Divila and Sokol (1993); Karlík (1993); Kaizrlík (1997); and Swain (1999).

Contraction

First, the newly post-communist economies in Central and Eastern Europe contracted sharply in the first few reform years. This is plain even when allowing for the statistical difficulties in measuring the level of economic activities[13]. GDP decreased in all Central and Eastern European countries in 1990 1991 and 1992 (except the Baltic states in 1990). Contractions, as expressed in annual GDP changes, were between 3 % (Slovakia) and 10 % (Albania) in 1990, 10 % (Slovenia) and 27 % (Albania) in 1991, and between 6 (Slovenia) and 35 % (Latvia) in 1993.

Thereafter growth returned to most countries outside the Baltic area. Here the slump came later and was more severe, but was also followed by sustained recovery. Central European countries also generally sustained their growth post 1993, but the Balkan countries lapsed into contraction again at later stages of the transformation – Albania because of its pyramid crisis early in 1997, Romania and Bulgaria because of postponed restructuring. Although estimating the precise extent of the decrease is problematic and the GDP data are only indicative, the contraction was certainly large by any standard. There are large differences between the countries, which reflect their different histories, location, and policies, but, except for Poland, none of them had returned to pre-reform levels by 1997.

Unemployment, Inflation, and Debt

Second, unemployment as a result increased considerably. Again, measurement of developments is problematic as unemployment did not exist under socialism, while in the transformation period, much unemployment remained hidden, showing in low labour productivity only (the Czech Republic is an example). Still, the trend in the official figures in the reform years is a strong increase in unemployment initially and a gradual decline or persistence later (here the Czech Republic is an exception).

Third, after consumer prices were liberalized, they typically shot up and continued to increase considerably, up till 1994 in most countries. High and volatile inflation proved particularly persistent in Romania and Bulgaria; in the latter country annual price increases ranged between 80 % in 1992 and 580 % in 1997. In the Baltics they peaked at around 1,000 % in 1992 and then continuously decreased to levels around 10 % in 1997. In the Central European area they persisted at around 10 % in the Czech Republic, around 20 % in Hungary and between 10 and 20 % in Poland. In Slovakia, Macedonia, Croatia and Slovenia inflation was kept at single digit levels after 1994. Inflation has been one of the main worries of policy makers throughout the region, although double digit levels were not always connected to a weak economic performance, as the example of Poland shows.

Fourth, in these years the annual budget balance was typically negative, and Central and Eastern European governments increased their debts. Still, annual deficits were mostly under 5 % of GDP in 1992-1997 (except Hungary up till 1995, and Bulgaria and Albania), while substantially lower in many countries and years (EBRD 1998). As important for policy as

---

[13] These problems originate in a switch in definitions and measurement methods, changes in reporting behaviour, changes in economic structures, and the imprecision caused by the large changes in virtually all relevant variables.

actual debt and deficit figures, however, was the high value that economic advisors, the international institutions, and most liberal politicians in the region placed on a balanced budget and on restricting the growth of the public debt. This put strong pressure on policy makers to cut spending and raise the level of taxes as well as the effectiveness of the tax collection system.

Income Inequality

Fifth, while income decreased on a *per capita* basis, it typically increased considerably for a minority of the population. Particularly in the first few transformation years, inequality measures based on real money incomes increased in all countries, sometimes dramatically. Many incomes, especially public sector wages, pensions, and other social security benefits, did not catch up with inflation. Moreover, many factors controlling the standard of living other than money incomes also changed for the worse for the majority of the population. Many goods and services previously publicly provided at no or low costs rapidly became expensive. These included medical care, housing, education, transport, recreation opportunities, child care, and meals provided at the workplace.

The overall change in standard of living due to the privatisation (sometimes an euphemism for disappearance) of many of these goods and services is hard to measure. The effect was, however, certainly negative and plausibly large for the majority of the population. One crude but indicative measure is the Gini coefficient, which approaches zero as income inequality decreases. Unweighted regional averages of the coefficient increased between 1987-1988 and 1993-1995 from .21 to .24 in Central Europe; from .23 to .34 in the Baltics; and from .24 to .30 in the Balkans (Milanovic 1998, 41; figures are allegedly based on disposable incomes including in-kind consumption).

TRANSFORMATION IN AGRICULTURE

An examination of the effects of these general trends in the agricultural sectors makes clear that typically, workers in the agricultural sector and their dependants were particularly hard hit by the perils of transition, compared to other sectors.

Agricultural Contraction

The contraction in the agricultural sectors was more than proportional to GDP changes. The level of agricultural output decreased dramatically in the early reform years, starting to increase again in 1993-1994. In 1997, none of the Central and Eastern European countries other than Slovenia and Romania had returned to pre-reform levels. In Slovenia this was because of political stability (compared to the rest of former Yugoslavia), high producer prices, and the historical dominance of individual farming in the sector which thereby suffered less disruption from reform. Romania stimulated agriculture extensively through various subsidy schemes.

The Baltic countries recorded the most dramatic fall over 1989-1997, of between 40 and 60 %, and experienced a turnaround only in 1996. Output recovered more in the Czech

Republic and Hungary (total decrease 30 % over 1989-1997), Bulgaria and Slovakia (15 %), and Poland (10 %) (Commission 1998a). In the histories of these countries there is no parallel for such a rapid and large contraction of food production, not even in the years of the collectivisation drives in the 1940s and '50s (see on this e.g. Pryor 1992, 110).

In consequence, the economic importance of the agricultural sectors in Central and Eastern Europe generally decreased both in terms of employment and in share in GDP. In the Balkans the contraction of the non-agricultural economy was in many years larger than that of agriculture, and the sector typically absorbed the newly unemployed. Agriculture in Central and Eastern Europe performed this buffer function only temporarily in the early and difficult transition years, and in some countries also later during an economic dip (e.g. the Czech Republic in 1998). But in most countries and for most of the time, relatively high rural unemployment was the result.

The contraction of the sector originated in the low technical efficiency and biased output mix of socialist agriculture, which necessitated extensive restructuring. Another general factor was the inherited structural imbalances in the economies, with too much agriculture and heavy industry relative to other consumer goods and services throughout the region. A set of more specific reasons would include the change in trade patterns, the decrease in state support, uneven market power relations in the agrifood chain, and the defective functioning of market institutions. Consider these in more detail.

Trade Patterns

First, trade relations in the region clearly deteriorated. In 1990 all Central and Eastern European countries except Romania were net food exporters. In 1997 all but Hungary and Bulgaria were net importers. Most imports came from the European Union, the share of which was between 40 and 55 % of all food imports in 1997 in the various countries. Poland, the Czech Republic, Hungary, and Bulgaria accounted for over 80 % of total Central and Eastern European exports and 75 % of EU imports from the region (Commission 1998a). Total exports decreased because of the collapse of the CMEA and the demand contraction in former export destinations (particularly the former Soviet Union). Imports, particularly from the West, increased because of the removal of many barriers to it. This occurred at a time when the European Union continued to have relatively high levels of import tariffs (and sometimes of export subsidies).

Trade liberalisation also changed the *composition* of especially food imports. In the pre-reform era, the rationale was to import products that were in short supply, as perceived by the central planners (e.g. proteins for livestock production). The post-reform structure became determined by a combination of consumer preferences, market power, and opportunities for re-export (OECD 1996).

The Role of the State

Second, the transitional imbalance in government budgets and the pressure on governments to cut spending were acutely felt by a sector that had largely relied on subsidies to keep afloat. In addition, political support for the sector was generally weak, certainly relative to its size. Farmers were typically not well-organized in the political arena during the first phase of the transformation. Moreover agriculture, in most countries the most conspicuously socialized sector, had a communist odium that did not appeal to liberal politicians and their constituencies.

Agricultural real wages decreased faster than the average. Partly this was because wages used to be paid by the state (either directly or via subsidies), not by private companies. (Such real wage rises as occurred during the transformation were typically concentrated in the private sector.) Moreover, there was no compensation for the output contraction by a comparable increase in the prices of the output or a decrease in input prices. On the contrary, the terms of trade for primary production during the first transformation years worsened considerably, leading to the operation of 'price scissors' not unlike that of the Soviet New Economic Policy years.

Terms of Trade

Taking 1986 as the base year, Czech price indices for agricultural inputs and outputs remained virtually constant till 1990. But by 1995, the input price index had risen to 265, while off-farm output prices only stood at 173. The 1995 ratio of input over output price indices (1.53 for the Czech Republic) was similar in other Central and Eastern European countries (e.g. 1.55 in Slovakia, 1.47 in Hungary), while higher in South-Eastern Europe, where inflation was higher and more persistent: for instance, 2.69 in Bulgaria and 2.21 in Romania (OECD 1996). After 1995, input and output price increases became of similar magnitude. The price scissors ceased to cut into farm profits, but the damage already done was substantial and was not compensated by later price developments.

This phenomenon was partly caused by the structural distortion in prices inherited from central planning, which had to be corrected sooner or later if liberalisation was to occur. Another part was caused by the fact that, for reasons of political economy, retail food prices typically remained under some degree of state control, rising only moderately compared to those of many other consumer goods. (Food outlays comprised between 30 and 60 % of household expenditures in Central and Eastern Europe by 1997, having risen compared to the 1989 level everywhere except in Slovenia.) But a major reason for the operation of the price scissors was the still large market power of 'upstream' and (particularly) 'downstream' industry.

Agribusiness Relations

After the major legal changes in the economy, enterprises involved in farm input manufacturing as well as those active in food processing, transport and trade started to operate on the basis of the profit principle (even though most of them were not quickly and completely privatized). They typically remained large and few, certainly in relation to the size and number of farms that delivered to them or purchased from them. Their market power was further enhanced by features of the production process such as product perishability and specific investments made by farms (the dairy industry being the outstanding example).

This uneven market power relation can be deduced from the size and number of such firms compared to farms; it is also evidenced by the development of the distribution of value added over the product chain. Not only did input prices increase relative to off-farm product prices; the latter, in turn, decreased considerably relative to retail food prices. For instance, between 1991 and 1995, the Czech off-farm price of milk rose from 4.96 to 6.57 (current) Crowns per kilogram, while retail milk prices increased from 5.31 to 9.56 Crowns. In those 5 years, inflation was 52, 13, 18, 10 and 8 percent, subsequently. In short, the profit margin of farms narrowed considerably more than those of the processing and wholesale firms directly following them in the chain. (More precisely, their 'loss margin' widened more.) Evidently, these oligopsonist enterprises started to skim off farm profits through low farm gate prices, delayed payment, and other methods.

Market Institutions

There were no, or only ineffective, checks on this in the regulatory, legal-economic environment. A more general reason, therefore, for the price scissors threat was the effective absence (or defective functioning) of institutions supportive to market transactions. Examples of these would include effective legislation against trusts, cartels, tacit collusion, and other forms of monopolies and oligopolies; effective (binding) contract legislation; impartial, knowledgeable courts that can decide quickly and consistently; and (price and quality) information dissemination mechanisms that would reduce asymmetries and render contract negotiations more competitive.

Formally, contract legislation was quickly introduced during reforms. In practice, problems arose both because of a lack of experience by businesses and the commercial courts, and because of the incompatibility of market practice and legislative provisions. The third-party (state) enforcement on which most market contracts implicitly rely was thus incomplete, and transaction agreements could be bent to the advantage of the stronger transaction partner – either by forcing a particular contract on the weaker partner, or by ex-post re-negotiation of the contract, i.e. hold-up (see e.g. Gow and Swinnen 1999, for a case study from Slovakia).

The enabling conditions for primary agricultural production, such as the availability of inputs and of financial means, had formerly been realized by the state (however incompletely). The market institutions replacing those socialist arrangements were particularly ineffective in rural areas, operating often to the disadvantage of primary producers. Hence the viability of farms was in general more threatened by the regime change than was the viability of productive units in other sectors of the economy.

Farm inputs were no longer always available at affordable prices. Producing and delivering outputs did no longer guarantee an adequate inflow of money. Losses were no longer compensated by the state through subsidies or agricultural credit. The newly commercial banks hardly extended loans to agriculture without state support or guarantees, while state support itself decreased and became more volatile. The joint effect of the above developments was that agriculture as a sector contracted more than the economy as a whole, and that farm workers' real incomes likewise decreased more than the national average (e.g. Milanovic 1998, 57).

EFFICIENCY AND STRUCTURAL CHANGE

The main economic rationale for the reforms had been the increase in efficiency that would result from changes in both the technical side of the production process and the organisation of production, i.e. through de-collectivisation of agriculture.

Efficiency

Technical efficiency indeed increased considerably, mainly through a decrease of costs. Labour was shed on a large scale, farms decreased their areas and herd sizes, the product mix changed, and investment all but came to a halt. These were intended short-term effect of reforms. At the start of the reforms, farms were generally seen as overstaffed and overly large, their products as not oriented towards consumer demand, and the sector as altogether too large due to the subsidy system.

In the medium and longer term however, the increase in efficiency was different from what had been anticipated because it hardly resulted from investments in new technologies and in new forms of farm organisation. In the absence of these, efficiency gains through cost reductions, though a necessary first step, did not sufficiently increase farm viability in the medium and longer term. For the typical farm, capital investments were typically ruled out because of the losses on production, the loss of subsidy, and the credit crunch. Moreover, restructuring of the sector on an individual-farm basis also did not significantly contribute to higher productivity, for two reasons.

Individual Farming and Efficiency

First, the supposedly higher technical efficiency of individual as compared to wage-labour farms was not clearly observable. One illustration is the situation in the Czech Republic. Efficiency estimates for the different farm modes calculated by Hughes (1998) indicate that individual farms did not appear to be more efficient than the other structures. In contrast, in a study by Mathijs et al (1999) based on efficiency measures different from those used by Hughes, individual farming is shown to be the more efficient farming mode. The difference in outcomes may be due to the different time of observation (1996 and 1998, respectively); to differences in the sample; and to differences in the efficiency measure applied (a Tornqvist index and an efficiency frontier analysis, respectively). However, in both studies efficiency differences seem more clearly associated with the product mix, farm size, transaction modes, or privatisation history, than with governance type as such (see also studies by Gow and Swinnen 1999; Mathijs and Vranken 1999; Sarris et al 1999; and Thiele and Brodersen 1997).

A second reason for the limited impact of individualisation of farming on the performance of the agricultural sector was that it did not, in general, occur on the scale and with the speed necessary for a significant impact on overall efficiency in the sector. Even if individual farms would have been clearly more efficient, there simply have not been enough commercial individual farms to make a clear impact during transformation up till now. As early as 1994 it could be noted that "already now it is clear that the process of farm restructuring ... is taking a course which appears to be different from the original expectations of many Western European observers. ... It is remarkable that farm enterprises ... choose to reorganize as whole entities, without dismantling the collective structure" (Csaki and Lerman 1994, 566, 573). Typically, new farming structures emerged which were based on individual property rights, yet in majority preserved features that had allegedly foreordained collectivism to inefficiency. These features notably include the use of wage labour and the complementary governance structure.

Structural Change in the Region

Table 1 shows the pattern of structural change in some Central and Eastern European countries where de-collectivisation was an issue (excluding Poland and former Yugoslavia, which had agricultural sectors dominated by family farms for most of the socialist era). Interestingly, the emergence of individual farming was most limited in some of the Central and Eastern European countries that have progressed most in the transition to capitalism: Hungary and the Czechoslovak successor states. But also in other countries, a considerable share of agricultural land was still worked by farming structures other than family farms.

Table 1: Much Farm Land Is Still Worked By Non-individual Farm Structures

Country	Year of observation	share in TAL worked by individual farms (%)*
Hungary	1996	28
Czech Republic	1998	24
Slovakia	1998	8
Estonia	1997	63
Lithuania	1996	67
Latvia	1997	95
Bulgaria	1995/6	52
Romania	1998	65
Albania	1995	95

* TAL is an abbreviation for Total Agricultural Land. The figures include (or largely reflect, as in Albania) household plots and part-time farming. Remaining land is mostly worked by co-operative farms, state farms, and farm companies.

Sources:

Mathijs, E. and J. Swinnen, 1999. 'The Economics of Agricultural Decollectivization in East Central Europe and the Former Soviet Union'. *Economic Development and Cultural Change*, 47 (1):24.

Cungu, A. and Swinnen, J. 1999. 'Albania's Radical Agrarian Reform'. *Economic Development and Cultural Change*, 47 (3): 607

This finding might, of course, be accounted for by the possibly disappointing efficiency performance of individual farms noted above. However, while equating efficiency to viability (via profitability) may be valid in analyses of longer-term trends in well-developed market economies, in the Central and Eastern European setting the observed limited individualisation seems more fruitfully investigated by considering the various dimensions of agricultural transformation.

To take just one example, the divergence between (formal) individual land ownership and (actual) individual farming is typically considerable in the post-socialist setting. In the Czech Republic, the share of agricultural land individually owned was from virtually zero in 1989 (counting collectively owned land as private, but not individual ownership). It rose to 94 % in 1994, and still further to 99 % in 1998. In comparison, the share of agricultural land worked by individual farmers increased from virtually zero in 1989 to 22 % in 1994 and to 24 % in 1998 (COST 1995; MACR 1998). According to a 1998 European Commission Report, the newly formed co-operative farms (then working 43 % of agricultural land), successor organisations to the old collectives, "showed a conservative and reluctant attitude to further restructuring and are to a large extent still run as in the pre-transition days" (Commision 1998b, 26). This was a deviation from the behaviour that the reforms were meant to induce. At the time of writing, World Bank researchers are starting to turn to this phenomenon. Lerman (2000, 10) notes that "the new organizational form is nothing more than 'a change of sign on the door': the new joint stock and limited liability companies continue to be managed and operated like former collectives."

Somehow, many farm managers have neglected the theoretical incompatibility of post-reform property rights and pre-reform organisation. They have been combining individually defined ownership and collective-era corporate governance structures. Currently, agriculture in the region is said to be structurally dual rather than homogeneous; it is often to a large extent corporate (i.e. traditional) rather than individual farming (Sarris et al. 1999, 306) [14].

Explaining Structural Change

Several general observations on the limited emergence of individual, or family farms in the region appear to follow from the above overview, which have perhaps not received due attention yet in the literature. A general reason for limited change in agricultural production structures appears to be that the transformation occurred in very difficult economic circumstances. Given the fact that change, and especially innovative change, is usually costly, one would indeed not expect vigorous efforts towards costly restructuring by farm managers during the years covered. Three elements from this overview lend further support to this observation.

First, the scale on which the conversion of wage-labour to individual farms occurred varies roughly inversely with general economic circumstances. It was most limited in Central Europe, and more extensive in the Baltics and Balkans. Without denying the importance of other factors, it appears a defensible generalisation to note that farms were disbanded in large numbers only when the entire economic system fell apart (rather than it being transformed) and/or when there was not much to lose by whatever change. In these conditions disbanding farms offered at least the option of household self-sufficiency in food. This observation invites critical consideration of the meaning of the 'individualisation' concept.

---

[14] See also Mathijs and Mészaros (1997); Debatisse (1999), Sarris and Gavrilescu, (1997); and Beckman and Hagedorn (1997) for country wise descriptions of dual agriculture. For an general overview of privatisation policies and outcomes, see Csaki and Lerman (1994, 1997) or Swinnen (1994).

For instance, in Albania and Latvia individualisation was almost complete – but the term individualisation (mostly used to refer to the creation of commercial family farms from traditional farms) is misleading in these cases. Traditional farms in both countries were most often replaced by gardens worked for own consumption and local barter rather than by commercial individual farms. In other countries, such as the Czech and Slovak Republics and Hungary, there was slimming and shedding, but not disbanding in large numbers of traditional farms. But the individual farms that were created there, were more often genuine, market-oriented enterprises rather than hobby or subsistence farms.

In sum, the destruction of the old system was more successful in the poorer countries that are less advanced in the transformation towards a market system; but its replacement by viable, market-oriented farms was very limited there. On the other hand, more advanced countries kept more of their traditional farms intact, but also allowed a larger (but still minority) share of agricultural production for the market to be produced by newly established, individual farms. Put differently, *formal* individualisation of agriculture was relatively successful in the Balkan and Baltic countries; *actual* individualisation was better accomplished – but still rather limited - in Central Europe. To capture both developments – destruction of the old, and creation of new productive structures - by the same term reflects the early belief that they would be complementary and could not exist separately. In understanding reality now, this terminology is confusing because it ignores the possibility of a third type of food production structures: subsistence farms or gardens.

This is true both for countries were individualisation of farming as rather limited – such as the Czech Republic – and for countries with, formally, almost complete conversion of traditional into individual farming structures, such as Albania. For instance, in the case of the Czech Republic, in 1998 there were, according to the 'Register of Economic Subjects', 92,845 agricultural businesses with the legal form of 'physical person' (*podniky fyzickych osob*), i.e. individual farmers, in the terminology used in this article. But the number of individual farmers also registered (this time in the 'Agricultural Register') as producing food (i.e. for the market) was only 32,365 (MACR, 1999: TA2.1/03;TA2.1/04). For 22,971 of these farmers, there is area information, indictating that over half (12,208) worked less than ten hectares and only 6 % (1,425) used over a hundred hectares. Plausible, the share of very small areas worked among the rest of the 32,365 individual farmers, for whom no area information was avaliable, is much higher.

In sum, the majority of food producers in the Czech Republic consists of operators of very small farms and garden workers. This obsrvation is true for agriculture in all the Central and Eastern European countries, were farming structures are often even more fragmented than in the Czech Republic. For instance, in the Albanian land reforms, almost all land worked in agricultural production co-operatives (473,514 out of 486,333 hectares) was allocated to 462,730 families. By 1995 (and afterwards), 95 % of arable area in Albania was worked by small-scale, individual farmers, with average farm sizes that were, unsurprisingly, below 1 hectare in some districts (Cungu and Swinnen, 1999, 607).

A second observation is that individual farms are relatively unimportant precisely in the countries were they were least actively promoted (the three Central European countries Hungary, Slovakia and the Czech Republic). This suggests that their prevalence in other countries is a result of policy and general economic conditions (intended or unintended) rather than primarily resulting from their innate superiority in terms of technical efficiency.

Third, restructuring, of which individualisation is the most far-reaching option, is costly in the short term while its benefits materialize in the medium and longer term. In view of the fact that economic hardship shortens time horizons for decision makers, it is plausible that restructuring was seen as a cost rather than a benefit by many of those directly involved. This would apply to both possible individual farmers-to-be and traditional farm management (although the latter in addition probably had several other reasons to oppose individualisation of farming).

This is supported by the observation that also in restructuring processes within existing traditional farm governance structures, the short term appears to have taken precedence over medium and longer term considerations. Such change as occurred in farming was almost entirely cost reduction rather than innovation in technical processes or organisation. As was the case in most industrial enterprises, 'deep restructuring' was avoided and 'defensive restructuring' implemented. Labour was shed, farm size decreased, loss making production (i.e. livestock) decreased. But investments and innovation have been largely absent. 'Deep' restructuring of firms in the post-socialist setting entails three elements: technical innovation, product reorientation, and reorganisation. In agriculture, the first and second elements have, by and large, been implemented only if it decreased costs, while the third has not occurred in large parts of the sector. This observation raises questions about the success of the reforms; or, alternatively, about the feasibility of reform objectives.

SUMMARY AND CONCLUSIONS

"The change we observe is seldom discontinuous", as Douglass North (1990) noted. Amidst the dramatic and sudden changes that ended the continuity of the Central and Eastern European socialist economies, this observation is true for the structure of farms in large parts of the region. This empirical overview concludes with a summary and an evaluation of the reforms.

SUMMARY

Agriculture was an important sector in the socialist economies of Central and Eastern Europe as measured by its share in employment, in GDP, in trade, and by food outlays as share in household budgets. In comparison to Western-type farms, socialist farms were large by any standard, used wage labour on a large scale, had a high degree of diversification both within food production and into other activities, were biased towards livestock (rather than crop) production, and were highly integrated with upstream and downstream industries in the agri-food chain. The socialist agricultural systems officially consisted of collective and state farms, but food production relied to a considerable extent on private plots.

The main economic goal of the post-socialist reforms was to improve the technical efficiency of farming. Reforms measures were applications on a sectoral level of what became known as the economics of transition, and included the abolition of state directives for physical production levels; the removal or decrease of subsidies; the abolition of the state monopoly on trade and the opening of borders; the privatization and de-monopolisation of agrofood businesses; and the definition of property right to farm land and other assets on an individual basis.

The collapse of the socialist systems and the ongoing reforms were accompanied by contraction of the post-socialist economies, mostly high levels of unemployment and inflation, increasing income inequality and poverty, and serious administrative failures. The 'transitional recession' lasted longer and was more severe than foreseen by most analysts. The agricultural sector was particularly hard hit.

One intended effect of the reforms was the emergence of family farms. Reform theories ascribed higher technical efficiency to this farming mode compared to wage-labour farms based on transaction-costs arguments. At the moment of writing, this superior efficiency is not yet clearly observable, while the emergence of family farms has been more limited than expected. Particularly striking is the very small scale, as measured in land, of family farms. This implies that the majority of them are not viable, market-oriented businesses but rather serve subsistence and part-time food production.

Evaluation of the Agricultural Transformation

The post-socialist transformation of agriculture was obviously necessary and beneficial in various respects. It was unavoidable politically, given the general desire for the introduction of a market economy and the particularly important, widespread perception of justice done in the land restitution and de-collectivisation processes. With respect to the economics of the transformation process, it clearly reformed a system that had been run on a non-sustainable basis. In addition, during the process allocational and technical efficiency in farming increased, the mix of food products available to consumers was adjusted and expanded, and the opportunity for private entrepreneurship was introduced in the sector.

But the reforms also generated (or did not address) several problems. The reform plans and (initial) implementation took little explicit account of the distribution of market power, of income inequality patterns, and of the political economy constellation that would evolve after privatisation. As one concrete result, exploitation by downstream industries became an important and unforeseen factor in the decline of farm viability. Perhaps the initial assumption was that privatisation would imply competition. Or perhaps political economy factors interfered with the implementation of reform plans that were actually designed to create or introduce competition and a level playing field. In either case, this particular development illustrates the one-sided theoretical basis of reforms in general. Mainstream economic theory did, and still does, incorporate power, inequality, and the political process only very incompletely in its analyses.

In connection with this, the wisdom of stimulating the disbanding and downsizing of traditional farms in favour of individual farms based on very small land properties must be questioned. It may still become unambiguously clear, in the future, that this policy has stimulated efficiency in the long term, as was its objective. In the short and medium term up till now, it has also served to undermine farm viability. It involved farm organisations that were in great economic difficulties in costly restitution and de-collectivisation procedures. It decreased their size and output levels and increased their number, thereby reducing their negotiation power *vis-à-vis* both the polity and downstream industry. And it replaced a large part of them with individual farms that suffered even more serious disadvantages in both arenas.

A final note is that the main economic objective of the reforms, an increase in efficiency, itself generates problems because it generates regionally concentrated unemployment. The post-socialist countries are experiencing a rural development problem within one decade of their reforms in a way that is similar, but compressed in time, to the one that Western Europe has been going through since the 1950s. With increasing technical efficiency, the agricultural labour force declines and rural populations decrease (or indeed dwindle to almost nothing, as currently in some parts of France). Rural physical, economic and social infrastructures may weaken to the point where the viability of rural communities and the quality of the countryside (in terms of both productive and recreative activities) are at stake. To note this is not to recommend a return to socialist-era overstaffing of farms, which was only hidden unemployment. But it does serve to question the early reform focus on farm efficiency, often to the exclusion of other economic and social parameters.

REFERENCES

Abel, I and J. Bonin, 1993. 'State Desertion and Convertibility: The Case of Hungary'. In *Hungary: An Economy in Transition*, ed. I. Szekely and D. Newbery. Cambridge, UK: Cambridge University Press.

Alchian, A. and H. Demsetz, 1972. 'Production, Information Costs and Economic Organization'. *American Economic Review* (62): 777-795.

Beckman, V. and K .Hagedorn, 1997. 'Decollectivisation and Privatisation Policies and Resulting Structural Changes of Agriculture in Eastern Germany'. In *Agricultural Privatisation, Land Reform and Farm Restructuring in Central and Eastern Europe,* ed. J. Swinnen,, A. Buckwell and E. Mathijs. Ashgate: Aldershot.

Blanchard, O, R.. Dornbusch, and P. Krugman, 1993. *Reform in Eastern Europe*. Cambridge, Mass: the MIT Press.

Brooks, K, L.J. Guasch, A. Braverman, A. and C. Csaki, 1991. 'Agriculture and the Transition to Market'. *Journal of Economic Perspectives* (5):149-161.

Commission, 1998a. *Agricultural Situation and Prospects in the Central and Eastern European Countries*. Directorate-General for Agriculture of the European Commission, Working Document. Brussels: European Commission.

Commission 1998b. *Agricultural Situation and Prospects in the Central and Eastern European Countries*: Czech Republic. Directorate-General for Agriculture of the European Commission, Working Document. Brussels: European Commission.

COST, 1995. *Agricultural Privatization, Land Reform and Farm Restructuring in Central Europe*. Preliminary Results from the COST research network. Leuven: Katholieke Universiteit Leuven.

Csaki, C., M. Debatisse, and O. Honisch 1999. Food and Agriculture in the Czech Republic. From a 'Velvet' Transition to the Challenges of EU Accession. *World Bank Technical Paper no. 437*. Washington: World Bank.

Csaki, C. and Z. Lerman 1994. 'Land Reform and Farm Restructuring in the Former Socialist Countries in Europe'. *European Review of Agricultural Economics*, 21: 553-576.

Cungu, A. and Swinnen, J. 1999. 'Albania's Radical Agrarian Reform'. *Economic Development and Cultural Change*, 47 (3): 605-19.

Debatisse, M. 1999. Hungary: A Successful Agriculture and Food Economy in Constant Search for Higher Competitiveness._*World Bank, Department of Environmentally and Socially Sustainable Development, Working Paper no. 9.* Washington, DC: World Bank.

Deininger, K. 1995. 'Collective Agricultural Production: A Solution for Transitional Economies?' *World Development*, 23, (8): 1317-1334.

Divila, E. and Z. Sokol 1993. 'The Conception [sic] Questions of Forming New Entrepreneurial Subjects in the [sic] Czech Agriculture'. *Prague Economic Papers,* 3: 261-274.

Ellman, M. 1979. *Socialist Planning.* Series Modern Cambridge Economics. Cambridge, UK: Cambridge University Press.

Ellman, M. 1994. 'Transformation, Depression, and Economics: Some Lessons'. *Journal of Comparative Economics*, 19 (1): 1-21.

Ellman, M. 1997. 'The Political Economy of Transformation'. *Oxford Review of Economic Policy*, 13 (2): 23-32.

Ferenczi, T., 1994. 'Some Aspects of Integration of Western and Eastern Europe'. *European Review of Agricultural Economics*, 21: 393-406.

Francesco, F., B. Laird and R. Laird, 1980. *Agricultural Policies in the USSR and Eastern Europe.* Westview Studies on the Soviet Union and Eastern Europe. Boulder, CO, and London: Westview Press.

Gow, H. and J. Swinnen, 1999. 'Up- and Downstream Restructuring, Foreign Direct Investment, and Hold-Up Problems in Agricultural Transition'. *European Review of Agricultural Economics*, 25 (3): 331-50.

Gros, D. and A. Steinherr, 1995. *Winds of Change. Economic Transition in Central and Eastern Europe.* London and New York: Longman.

Hobbs, J., W. Kerr, and J. Gaisford, 1997. *The Transformation of the Agrifood System in Central and Eastern Europe and the New Independent States.* Wallingford, UK and New York: CAB International.

Hughes, G., 1998. *Total Productivity of Emergent Farm Structures in Central and Eastern Europe.* Report on the EU DG VI FAIR project, task 2. University of London, Wye College, Kent, UK.

International Monetary Fund, World Bank, Organisation for Economic Co-operation and Development, and European Bank for Reconstruction and Development, 1991. *A Study of the Soviet Economy.* Volume III. Washington, D.C.: IMF.

Kaizrlik, V., 1997. 'Zur Transformation der tschechischen Landwirtschaft'. In *Privatisierungsprozess, Rechtsformen und Betriebsstrukturen im Agrarbereich der mittel und osteuropäische Länder*, ed. P. Tillack and E. Schulze. Halle: IAMO.

Karlík, J., 1993. 'Questions of Ownership and Use of Land and Other Agricultural Means in Agricultural Co-operatives'. *Prague Economic Papers*, 3: 264-283.

Lavigne, M., 1995. *The Economics of Transition.* Houndmills and London: Macmillan Press.

Lerman, Z., 2000. *Perspectives on Future Research in Central and Eastern European Transition Countries.* Paper presented at the KATO symposium, Berlin, November 2-4, 2000.

Lindemans, I., 1997. 'Process and Politics of Agricultural Privatization in the Czech and Slovak Republics'. In *Political Economy of Agrarian Reform in Central and Eastern Europe*, ed. J. Swinnen. Aldershot, UK: Ashgate.

Machness, Y. and A. Schnytzer, 1993. 'Risk and the Collective farm in Transition'. In *Agricultural Co-operatives in Transition*, ed. C. Csaki and Y. Kislev. Boulder: Westview Press.

MACR, 1998, 1999. *Zpráva O Stavu Zemedelství CR Za Rok 19.. "Zelená Zpráva"* (Annual Agricultural Reports). Prague: Ministry of Agriculture.

Marshall, A., 1930 ed. *Principles of Economics. An Introductory Volume*. Eighth Edition. London, etc.: MacMillan

Marx, K., 1961 ed. *Capital*, Volume I. Moscow: Progress Publishers

Mathijs, E., 1998. *Essays on Land Reform and Farm Restructuring in East Central Europe and the Former Soviet Union*. Ph.D.Thesis, Katholieke Universiteit Leuven.

Mathijs, E. and M. Mészaros, 1997. 'Privatisation and Restructuring in Hungarian Agriculture'. In *Agricultural Privatisation, Land Reform and Farm Restructuring in Central and Eastern Europe*, eds. J. Swinnen,, A. Buckwell and E. Mathijs. Ashgate: Aldershot.

Mathijs, E. and L. Vranken, 1999. *Farm Efficiency and Restructuring: Evidence From Hungarian Crop Farms*. Leuven: Department of Agricultural and Environmental Economics, Katholieke Universiteit Leuven.

Mathijs, E. and J. Swinnen (1999) 'The Economics of Agricultural Decollectivization in East Central Europe and the Former Soviet Union'. *Economic Development and Cultural Change*, 47 (1):1-26.

Mighell, R. and L. Jones, 1962. *Vertical Coordination in Agriculture*. Washington: United States Department of Agriculture.

Milanovic, B., 1998. *Income, Inequality, and Poverty During the Transition from Planned to Market Economy*. Series Regional and Sectoral Studies. Washington, D.C.: World Bank.

Mill, J.S., 1965 ed. *Principles of Political Economy With Some of Their Applications to Social Philosophy*. Series Reprints of Economic Classics. New York: Kelley.

North, D., 1990. *Institutions, Institutional Change and Economic Performance*. Cambridge: Cambridge University Press.

Nove, A., 1987. *The Soviet Economic System*. London: Allen and Unwin.

OECD, 1995. *Review of Agricultural Policies: Czech Republic*. Paris: Centre for Co-operation with Economies in Transition of the OECD.

OECD, 1996. *Agricultural Policies, Markets and Trade in Transition Economies: Monitoring and Evaluation 1996*. Paris: Organization for Economic Co-Operation and Development.

Petit, M. and K. Brooks, 1994. 'The Role of the West in the Reconstruction of Agriculture in Eastern and Central Europe and the Former Soviet Union'. *European Review of Agricultural Economics*, 21: 477-492.

Pollak, R., 1985. 'A Transaction Cost Approach to Families and Households'. *Journal of Economic Literature*, 23: 581-608.

Pryor, F., 1992. *The Red and the Green. The Rise and Fall of Collectivized Agriculture*. New Jersey: Princeton University Press.

Sarris, A, T. Doucha, and E. Matijs, 1999. 'Agricultural Restructuring in Central and Eastern Europe: Implications for Competitiveness and Rural Development'. *European Review of Agricultural Economics*, 26 (3): 305-329.

Sarris, A. and D.Gavrilescu, 1997. 'Restructuring of Farms and Agricultural Systems in Romania.' In *Agricultural Privatisation, Land Reform and Farm Restructuring in Central and Eastern Europe*, eds. J. Swinnen, A. Buckwell and E. Mathijs. Aldershot: Ashgate.

Schmieding, H., 1993. 'From Plan to Market: On the Nature of the Transformation Crisis'. *Weltwirtschaftliches Archiv*, 129 (2): 216-53.

Schmitt, G., 1993. 'Why Collectivization of Agriculture in Socialist Countries Has Failed: A Transaction Cost Approach'. In *Agricultural Co-operatives in Transition*, eds. C. Csaki, and Y. Kislev. Boulder: Westview Press.

Smith, A., 1976 ed. *An Inquiry into the Nature and Causes of the Wealth of Nations*. Oxford: Clarendon Press.

Swain, N., 1999. 'Agricultural Restitution and Co-operative Transformation in the Czech Republic, Hungary and Slovakia'. *Europe-Asia Studies*, 51 (7): 1199-1219.

Swinnen, J., ed., 1994. *Policy and Institutional Reform in Central European Agriculture*. LICOS Studies on the Transition in Central and Eastern Europe, 1. Aldershot etc.: Avebury.

Swinnen, J., ed., 1997. *Political Economy of Agrarian Reform in Central and Eastern Europe*. Ashgate: Aldershot.

Thiele, H. and C. Brodersen, 1997. 'Anwendung der Nicht-Parametrischen Data Envelopment Analysis auf die Effizienz landwirtschaftlicher Unternehmen in der Transformation Ostdeutschlands.'*Agrarwirtschaft*, 46: 407-416.

Tracy, M., 1993. *Food and Agriculture in a Market Economy: An Introduction to Theory, Practice and Policy*. La Hutte: APS.

Wädekin, K.-E., 1982. *Agrarian Polices in Communist Europe*. The Hague and London: Allenheld/ Martinus Nijhoff.

World Bank, 1995. Farm restructuring and Land Tenure in Reforming Socialist Economies. A Comparative Analysis of Eastern and Central Europe. *World Bank Discussion Papers* 268. Washington, D.C.; World Bank.

Chapter 8

SOCIAL POLICY IN EAST EUROPE[1]

Ludmila Dziewiecka-Bokun

The main object of this chapter is to present some of the social policy problems encountered by post-socialist East European countries. It refers mainly to the Polish experience in its current phase, and only to a small degree to the experience of other post-socialist societies.

The real dilemmas of the transition stem from the process of intensifying social conflicts, which justifies the following questions: to what extent did the socialist burden influence new governing elites' thinking about social policy? How do economic and political reforms shape social policy? What kind of social reforms and institutional changes are needed if a new and more democratic but still weak bargain is to be sustained? Who is to carry out what actions under social-conflict circumstances? When answering these questions I would like to find a fruitful meeting point between the legacy of the old system and the needs of a new one.

A model reconstruction of the social policy problems that post-socialist societies have to face at present, in view of the lack of a theory, requires some introductory explanation.

The first thing to be discussed is connected with a post-socialist vacuum, which means a relatively permanent situation where the basic structures of the existing system have disintegrated, but where this disintegration was not followed by an emergence of social forces which could, in a short time, create the structures of a new system. In the social policy area this vacuum is rooted in the fact that the state tries to keep social interventionism at the lowest possible level but at the same time the foundations and mechanisms of the state's old policy have not been replaced by new social mechanisms.

Another problem is the new shaping of the state's social functions expressed by a rejection of the state's monopoly in the social sphere and a privatization of social policy, that is, a commercialization of the process of satisfying the majority of social needs. Actually one can already notice the gradual withdrawal of the state from responsibility for particular welfare policy subsystems, such as the job market, housing, medical care, education and culture. A sharp drop in state expenditure on the socio-cultural sphere and a reduction in the

---

[1] A more detailed version of this article can be found in S. Nagel and Vladimir Rukavishnkov (eds.), *Eastern European Development and Public Policy* (St. Martin's Press, 1994).

social functions of state enterprises are evident. This has been accompanied by a noticeable decrease in the real income of individuals, increased unemployment, decapitalization of the social infrastructure and increased emigration, especially among younger people. Also, in an unequal struggle, the work ethic is losing out to cunning, scheming and plain deceit. People's attention seems more and more to be directed at exploiting loopholes and inefficiencies in new laws and in the economic system for individual short-term benefits.

The declared or demonstrated indifference of post-communist governments toward the conditions of life and work and the social consequences of the liberalized economy have resulted in many conflicts between state and society. The increasingly evident discrepancy between promises and reality has led to the growing difficulty of state policies in gaining popular acceptance, a necessary precondition for legitimizing the rules upon which political power is based. Paradoxically social policy - the weakest point of the real socialism - social policy remains the weakest point of the post-socialism, as is shown by current debates on a developmental strategy.

The market is rarely seen as a social institution itself, and it is necessarily supported by a network of other social institutions. Such an institutional framework includes, among other things, scope for government intervention in economic and social processes, the extent of local self-management, the creation of organizations to represent the interests of different economic agents and social groups and procedures to coordinate the actions of such organizations. Although some spectacular transformations towards a market economy and democracy have already begun, it is obvious that democratization and marketization of the Eastern European economies requires extensive institutional change over a long period.

To ease the transition into a world of greater economic success and social security the most obvious and elementary of steps is to appreciate and use social policy, which is understood both as a means of restructuring society and as a way of managing social conflicts, in such a way that they do not disturb the balance of the socio-economic and political system. This means that in Eastern Europe, politics must be constructed anew, in short a shift from state-centered to society-centered politics.

An important part of this process should be creating an appropriate institutional framework for a new social policy, a prerequisite of which is a network of organized social interests. The weakness and inadequacy of the system of interest representation is a permanent structural cause of the combination of passive expectation and anarchic defensive behavior that characterizes post-socialist society.

In order for society to govern, particular groups must put forth their own representations. For politics to be decided by competing societal interests, those representations must forthrightly articulate their claims. Currently, however, such social self-representation is markedly absent in post-socialist Eastern European societies. The socialist system, by making all social groups dependent on the state, did not facilitate the creation of the kind of autonomous, self-conscious social groups that are indispensable to a liberal polity, and that tend to exist naturally in market societies. Social groups in Eastern Europe today do not have a clear sense of where their interests lie. Workers do not know if it is in their interest to support a reform program that causes them to lose their jobs. On the one hand they do not want to become unemployed, on the other hand they desire the better life they are told a market reform program will make possible. Intellectuals know that it is in their interest to enjoy the intellectual freedom that comes from removing the state from the universities.

However, when the state withdraws its long arm, it also removes its wallet and so intellectuals are divided on how far the removal of the state should actually go.

Although everyone supports the idea of a transition to a market economy, few people know where and how they can fit into such an economy. They support the idea of a market economy, but they are reluctant to organize against the many inevitable ill effects of marketization. On the one hand they would like to be protected by a kind of the welfare state, on the other hand they fear that the welfare state has the potential to become politically repressive though its administration of an omnipotent bureaucracy, transforming citizens into dependents, whose behavior can then be manipulated to fit the state's own principles. These feelings are on a par with the value premise of new Eastern European political elites, which is expressed in the old saying, the government which governs least, governs best.

A government's declared indifference to social issues raises many doubts for two basic reasons. First, it proves that the thinking of present day reformers is tainted by the old sin of a one-sided, narrow-minded perception of the socioeconomic system, in which satisfying social needs is mainly perceived in cost terms and is understood as an economic loss. Second, its advocates reveal a surprising affinity with yesterday's communists on social issues. They are strongly bound by trust in the omnipotence of the economy. Fifty years ago the most important objective for the communists was the creation of a new socialist economy, regardless of the social costs. At present a similar determination is displayed in reviving capitalism. Nothing is mentioned of the social costs involved in this undertaking. The only thing widely known is that the costs are high and will become higher.

The idea of an economic recession, the size of which nobody can estimate, for a society tired by years of stagnation is, in my opinion, socially and politically unacceptable. Socially, recession as a program is discouraging and in practice it can even become a destructive force. It is always accompanied by social pathologies and by a phenomenon known as the "vicious circle of poverty," the consequences of which are generally unknown and ignored by politicians in Eastern European countries. Politically, the results of recession threaten social peace, the most precious political attribute in a time of transition. Under socialism it was always disturbed when the discrepancy between economic efficiency and consumer expectations outstretched social patience.

One cannot forget that Eastern Europeans rose up against socialism not because they could no longer stand the lack of democracy in the "socialist welfare state," but because the communist system was incapable of creating such a welfare state. In other words, they revolted when the gap between the expected and actual degree of satisfying their needs and interests exceeded that which was socially tolerable.

A large part of society put the blame for the present economic and social crisis on the previous state-party organization, in which the state gave too little and blocked too much. The omnipotent state monopolized decisions pertaining to the division of national wealth and controlled large portions of public life, bearing no heed to societal activity. This resulted in a decreasing belief in the possibility and effectiveness of society's self-organization and self-defense, which furthered the spread of passive and demanding attitudes, a deepening atomization of society and increasing social aggression.

In the immediate post-socialist period still too much depends on the state. It is the state that has to organize the withdrawal of the state from the economy and create the conditions for "building" civil society. This makes the process of Eastern European transition different from all patterns that have existed till now. One can say that as the market mechanisms and forces are very weak, necessary restructuring requires administrative intervention. Practically it means that state's control over the economy and social subsystem has to be maintained. New structures are gradually emerging. However they do not yet constitute a system because the links between them do not exist. These links will emerge in the co-evolution, mutual penetration and reciprocal adaptation of the various structures.

In the absence of these relations and relevant mechanisms various segments of society function according to their own separate rules, provoking many horizontal and vertical discrepancies in the functioning of society (Hausner, 1991, p. 7), from which different conflicts emerge. The ability to solve conflicts and to manage them before they intensify and endanger social, economic and political stability has become in modern democracies the main evidence of their political vitality. It means that in rebuilding the economic and political system a coherent social reform strategy is necessary. However, governments in postsocialist countries do not yet have a strategy for social reforms. Instead there is an implicit hope that the free market and democracy, once achieved, will automatically satisfy the true needs of society.

One of the main features of the post-socialist debate in Eastern European countries is that there is hardly any discussion on social policy. However one may draw some ideas from debates on economic reform. There are three basic tendencies connected with political choice and economic strategy that are shaping the general image of a social policy for today's Poland. They are (1) liberal, (2) populist and (3) social-democratic corporatist.

The neoliberals say that the state socialist economy has to be transformed as quickly as possible into a capitalist market economy, regardless of the social costs. The first step is to attract private investment by abandoning state price control, job security, subsidies on basic goods such as food, housing, health care and different social services. Because such an economic policy creates budget deficits, shortages, inflation and low labor productivity they propose tax breaks for everyone in order to erase budget deficits. The main goal is to disaccustom citizens from turning to the state for assistance. The sooner this is accomplished, the better.

Populists would like to try to use the state to build up the country's economy on the basis of what already exists. Their proposals include promoting small-scale business and peasant entrepreneurship, and creating a domestic bourgeoisie before inviting in a foreign one. They fear being losers in the European/world economy for a long time to come. In order to avoid the poverty and social dislocation that the liberal program entails, the populists propose a slow transition to a full market economy. They are not opposed to a strong state, especially one that serves society and takes care of social welfare.

The social democrats strongly favor marketization in general. However they share with the populists a commitment to minimizing social costs and a concern for those the market leaves behind. They reject the liberal's view that workers should be left out of the transition process. Their belief in the value of worker participation leads them to support strong social-welfare provisions on economic as well as moral grounds. On economic grounds they argue that neither labor production nor crucial exports can be increased without worker participation. On a moral basis they argue that those who paid the costs for so long, and who made possible the revolutions of 1989, should not once again be sacrificed in the interests of future generations, which is what happened under communism. Against liberals and populists they say that the market in a post-communist society cannot be returned to the way it was in precommunist times because current conditions are completely different.

In the immediate aftermath of communist rule, neoliberalism had the greatest credibility and became the basic framework for economic discussions. One should keep in mind that adopting economic liberalism was increasingly a precondition for receiving Western aid. However despite neoliberalism's ideological predominance, only Poland chose to embark on the neoliberal program with the Balcevowicz Plan in January 1990. Hungary and Czechoslovakia have proceeded more slowly. Populism is prominent in Bulgaria, Hungary and Romania as well as in Poland and Slovakia. It is less prevalent in the industrially developed Czech lands. Post-communist transition is likely to involve aspects of all three tendencies. Neoliberalism is where East-Europe would like to go, populism will be increasingly demanded by state sector workers, especially because the state sector will survive longer than was initially expected.

However all Eastern European governments will sooner or later be forced to introduce a large degree of economic liberalism, since no Western aid will be forthcoming without it. The practical political problem for the various governments will be how to legitimize such politics. By dictatorship? What about democracy, to the principles of which most Eastern Europeans are so attached? The introduction of a market economy in the post-socialist societies as a political project has prospects of success only if it results in strong, democratic legitimation. For Eastern European countries democracy is a necessary precondition of economic transformation.

The legitimation of modem developed societies stems from the fact that an efficient economic mechanism serves the overall interests of society, at least in the long run. This means that, first, the role of social policy as an efficient instrument of solid democratic mandate for economic and political reforms can not be overestimated, and second that social policy would make it possible to make the individual costs and risks of the economic transition a subjectively acceptable burden and guarantee that the pains of the transition would be compensated for by equitable returns.

The most important differences between classic and post-socialist models of marketization and privatization are that the former was rights-driven, class-based, creeping and halting, and supported by moral and ideological arguments, whereas the latter is outcome-oriented, highly visible and defended in the name of economic benefits for all.

The paradox of the transition in Eastern Europe is that it is being carried out in the name of a class that does not exist. Moreover, there is no social group, apart from the old communist elite, that has a real interest in implementing a market economy. The new private entrepreneurs still have an interest in the continuation of an inefficient state sector, since they have traditionally profited so well from that sector's deficiencies. Even this group is politically quite unorganized.

What seems to be important is that, after a short period of psychological shock following the fall of the communist system, the workers in enterprises have increasingly begun to resist the challenge to their previous positions in society, that is mainly as wage-earners. Having been the first group in society for almost half a century, they object to being the last one now. They feel cheated once again.

It must be made clear that what post-communist societies in Eastem Europe view as the alternative to socialism is not necessarily capitalism. Societal majorities in Eastern Europe are interested in the revival of capitalism inasmuch as its national version can ensure material progress for society as a whole, or at the least for its majority, in a relatively short time. Proposals in which this progress is offered to only a few cannot count on broad support. And this is the great difficulty confronting Eastern European governments at present. In general, the rebuilding of capitalism is a proposal that will benefit the still non-existent capitalist middle class. This is the Achilles heel of such a strategy, because farmers, workers, intellectuals and artists feel ignored and humiliated.

Weak and inadequate representation of social interests (one of the most significant causes of the defeat of socialism) remains a valid structural reason for widespread attitudes of passive expectation and anarchic defensive behavior in Polish society. Societies trained in passivity are unable to carry the burden of the system's rebuilding without state assistance. A condition *sine qua non* for functional change is a radical restructuring of social bonds.

A crucial weakness of the old system reflected itself in the establishment of vertical social bonds. Associative ties, based on the rule of a horizontal, cooperative system, comprised only a small fraction of the many regulators of social life. This situation resulted in the destruction of community spirit and encouraged apathy. However, lack of tradition concerning democratic local self-government and minimal understanding of how it would actually function have combined to create an unbearable burden for reform efforts.

In post-socialist countries, because of the ideological discreditation of socialism, societies have convinced themselves that a liberal democracy and a market economy are the answer to their particular problems. For an average Eastern European citizen both of these symbolize the Western standard of living rather than a specific form of social and economic organization. Almost everyone wants to believe that a liberal market will make them rich. However, the post-socialist legacy gives grounds to suspect that privatization will enrich the powerful and that the powerless will fall victim to the market.

That property rights and market mechanisms are actually introduced in the interest of society as a whole is not reliably recognized and appreciated by the majority of the population. People are very reluctant to believe in the beneficial outcomes promised by reform elites. Therefore it must be stressed that public support for the first noncommunist governments was mainly based on symbols, not on definite social interests, and it reflected hopes and notions, not attitudes resulting from knowledge and experience. Support built on such fragile foundations was bound to dwindle.

In order to assess current political, social and economic processes and the role of social policy in system transformation, identifying the sources of emerging conflicts is of fundamental importance. Various conflicts within Polish society are now seen to be intensifying and spreading. Their characteristic features are, first, they have mostly economic roots, and second, they mainly stem from events within state-owned enterprises, which are the main source of income for society. The most widespread are conflicts associated with privatization, conflicts over wage increases and conflicts over unemployment.

Wages and unemployment are particularly vulnerable areas for emerging conflicts because of both the social response and the economic implications. The decrease in real wages in the first year after the soft revolution was enormous. January 1991 real wages dropped to 83.9 percent of their level in December 1990. Such a decrease in the standard of living was bound to trigger public discontent and cause conflict between enterprise employees and the government. But cash-flow problems and the debt burden on the state-owned enterprises changed the situation during 1991. For the first time there were strikes not for increased wages but simply for the payment of the wages due.

The new economic policy abandoned the basic principle of full employment, but the reality exceeded all government forecasts. Between January 1990 and December 1991 unemployment rose from 55,000 to 2,155,000, that is, the unemployment rate reached 11.4 percent in December 1991. What is distressing is that two thirds of the unemployed are young people between 16 and 34.

One can also notice a widening gap between the feeling of privation in material things and the expectations aroused by the "soft revolution" of 1989. This subjective aspect of transition is created by the following factors:

1. Objective privation, that is, distance from the social minimum.
2. Relative privation, that is, in comparison with other social groups or the average situation in the country.
3. The state of the lost standard of living, no matter what the current level is (for example in comparison with the situation before 1989, before economic crises).
4. The distance between the current situation and consumption ambitions.

An evaluation of this situation shows that in the early 1990s 37-75 percent of various groups in Polish society felt that their living standards were falling. In the crisis situation due to "bolt effect", previously realized consumption patterns became the reference point for the minimum income level. The lost consumption level became the mark of basic needs, which actually denotes a widening (and not a narrowing) of the range of needs considered as basic.

According to the surveys of the Institute for Social Analysis at Comenius University (in Bratislava) only one third of adults in Slovakia are convinced that the present regime has more advantages than the communist one. Among the positive traits of the communist system, full employment, and stabilized price levels and living standard were most appreciated (among the negative, the lack of political and religious freedom, nepotism and the privileges of communists were deplored). Growing unemployment is considered a pathological phenomenon by the majority of the population. Thus, now that the euphoria from the silent or velvet revolution has faded away, pessimism and fear of the future are prevailing.

All these factors are causing not only social tension and conflicts but also indifference to the new politics. In Czechoslovakia and Hungary as well as Poland there is popular disgruntlement. It is not only about the costs of economic transition, such as unemployment, reduction of subsidies, price rises, wage reductions, or about new injustices and the slowness of visible change. It is also about the processes of parliamentary democracy, which are themself held to be responsible for the slowness of change. Apparent indifference to the new politics (reflected in the very high abstention rates in Poland and Hungary in 1990 and 1991) and revolutionary impatience are, in fact, two sides of the same coin.

The processes of the fledging and flawed democracy are accompanied by very low popular tolerance and understanding of political conflicts and also by an abnormally high level of political conflict inside the new political elites. This is because there are no clear dividing lines, no proper parties and few rules of the game (or the players decide on the rules of the game they are playing, as well as the scope of what the game is about because the new leaders, too, are unused to living with routinized, multilateral conflicts and have difficulty moving from antipolitical to ordinary political language.

Thus the period of transition from totalitarianism to democracy has been transformed from an intellectual debate to a social struggle and socio-political conflicts. The most striking feature is that the social conflicts are (when possible) ignored or "solved" in the old socialist way, that is, they are either blocked or suppressed. However conflicts have always reappeared and they will inevitably emerge in the future. This means that the system of social policy is in desperate need of reform. It cannot be replaced by encouraging people to be active and self-sufficient, which has become the main element in official rhetoric. A market economy produces, along with a growing output of goods, a growing inequality - a tendency that is met with strong resentment.

An active social policy is needed not only to prevent the massive economic deprivation of the majority of the population, it is also desirable because the process of progress, causing the intensification of contradictions, is both costly and risky. The main reason why active social policy is urgently required is that nowadays processes of economic and political transition need growing societal support. Consequently the reformers have to acquire the institutional mechanisms necessary for mobilizing winners (such as intellectuals, professionals, businessmen and technocrats) and compensating losers (such as government workers, the jobless, students or the unemployed).

The main empirical question of how to construct a new system of social policy remains to be answered. To put such a system into practice will take yet more time and yet more planning, both of which are politically unpopular these days.

The declarations of various political groups indicate that the idea of abandoning the overprotective social policy of the socialist state is seen as a necessary element of system transformation. At the same time the major problem of transition for post-socialist societies seems to be the fact that it is the state which must pursue a definite policy. Social policy in post-socialist states cannot rely on a blind evolutionary process, which has been the predominant pattern in the history of Western capitalism.

The fundamental premise lying behind current changes is to make it easier for citizens to participate in public life. Such a redirection requires modernization of the civil administration's organizational structure and a definition of an individual's status within a state. Civil rights and duties must be reformulated and reconceived in such a way that they comprise two sides of the same coin. Attention must also be directed at determining the means by which group interests can express themselves, a task that involves, in addition, a general reassessment of the principles upon which organizations and social associations function. It is also necessary to present the assumptions upon which individual recommendations are made and to point out the different alternatives and their respective costs. Additionally, it is important to take into special consideration the fact that social rights require complex programs, policies, implementation procedures, coordination and eligibility criteria for them to be utilized by citizens.

However, until now, post-socialist government thinking has been very limited and represents a simplified image of the market economy. Discussions on social policy problems are not the outcome of strategic analyses but rather are reactions to short-term tensions and conflicts, which usually take the governing elites by surprise. They are side issues in political disputes, exactly as they used to be in socialism, and they testify to the instrumental treatment of various groups and organizations in the political struggle.

In my opinion state activities directed at providing societies with some kind of security and social welfare are indispensable for the immediate future. We Eastern Europeans cannot ignore the fact that contemporary democratic societies are almost by definition also welfare-state societies. The welfare state's multifunctional character and its ability to serve many conflicting ends and strategies simultaneously, which made the political arrangement of the welfare state so attractive to a broad alliance of different forces in non-communist countries, is not very well known to us. The social welfare state would be recognized as the presupposition for both the market and democracy. I am perfectly aware that so far this has succeeded nowhere, but also, to date, the transition from socialism to democracy and a market economy has taken place nowhere.

INDEX